Contents

Ann Belford Ulanov

Religion and the Spiritual in Carl Jung

PAULIST PRESS
New York / Mahwah, N.J.

Cover design by Jim Brisson

Copyright © 1999 by Ann Belford Ulanov

All rights reserved. No part of this book may be reproduced or transmitted in any form or by any means, electronic or mechanical, including photocopying, recording, or by any information storage and retrieval system without permission in writing from the Publisher.

Library of Congress Cataloging-in-Publication Data

Ulanov, Ann Belford.
    Religion and the spiritual in Carl Jung / Ann Belford Ulanov.
       p.   cm.
    Includes bibliographical references.
    ISBN 0-8091-3907-3 (alk. paper)
    1. Psychoanalysis and religion. 2. Jung, C. G. (Carl Gustav), 1875–1961.
I. Title.
BF175.4.R44U43 1999
200′.92—dc21   99-41154
                                                        CIP

Published by Paulist Press
997 Macarthur Boulevard
Mahwah, New Jersey 07430

www.paulistpress.com

Printed and bound in the
United States of America

FOR BARRY

Introduction:
The Spirit in Jung

I wanted the proof of a living Spirit and I got it. Don't ask
me at what price....Why not spiritual welfare?...Spiritual
adjustment is *the* problem.[1]

Jung looked for the Spirit in all things, even in neurosis or psychosis. He was driven to do so by some inner "glowing daimon."[2]
Thus he brought to therapeutic treatment an approach that valued the numinous above all, and he conceived of health as finding life's meaning. Freud could not let religion alone; he wanted
to replace it with his brand of psychoanalysis. Jung wanted to
reconnect people to their religious traditions (Western and Eastern) by making a bridge "between the sacred figures and their
own psyche," because, as he saw it, "we cannot understand a
thing until we have experienced it inwardly."[3]

Jung saw the instinctual basis of human life expressing
itself in many different forms. He called the patterns he found
"archetypes." Just as birds submit to forms that force them to
build their nests in a certain way, so we humans find our
instincts taking specific forms because "unconscious thought
expresses itself mythologically."[4] To Freud's emphasis on sex
and aggression, Jung added a new emphasis on archetypes that
manifest the psyche's mysterious origins in reality beyond
itself. To the object-relations school of psychoanalysis, which
stresses our dependence on others, Jung added his insistence
on our directly connecting to this generative energy that fuels
human relations and their surrounding culture. To the emphasis on the overarching sense of self of the self-psychology school
of psychoanalysis, Jung added his underlining of the archetype

1

of Self, which acts to order and center the whole psyche, conscious and unconscious.

Jung brings his insights right into the consulting room. We cannot get well unless we get in touch with the deep energies that are there, always touching us. We need to humanize archetypal symbols into livable forms in our ordinary lives as they are mediated by other persons and by human culture. Thus we can come to see, for example, through a father complex to the form of fathering per se, from the generalized father to *my* father, understanding my parent's faults and finitude. But then we go back again, from my father to *the* father, so that the parent I began by holding responsible for my problems, I come to see as a fellow sufferer trying to work out his life in relation to the primordial human experience of being a parent. He may have given me a specific conflict through his own faults or choices, but now it is up to me to work it out in my body, in my time and place in relation to others, in my life, and in relation to life itself.

This direct relation to life itself, in all its forms, is the way we approach the numinous. We see through the visible to the invisible, and try to name what we find and our relation to it. Otherwise, we get stuck in an endless tug-of-war with the mediator of this transcendent dimension—the parent who failed us, the analyst who made it just enough better so that we cannot end treatment. Stuck in blaming or idealizing, we look for another person or institution on which to transfer our dependence and thus repeat the past instead of opening to the ever-new. Jung urges us to see through the mediator to the interconnectedness of the reality that we experience directly in our psyches. Jung wants us to be conscious of that reality and enter into a devoted relationship with it. Then even our pathologies change. For we see in them now a germ of the numinous trying to reach us, to grow alive in us. For Jung, relating to that is the whole point.

In this collection of papers, written and delivered over some twenty years, like Jung, I can say my thoughts have circled around God, as planets revolve around the sun. At this end of the twentieth century, a major shift in religious life has occurred. No longer is God way up above us, as if in high heavens, in stark contrast to the lowly Earth below, so aptly symbolized by the opposed positions of the fish of Pisces, the astrological age now coming to its close. Rather, as I understand it, the human psyche is a major locus within which to discern the workings of the Spirit, that psyche which is in us and between us and among us across societies, speaking from deep within us, in confounding symptoms, in startling dreams, addressing us directly with questions about what life means, to what are we to be devoted. For many people, there are no hallowed answers easily available to us from our religious traditions. Ready-made answers do not convince—though some of us do take a long regressive route to try to shoehorn ourselves back into an age where clerical pronouncements carried the authority of God. So we see many kinds of fundamentalism blooming across the globe, presenting in their doctrines and actions the very problems they are trying to solve. Whether the Taliband insistence on putting women back into a closet under their husbands' lock and key, or the Southern Baptists' dismissal of all interpretations of the Bible and of all the learned faithful professors who do not subscribe to biblical inerrancy, the same psychological move takes place: regression. It is regression from real symbol—a symbolic life where finite things point to the infinite mysteries, and only point to them, do not define them—to symbolic equation, where finite doctrines or political positions are identical with infinite mysteries. Truth becomes a weapon of power—and power over others.

The cross that we could once envision stretching up into the heavens and across the continents, it seems to me, is better envisioned now as planted right down in the depths within each of us, and thus stretching far and wide across the world's societies. We feel pulled apart by the mysterious and unthinkable repetitions of events that baffle our understanding—little boys taking guns to school to kill their playmates; ethnic cleansing possessing whole countries, as if they had learned nothing from the Holocaust; tribal genocide destroying the land and children in large parts of Africa; economic collapse in Japan threatening her near neighbors; nuclear bombs set off in India and Pakistan. All these events speak to and about our psyches, bespeak our incomprehension of how to live together in a shared existence. We bear the cross individually. We bear it globally.

Jung sees the answer to all of this in reclaiming the spirit, and knowing that it claims us. Inner and outer go together. If we lose one, we lose the other. Religion is an effort to describe the inextricable binding of self and other, including all the inner others—all those parts of us we so easily turn from and come to despise. And so in Part I, I take up the psyche as one locus and medium of religious life (chapter 1), and the efficacious effects of prayer, including Jung's own prayers (chapter 2). We confront the psychological roots of anti-Semitism that lead us to a religious root—fear of the Holy right there in our communal and personal life (chapter 3), and the hidden ways of desire that can bring persons to face their own particular conflicts only because they see working in them a desire for something of their own, for their participation, for their individual beings to show the love of being (chapter 4).

How do we communicate this desire of being for us? Jung suffered all his life long feeling others did not understand the precious connections he uncovered. Part II addresses this task through a question: What do we do with the unconscious in the nontherapeutic setting? In the educational setting? Therapy is a modality of treatment. To discover the center of reality seeking us in and through our little problems and our large international conflicts, which so clearly reflect our inner splits and repressions in worldwide terms, is to make a very considerable discovery indeed. Chapters 5 and 6 address the specifics of explaining Jung and understanding the unconscious in relation to religious texts and to those preparing for religious professions, those willing to work in the trenches. Surprisingly enough, fear of the unconscious exists in religious persons and often with resistance to acknowledge its presence in me, in you, here and now. Chapter 7 lays out the way Jung went into this fearful country and mapped it for himself and for the rest of us, and relates his method to our present-day world.

Religious and psychological issues mark our century. Part III addresses the psyche in our times by setting Jung in relation to other seminal thinkers in psychoanalysis (chapter 8), and examining how some of the great souls of our century battled with their own psyches and how their battles proved the source of their most creative ideas (chapters 9 and 10 on Paul Tillich, chapter 11 on Thérèse of Lisieux). I conclude with an exploration and illustration of the way God touches us (chapter 12, especially in relation to Buddhism), comes to us in the small space, so tiny and so necessary, of our own incarnate being (chapter 13).

Ann Belford Ulanov
Woodbury, Connecticut 1998

Notes

1. C. G. Jung, *Letters*, 2 vols., eds. G. Adler and A. Jaffé, trans. R. F. C. Hull (Princeton: Princeton University Press, 1973 and 1975), I, 30 January 1948, 492, and 23 September 1949, 537.

2. See C. G. Jung, *Memories, Dreams, Reflections*, ed. A. Jaffé, trans. Richard and Clara Winston (New York: Pantheon, 1963), 357.

3. C. G. Jung, *Psychology and Alchemy, Collected Works* 12, trans. R. F. C. Hull (New York: Pantheon, 1953), pars. 14–15.

4. Jung, *Letters*, I, 29 March 1949, 526.

Part I
JUNG AND RELIGION AND POLITICS

Chapter 1

Religion: Jung's View

The religious person, from Jung's perspective, is one who has immediate experience of the "numinous," an awe-inspiring confrontation with a "dynamic agency or effect" over which the subject's will exerts no control. After such an experience, we pay close attention to this powerful dimension of otherness that has seized hold of us, and place confidence in its meaning for our life. Jung contrasts the immediacy of such personal experience of the numinous with the more remote allegiance to a religious creed. Creeds may serve as valuable protection against the searing nature of the experience by channeling its effects into the conventional lines of religious tradition. Too often, however, and for too many, Jung says, creeds serve as substitutes for authentic religious experiences. In describing the psychodynamics of such a numinous event, Jung substitutes his own vocabulary for traditional religious terminology. In religious experience, the ego, the center of consciousness, is gripped by the autonomous manifestation of the Self, the center of the whole psyche, conscious and unconscious. Consciousness is invaded by contents rising from the deepest layer of the unconscious—the "collective unconscious" or "objective psyche." These contents are archetypes, primordial images that arrange behavioral and emotional reactions of people of different cultures and historical periods into patterns and motifs that operate in the psyche in certain typical and thus predictable ways. The archetype of the Self, for example, makes itself felt to the ego in the form of powerful "God-images." These act in the psyche as centers around which everything else revolves. They may evoke in the recipient a positive feeling of being "healed" and made free of psychic splits, "blessed" by a life-changing vision, or a negative feeling of such power that the

9

ego seems about to be invaded and overrun by an alien force bringing destruction and psychosis.

SACRIFICE

Jung analyzed religious ritual, spiritual exercises, and dogmas as descriptions of the way a person's ego comes into right relation with the transpersonal Self-archetype. In the mass, for example, Jung focuses on the transformation worked by the double sacrifice of ego to Self and of Self to ego. The ritual act of confession of sin prior to mass brings worshipers to consciousness of their possessive ego claims upon others, projecting their ego as the principal authority to be obeyed. Thus, in the offering up of the bread and wine, the congregation must acknowledge its own ego identification with the gifts it sacrifices. Through bread and wine, the worshipers also offer up themselves—their claims to self-possession and ego authority—and surrender to a higher, more encompassing authority. In giving up what we identify as "mine" or "ours," we sacrifice our own ego claims without expectation of repayment. In so far as we are identified with our gifts, we give ourselves away.

The ego resists total sacrifice at the same time that it meets another claim, and one of superior value and authority: that of the Self. The Self demands the obedience of the ego to its higher call, even when that obedience requires the destruction of the ego's whole system of values. As examples, Jung cited Abraham's sacrifice of Isaac, Hosea's marriage to the harlot, and Jesus' agony at Gethsemane. When we feel our ego's claim to assert its own authority conflicting with a stronger power that challenges that claim and demands its sacrifice, we directly experience the power of the Self. The Self in us causes us to sacrifice the ego; we are the human sacrifice, just as Abraham must have felt himself even more the victim than Isaac, when he was summoned to give up what he loved most, his only son. In this double experience, as both sacrificer and sacrificed, we participate in the mystery of God's sacrifice in the mass. In such an experience we find what we had given up for lost. Because we can give only what we have, we gain a surer sense of the ego. The Self in turn comes more into conscious awareness, as it is differentiated for us from its unconscious state where it lives only in projection onto other objects. As the Self comes more into human form, we experience it as a direct part of our own persons.

PSYCHOLOGY OF RELIGION

Jung viewed the function of his psychology for religion as a means to help persons see direct connections between their own personal experiences and the archetypal symbols contained in religious tradition. The forging of these connections is crucial for psychic hygiene. Much of the anxiety, restlessness, and destructiveness of twentieth-century persons, Jung believed, results from the fact that their psychic energy no longer flows into religious symbols that can give them a picture of their place in the universe. Instead, traditional symbols are for many people obscure anachronisms that no longer command any quickening of spirit. Thus psychic energy often has nowhere to go, and either falls back abjectly into the psyche, creating psychological problems there, or it is projected onto substitutes for a value system, such as political causes, that dangerously inflate them out of all proportion. In such a situation, Jung says, we do not need new symbols or new religions as much as we need to find fresh personal connections to the old ones. Jung is opposed to people raised in Western culture who seek in Eastern religions the ultimate answers to their psychic dilemma. Jung studied Eastern religious thought, as his work on the *I Ching, The Secret of the Golden Flower,* and the *Tibetan Book of Liberation* and *Book of the Dead* indicate, but he did not think we can simply incorporate into a personality conditioned by one set of traditions a religion developed out of an entirely different cultural set. Religion is not a substitute for life, but rather the symbolic expression of the process of integrating the Self into a life lived in relation to the unconscious and to others. We must pay close attention to what our individual unconscious experience says to us through dreams, "God-images," and even neurotic symptoms.

Neurosis, Jung wrote, often results from our direct refusal or inability to find the right direction for our religious instincts. The religious instinct presents itself as a drive for significant relation of the personal self to the "numinosum." If this instinct is frustrated or repressed, we fall ill just as surely as we do when other basic instincts are obstructed. For Jung, neurosis is the suffering of human beings who have not yet discovered what life means for them. Jung described the human soul as the capacity for relation to God. Failure to develop that capacity means loss of soul, in the sense that meaning goes out of life; we lose the center.

Jung used his own vocabulary interchangeably with traditional religious terms. He stressed, however, that he confined himself to the examination of what is empirically observable in the human psyche. Thus "God-images" are clusters of emotion-laden symbols that operate within the psyche as the unifying centers of psychic life. Inherent in any of these is the Self-archetype—the principle of "orientation and meaning." Jung stated that God is not the Self and cannot be reduced to the Self-archetype, but we can study the psychic effects of belief in God by means of such terms. Of his personal conviction about God's existence, he said emphatically, "I do not believe; I know." In this archetypal world, our personal religious symbols increasingly appear as clues to collective human experience, suggesting a personal coming to terms with human problems that contribute to collective value systems, ritualized worship, and all the other primary materials of religion.

RELIGIOUS EXPERIENCE

To come to terms with the impersonal world of the objective psyche, our egos must be strong enough to withstand the emotional impact of archetypal imagery. We must not get lost in our own private religious experience. We must also understand, according to Jung, how puny our own experience is in comparison with the range and depth of meaning contained in religious dogma. Thus we must connect our own insight with the accumulated religious experience of the human family. Jung himself organized his own experience of the numinous power of the unconscious into his theory of individuation. He saw parallels between the concept of individuation and seventeen centuries of alchemical studies. Through a complicated series of chemical and psychological operations, the alchemists sought to turn lead into gold. By taking the basic *materia prima* and subjecting it to various transforming procedures, alchemists projected into their physical material the stages of psychological transformation. In contrast to the descending direction of Christian revelation, which proceeds from the divine down to the human, Jung saw in the upward direction of both ancient alchemical procedures and modern psychological rites of transformation attempts to build up from the human, whether releasing the spirit contained in matter or in the human unconscious. Both represent efforts to construct an indivisible wholeness, whether of metal or of the human personality. Jung did not offer the psychological process as a substitute for the revelations of grace, but said that we have lost the means to receive grace. We need to ready ourselves for its reception by moving toward it from our human side as it moves toward us from its own otherness.

Jung talked about living the Christian myth fully and participating in the ongoing process of the incarnation of the divine in the human. As his own particular contribution, Jung offers individuation, a lifelong process involving the differentiating of the ego from the unconscious Self-archetype and the crafting of a conscious relation of ego to Self. It is precisely here that Jung collides with Christian theology. Jung observed that at certain points traditional Christian symbols seem to leave out central and unavoidable elements of human experience. The two upon which Jung concentrated, the feminine and evil, emerge vigorously out of the life of the instincts. In the symbolism of the dogma of the Trinity, for example, Jung noted the absence of a feminine element in the Godhead. To deal with this, he formulates a feminine principle called *Eros*. This is the principle of relatedness, the human tendency pronounced in the consciousness of women and usually present more unconsciously in men—to go down into the intensity of experience and to participate in it directly. The opposite masculine principle of *Logos* describes the tendency to stand aside from experience and abstract from it salient points which then can be generalized into universal truths to be applied to experience, which is a way of imposing ego purposes on the flow of life. This masculine principle is overemphasized in Western

culture, which stresses the rational ego-consciousness to the neglect of a more feminine style of ego-consciousness.

EROS

The neglect of the feminine principle, Eros, has clear negative
results for the religious life, the principal one being discrimination against women, both as themselves and as agents of the
unconscious side of life. In the Eros principle, more than an
organic relation to the unconscious is proclaimed. It carries with
it an injunction to include in our awareness the entire human
experience, such as aggression, conflict, sexuality, failure, or
evil, toward a search for greater truth in human relationships.
Christian myths could aid in the psychological and cultural
transformation that an attention to the feminine principle must
bring. Jung heralds the promulgation of the dogma of the
Assumption of Mary as a significant step, because it symbolizes
the acceptance of the feminine and the mortal, human element
in the Godhead.

EVIL

Jung saw his patients struggling to bring themselves to accept,
without bitterness or elation, impulses, drives, and wishes in
themselves that appeared to be "evil." Christian tradition, Jung
believed, put up unnecessary obstacles to this process of integration of the split-off sides of the psyche that either conflicted with
personal values or with collective moral standards or presented
themselves as clearly destructive urges. Christianity, Jung said,
seems to leave no place for the dark side of the human person.
Even the doctrine of evil as the privation of good failed to recognize the actual existence of evil as a force to be contended with.
The figure of Christ, for Jung the most visible and complete symbol of the human self, fails to include the dark side of experience
and splits off into the figures of the Devil or the Antichrist.
According to Jung, God depends on humanity to live the Christian myth further and to carry it beyond its limitations into a
greater psychic reality. Humans possess consciousness that can

wrestle with evil and strive to integrate it into larger wholes, thus rendering the negative side less destructive. God has a negative side. In the process of individuation, the person wrestles with the conflicts of good and evil, thus continuing the process of incarnation begun by Jesus, slowly bringing into acceptable human form the rampant energies of the unconscious.

Notes

This chapter was originally published in 1978 in *The International Encyclopedia of Psychiatry, Psychology, Psychoanalysis and Neurology*, IX, ed. B. B. Wolman (New York: Human Sciences Press, 1977), 429–32. References follow.

C. G. Jung. "The Development of Personality." *Collected Works* 17. Trans. R. F. C. Hull (New York: Pantheon, 1934/1954), pars. 284–323.

C. G. Jung. *Psychology and Religion: West and East, Collected Works* 12. Trans. R. F. C. Hull (New York: Pantheon, 1958).

C. G. Jung. *Psychology and Alchemy, Collected Works* 12. Trans. R. F. C. Hull (New York: Pantheon, 1953).

Chapter 2

Jung and Prayer

The interrelationship of religion and the psyche, particularly in prayer, is complex and primordial in its roots. Prayer touches us all so deeply and intimately that it is harder to talk about than our sexual life or our bank balance. This is our experience of prayer when we wake in the night full of anxiety—the wolf hour; it is what spills out of us in gratitude in moments of joy. Prayer expresses what we fear, and often reduces us to utter silence, held in awe by its ministrations. It is with us when we die, or even begin to approach death, in the images we have of bridges to the other side.

It is this set of religious and psychological connections that is at the center of Jung's special work with the psyche: He is concerned with the numinous, not in the abstract, but in all its concretions, wherever it touches us intimately. The abstract God "beyond all human experience leaves me cold," says Jung. "We do not affect each other. But if I know that he is a powerful impulse of my soul, at once I must concern myself with him...."[1]

No, nothing general, abstract, or distant here—Jung brings the issue right home to us where we live. He wants to know more and more about what his and our immediate experiences of God amount to. There is no substitute for this understanding, this experience, this knowledge. Our community, our environment, our society cannot give it to us.[2] In this reading, dogma and our shared religious traditions are at their best a collective dreaming of such experiences of spiritual immediacy as prayer. Like a great river, dogma runs beneath our societies, watering and nourishing them. Hans Urs von Balthasaar says something similar about contemplatives: "Contemplatives are like great rivers which, on occasion, break out into springs at unexpected points, or reveal their presence only by the plants they feed from

16

below."³ Despite our "fear of primordial experience," Jung says, "I consider it my task and duty to educate my patients and pupils to the point where they can accept the direct demand that is made upon them from within." From his study of early Christian writings, Jung continues, "I have gained a deep and indelible impression of how dreadfully serious an experience of God is. It will be no different today."⁴

What is no different today is the placing of ourselves in prayer under the authority of the transcendent. In a curious way, the theologian Karl Barth and the psychiatrist Jung are brothers here. Barth starts his theology from God's side, so to speak, saying we cannot even know who we are without first looking to God. Only by seeing God's judgment and mercy do we realize we are sinners, for really we see our sins only when they are forgiven by God in Christ. Jung uses a different language, but the movement of soul is the same. Jung places the ego under the authority of the Self. Only looking there, in the Self's demands, do we find all the ego-life we are to live here: "If that voice is listened to, one will have a chance of a more complete life, because one lives then almost as if one were two people, not one alone, and there will be a whole sphere of knowledge and experience in which all functions, all ideas, will enter besides our ordinary consciousness."⁵

We discover that trying to become ourselves, consciously to enter the process of individuation, means to be on the receiving end of a conversation with an Other who addresses us. In and through the various psychic complexes that address us from within—shadow, anima, or animus—this greater center of the whole psyche that Jung calls the Self puts us into relationship with itself. We may find, further, that in conversation with the Self we enter a discourse that transcends the Self. We thought we were one person only to discover that we are two—conscious and unconscious, ego and Self, Jung's famous Number 1 and Number 2 personalities—only to discover further the stunning fact that what we thought was a two-way conversation is in fact a three-way discourse. The conversation going on all the time is between ego, Self, and that which the Self knows about, God.

Jung speaks out of the concrete facts of his own experience. His kind of empiricism is fundamental in any discussion of prayer. See how *in fact* life is affecting us. Admit it, wherever it is, and pay close attention to it and everything in and around it; this is the only useful approach. Jung wants to understand in the most concrete terms the depths of our experience of the primordial and to identify the reality of what is touching us there. Thus Jung puts himself in the place of the ordinary receiver. He can be himself touching about prayer, because he himself is touched and honest and aware of his limits. He begins, and always counsels us to begin, in the midst of life, in immediate experience.[6]

Prayer is to religious life what dreaming is to psychic life: experience at the source, in its narrowness and breadth, its daily fare, its interior space. It reveals that what lives most privately, hidden inside us, opens us far outside ourselves to shared living with others and with life itself. What Jung says about dreams could as well be said about prayer: "In the deepest sense we all dream not *out of ourselves* but out of what lies *between us and the other.*"[7] When we pray we speak not only out of our truest self but also into and from a space we are surprised to discover is inhabited by an unmistakable Other, clearly there before us. In the language of Judeo-Christian tradition, it is the Holy Spirit moving in us that moves us to pray in the first place. What we thought was all in us is also the Other and many others like us, too, who are similarly moved to bow their heads and bend their knees.

RELIGIOUS INSTINCT

Jung stands out from other depth psychologists in his positing the existence of a religious instinct. Operating in us, independent of our will, this instinct is a capacity for and urge toward conscious relationship to transpersonal deity.[8] We can fall just as ill from disorder in our relationship to this instinct as we can to any other. Repression of sexuality leads to all sorts of outbreaks of complicated symptoms. The splitting off of our aggression leads to schizoid disorder and variations of a passive-aggressive character. Efforts to control our hunger instinct land us in eating disorders of all kinds. So too with the religious instinct: when frustrated or thwarted it has its own unmistakable pathology.

I have seen the disease of alcoholism contain a massive psychosomatic defense against facing the inner emptiness that stands behind the disease. One man poured all his energy into persona performance to flee from an engulfing sense of lack to which he simply refused admittance. He knew meaning existed, but he could not house it in his own living. He needed more and more drink to keep his persona—the mask he showed to the world—intact and adequate to present his usually high level of performance. Meanwhile behind the mask, when he faced inward to his own private and unconscious life, it was as if another part of him that felt both like and unlike himself, and turned up in dreams and fantasy as a hated woman (his anima), was raising more and more hell. Sometimes he dreamt of various women who were standing up in public to expose his drinking. Other times he dreamt of a female wanting to trap him into life-long dreary servitude. Another dream theme presented women in various stages of illness, hysteria, or maudlin moping. He put it poignantly: "Drink is my fuel to perform and my reward when alone, but it does not allow me to do two necessary things—to pray and to do this analytical work." He might have added, "Dangerous analytical work." The analysis was dangerous. When we worked successfully, we inevitably came to the mangled and dreaded woman-part that enraged the man. His psyche would use me in the transference to carry it. He would say, "I love you as an analyst but I don't want you to be a woman. Whenever I think of you as a woman I want to slap you!" When we reached this pivotal point, this point of breakthrough, where we could look at and talk with this anima, the drinking defense overcame him and interrupted therapy, sometimes for as long as three months. All the work seemed to wash away in alcohol.

We can repress the religious instinct, and the power of the primordial can fall into drink and make it an idol that enslaves us in addiction. It can get identified with other things, too, and then we find our usual idolatries—money, work, food, drugs, family, love relationship. Or we can fall into identification with this power of the primordial and see ourselves as gurus, wise beyond telling, inflated beyond our small human size. We can always spot an idol because it apes the ways of God. Everything in us revolves around, say, food, or an inferiority complex, or identity crisis. We think of it all the time, in every situation, devote enormous amounts of energy to it. We are distracted from listening to others because of our thinking and fantasizing all the time about what we can eat and when, or how the other sees us and why. Inside our compulsion hides the religious instinct, bending us to masochistic enslavement, which is the shadow side of veneration.[9]

We can also dodge the religious instinct by substituting our map of it for the territory it describes. Then we use our theories as convenient places in which to hide; Jung's map of the numinous, for example, becomes our pseudo-religion. Reveling in it, we avoid our own immediate experience of the religious territory, living at a great remove from our creative center. Our unreceived primordial power puffs up our interest in Jung; we become fanatical—and boring!

We can also put another person in place of our religious instinct. A woman whose love and money were entangled with a man who had been central in her life for three decades thought it was essential to separate her life from his, but found this extraordinarily difficult to do. She lost hundreds of thousands of dollars because she could not move quickly or decisively enough to make the break. She felt both homicidal and suicidal. Disentangling her connection to him involved identifying and separating many strands—giving up her idealization of him, ending her long practice of denying the bad in him and between them, withdrawing from all the demands and displacements and projections to claim in herself the power she had put onto him. The crucial piece was her projection of the religious instinct so fully onto him that she then identified him as the authority in her life. What made her feel conscious of her capacity for relating to a center that gave her hope and a sense of living creatively and unified within herself was all caught up with him. God came in a wrapper made up of this man's parts. Her belief was not clearly expressed, but was deeply felt. She hated official religions and traditional religious process and saw them as coercive and controlling. The values she held, she had discovered with this man when younger, and those too she identified with him. She believed in humanness and humaneness, in the rock-bottom goodness of people, in their simple acts of kindness and respect. As she struggled to express all of this, I asked her about what had surfaced: "You believe in this, don't you? This is your value, isn't it?" She saw for a moment how she had wrapped her sense of value around this man like a coat that now would not come off. She saw then why she had felt that if she separated from him, she would be separating herself from all she had ever believed made life worthwhile. She saw she could not leave him, because that meant living away from the primordial. To see that this sense of value was like indispensable protective clothing (like a good rain-coat), but was not the man himself and was not carried only by him but was really *her own* coat of values, became a little epiphany for her. It was an immensely moving moment for both of us, a little bit of numinous fire suddenly flaming up in the office on an otherwise average Wednesday morning.

Jung writes early on that the soul "is a function of relation between the subject and the inaccessible depths of the unconscious. The determining force (God) operating from these depths is reflected by the soul, that is, it creates symbols and images." The soul is then "both receiver and transmitter," perceives unconscious contents and conveys them to consciousness by means of these symbols.[10] The soul lives, as it were, midway between the ego and the primordial unconscious, which expresses itself through the archetypal images that the soul receives, creates and transmits. Jung continues, "When God is in the soul, i.e. when the soul becomes a vessel for the unconscious and makes itself an image or symbol for it, this is truly a happy state...[which] is a *creative* state...."[11] The soul gives birth to images—like the wrapper, like the overcoat which really is removable from the man and must be acknowledged and donned by the woman herself—but we can lose these images in licentious behavior, aesthetic indulgence, quasi-religious enthusiasm, and addictive compulsion where we project them into various substances where they soon lose their identity and disappear. To realize these images consciously and relate to them is to be free to adapt to reality and promote our happiness and well-being.

Depth psychologists other than Jung aim toward this same understanding. It is interesting to see how this one-hundred-year-old discipline, as it advances toward the end of our century and millennium, increasingly takes up religious questions, even if only implicitly. For example, in our therapeutic theorizing, we reach farther and farther back in a child's life for the origin of being, for signs of the existence of any self at all. We seek that intrasubjective space where we feel alive, real, in a creative living of life that sustains hope and joy and makes for some sense of meaning even in the most wretched of circumstances. This is the space Winnicott calls "transitional," from which our symbols spring;[12] the space that Freud finds between the free-associating ego and the observing ego that allows us freedom from instinct at the same time that we channel it into life projects.[13] In this space Kohut locates the cohesive self, so elusive of definition but also central to living.[14] Bion talks about this space as the ultimate O, the truth of the moment;[15] Klein finds in it the mysterious triggering of our reparative efforts to make things better and to express gratitude.[16] Such moments spring from facing the ambiguous mixture in us and in those we love of good and bad, love and hate. Christopher Bollas writes of an evocative space where we receive news from within, and Masud Khan of our lying fallow and finding the self from which to live.[17]

All workers in analysis aim for this space, but Jung speaks of it explicitly as the space of our religious instinct—a force archaic and immediate, insistent and commanding. We may turn away from the instinct, put it to wrong use, deflect it, or fall into identification with it, but we cannot escape it. Jung brings the primordial right into the consulting room this way, and asks of every symptom or depression, or even trauma: What is the Self engineering? What is being made manifest here to which we must pay close attention?

For example, the woman who could not free herself or her money from the man she used to love discovered a radically different way to look at her entrapment. She still saw her unsuccessful struggle over several decades to liberate herself in terms of her accusations against herself—as a product of illness, of fragmentation, of excessive projection of power onto him, of her tendency to be cowardly and too easily bullied. But now she also saw that she had equated leaving him with abandoning what she believed in, with perjuring the good as she knew it.[18] She saw now that her not getting free from this man did not just manifest her sickness but also her faithfulness to the good where it had found her. Her addictive attachment to him did indeed reflect her woundedness—the result of never knowing a container, of having a mother who had been afflicted with psychotic episodes and a stepfather who had tyrannized and molested her. It was not easy to give up the home base she had established with this man. But this relationship also contained serious and ugly abuses of many different kinds, all mixed in with the goodness she and he had created together, and the goodness in which she believed and which she had identified with him as if it had originated there.

The epiphany of the image of the wrapper—of the coat draped on this man—was no less for her than a discovery that God is portable. The good was not grafted onto this man, but removable. She could see it itself between them, between her and other people, on its own, existing in its own right. Like Yahweh's priests who carry the Ark and know it is not identified with just one particular place, or like Yahweh's words of self-revelation—I am who is, I am who is with you—she now saw her responsibility and devotion was to goodness, not to the man upon whom she had grafted it. It lived. For her, this was where Being was and is.

Such seeing redeems suffering as it did in this case, not by denying the woman's fragmentation or woundedness, but by revealing that hiding in her illness was also a persistence to stay close to goodness, to the transcendent, and not desert or abandon it. This may sound like a mere shift of accent, or even a verbal sleight of hand. But not to the person involved: to him or to her it makes all the difference in the world, for here, found for us, is the deeper meaning of suffering that makes it bearable and forgivable. Redeemed, the woman's suffering opened a future to her.

Jung, it is clear from these examples, works to reconnect religion to its archaic instinctive roots, from which the symbols of theology and ritual spring. When we reach and link ourselves to the primordial religious impulse deep within us, we fashion a formidable hermeneutic for ourselves. We can now interpret religious doctrines, symbols, and rituals in terms of their analogies in our own psychological experiences and those of the collective human psyche. Religion ceases to be merely an intellectual activity or a systematic exploration of abstract principles of being. Instead, it reaches right into our hearts, our souls, our bowels. It helps uncover the meaning hiding in our experiences. This hermeneutic does not replace such interpretive methods as literary criticism, historical criticism, or sociological analysis, but rather adds to them the psychological. We ask, for example, about the psychological equivalent of the visions of Ezekiel, or of the parable of the sheep and goats.[19]

To address the psychological meaning of symbols, both for ourselves and in the history of symbology, does not equate the psyche or any of its parts, and especially not the unconscious, with the deity. The unconscious is not God, but it is another medium through which God speaks to us.[20] God addresses us through images that arise from the deep unconscious just as much as God addresses us through national events, historical moments, other people, a sermon, another's pain or generosity, and especially through the witness of scripture and the believing community. Jung reminds us with great force of God's freedom. He also reminds us that we tend to ignore the human psyche as another central way through which God touches us—in dreams, visions, symbols, even in symptom and complex. It behooves us to keep all this in mind when working with the unconscious. We have in hand an empirical method for studying living religion.[21]

PRAYER

Prayer opens a psychological and religious reality to us. We must look at the ways prayer functions in the psyche, whether for illness or health, and we must look at whether or not prayer points to real transcendence. Jung devotes most of his attention to prayer as it functions psychologically. He says, for example, that the God-image is an archetypal idea which is everywhere, which "I observe but I do not invent."[22] God is a "psychic fact of immediate experience....God has general validity in as much as almost everyone knows approximately what is meant by the term 'experience of God.'"[23]

Our image of God is thrown up spontaneously from the unconscious like "a being that exists in its own right and therefore confronts its ostensible creator autonomously."[24] We have a dialectical relationship with this figure. In naive moments we experience it as existing in and for itself and feel that we did not fashion it; it fashioned itself in us. We cannot really decide "whether the God-image is created or whether it creates itself."[25] In religious language, this paradox is to be found in the creed, where in referring to Jesus, the God-image that God gives us, he is defined as "begotten not made...." We put this dialectical and paradoxical relationship to practical use when we pray.

We call upon the "divine presence in all difficult or danger-ous situations, for the purpose of loading all...[our] unbearable difficulties upon the Almighty and expecting help....In the psy-chological sense this means that complexes weighing on the soul are *consciously* transferred to the God-image."[26] Such praying ben-efits us because we then can carry our complexes consciously. Repression enacts an inversion of this prayer, a sort of dumping into the unconscious all that we want to forget about. Here, instead, in prayer, we carry what belongs to us, and are able to do so because we are not all alone.

Jung goes further. Not only does he recognize that any dis-cipline undertaken for religious reasons aids us in remaining conscious of our difficulties, but also enables us to confess our sins; for it "effectively prevents...[us] from becoming uncon-scious."[27] Confession brings us into a new community, because it is an enlarging enterprise, undertaken "for the sake of collectiv-ity, for a social purpose....Through sin and secrecy one is excluded and when one confesses one is included again." This builds up a new society: "The idea of confession being a collec-tive duty is an attempt on the part of the unconscious to create the basis of a new collectivity."[28]

By such a fullness of confession as we find in prayer, where we prevent "a known suffering from turning into an unknown one," we join with others, both in keeping the conflicts of oppo-sites within us conscious and in recognizing a superior power that lightens our burdens because we surrender them "to God to whom all solutions are known."[29] It is crucial to note that all this enlarging and joining and recognizing occurs where we are most wounded and divided in our nature, just where we are "weakest and lowest; there intercession takes place."[30] Could this be the sta-ble in us where Christ gets born? Where the soul comes alive? Where we need and desire the most and wish most strongly, because we are so poor in our own resources? There God arrives.

One man, for example, long practiced in the skills of analy-sis, nonetheless felt powerless in the grip of a compulsion. He put its power in psychological terms: the ego is not in control of everything in life; therefore my compulsion is a defeat for my ego. He knew that with certainty, he felt. But in the middle of the night he woke and could not return to sleep. Thinking on these things, he said, "For the first time in years I earnestly got down on my knees to pray to the Self or to God for help. This I experienced as an act of humility and admission that something besides my ego was running the show. Maybe my compulsion is *its* way of letting me know of *its* presence and my tendency to think my ego can run my life." Yielding to the impulse to get at the primordial root of his compulsion gave this man a glimpse of what purpose the compulsion might be hiding.[31] This is risky business. As Jung puts it:

> Surrender to God is a formidable adventure....He who can risk himself wholly to it finds himself directly in the hands of God, and is there confronted with a situation which makes 'simple faith' a vital necessity;...the situation is so full of risk...that the deepest instincts are aroused. An experience of this kind is always numinous, for it unites all aspects of totality....Christian faith insists on the deadly danger of the adventure....[32]

We begin a conversation, or continue one in the open, when we pray. From a psychological point of view, we concentrate libido on the God-image. By emptying our conscious mind and transferring its energy and expectation to this primordial image, we allow it to activate, to change us. Jung describes it thus: "The libido...is immersed in introversion and is allegorized as God's kingdom. This amounts to...living in his kingdom, in that state where a preponderance of libido lies in the unconscious and determines conscious life."[33] What happens as a result is that we know a precious "childlikeness" where we feel "borne along by the current of life, where what was dammed up can flow off without restraint....'Things go of themselves....'" This is "that unique inner condition on which blissfulness depends....[It] means to possess a treasury of accumulated libido which can constantly stream forth."[34]

When we pray, we give over and we invoke. We surrender our ego control and enter into conversation with a power greater than ourselves that nonetheless inhabits us and strongly influences our lives. We grow more conscious and less repressed; our energy flows unblocked, and we confess—that is, become aware of—our weakest places where our fabric has worn the thinnest and our wounds still bleed. There God meets us, binds up our wounds and unites us with others in new community. In psychological terms, we describe all this as our giving over to the primordial, opening to the power of archetypal images that come from the deep unconscious, and seeing through them to the transcendent they point to.

To do this opening and seeing, Jung says we need the "concrete reality of religious figures," for they assist in "the canalisation of libido into the equivalent symbols provided that the worship of them does not get stuck in the outward object."[35] Here we see Jung looking at prayer from a religious point of view: "It is not a matter of indifference whether one calls something a 'mania' or a 'god.'...When the god is not acknowledged, ego mania develops and out of this mania comes sickness."[36] We cannot pray to a concept or a psychological term. We pray to a Subject, an "I" for whom we are the "thou." We pray from our weakest places, for there we stay most open and accessible. But we can only show our weakest place to One who knows us and holds us in that knowing. Jung writes:

> Only on the basis of such an attitude which tries with charity and forebearance to accept even the humblest things in one's own nature, will a higher level of consciousness and culture become possible. This attitude is religious in the truest sense and therefore therapeutic, for all religions are therapies for the sorrows and disorders of the soul.[37]

JUNG'S PRAYERS

Scattered through his letters and autobiography, we find Jung's own prayers. They give us a sense of his relationship to God and the questions in him that reached down to his weakest places. He writes, "I thank God everyday that I have been permitted to experience the reality of the *imago dei* in me. Had that not been so, I would have been a bitter enemy of Christianity and of the Church....Thanks to this *actus gratiae* my life has meaning, and my inner eye was opened to the beauty and grandeur of dogma."[38]

Prayer is getting down to basics. We stop before the fact that Being is. We experience the primordial as fact. Jung found prayer necessary "because it makes the Beyond we conjecture and think about an immediate reality...." We enter a dialogue, a "duality of the ego and the dark Other." This changes us; we cannot doubt the reality of the "That" whom we address. But, says Jung, "The question then arises: What will become of Thee and of Me? Of the transcendental Thou and the immanent I?"[39]

This relationship between the Thee and the me preoccupied Jung from his earliest years to the end of his days. He knew from his early experience of grace after his intense fantasy about the destruction of the Basel Cathedral, "that one's duty was to explore daily the will of God."[40] But, like most of us, Jung did not do this. Everyday concerns, duties, problems—all that makes up the life of what he called our "Personality Number 1," the ordinary self—took up too much time. Nevertheless, Jung asked of these experiences: Who makes me do this? Who makes me think these thoughts? Who poses this problem to me? And he responded, "I knew I had to find the answer out of my deepest self, that I was alone before God, and God alone had asked me these terrible things."[41]

Out of that deep aloneness Jung discovered that "the Divine Presence is more than anything else....This is the only thing that really matters....I wanted the proof of a living Spirit and I got it. Don't ask me at what price."[42] For what confronted Jung in that space between the transcendent Thou and the immanent I was the "beatific vision," and with it a God who sometimes "kicks us, as with Jacob, and you punch back," a God who might, as with Job, slay our firstborn, cause all our cattle to die and dump us in heap of suffering among the potsherds.[43] This other side of the deity Jung called "the dark side" of God. He meant it concretely, giving voice that way to a great many of the questions of others: Why does our child die in such pain from disease? Why does a hurricane wipe out everything families have worked for all their lives? Why do some of us know endless, repeated suffering and very little joy? What could this mean, this dreadful catastrophe falling on us? Why do the innocent suffer? How can God be good and loving when there is so much hurt and hate in the world?

What Jung calls "the dark side" of God refers to the hard, painful experiences that break apart the frames of our lives so that we cannot hold together anymore. It might be war, the loss of our ideology, or its exposure as bogus after we have given our whole life to uphold it. It might be the destructive impact of climate and environment, so that for all our days we live with dust in our mouths and noses, unable to survive decently and yet unable to leave where we are. It might be the brutal impact of another's psychic disturbance that maims us before we have achieved secure connection to our body and a sense of self. These experiences engulf a child born into prison or crack addiction, a citizen left to starve in a barren land, the Holocaust victim left to die alone a horrible death. These examples, alas, are countless; the questions, persistent: How? Why? What can this mean?

I would suggest that the dark side of God experiences are those that fall outside the light of our God-images, that exceed the grasp of our understanding, that confound our images of God. If we pray and keep on praying, this kind of experience always comes. The more converse with God grows, changes, the closer we come upon the God who surpasses all images of God. The Holy refuses to stay put in a box. Inevitably we will be led to experiences of God that are bigger than our pictures of the divine.[44] Such events come out from the shadows, beyond the light of our God-images. They break in, steal into us like a thief in the night, and they fall upon us. These meetings with God well beyond our images of God comprise great religious moments that can smash us, or open us further to the transcendent, or both. Mystics write of these moments. In Jung's terms, these are the moments that comprise the mysterious exchange between ego and Self. If we really want God as God is, then a God who is so much bigger than any of our concepts or imaginings about God will cast everything in the darkness the nearer God comes.

MYSTERY

To be brought to glimpse something of this God, so different from our pictures of God, leaves us breathless with surprise, fear, awe, gratitude. Jung knows such encounters: "The deity is always preceded by terror, fear, or a feeling of divine presence, a special atmosphere...."[45] Archaic emotion grasps Jung, leaving him ambivalent about the exact nature of the divine presence. We always must keep a sharp eye on God, pay close attention and observe who this is: "There is no prejudice, there is supreme submission. God can appear in any form he chooses...to prescribe to that phenomenon which it ought to be, and not accept what it is, is not submission."[46] Or, to put it more boldly: "The real Christ is the God of freedom."[47]

In our littleness, we feel this freedom as dread. Prayer becomes a risky business. The problem is not that we receive no answer, but that we might get what we prayed for. Worse, we may pray for the wrong thing, instead of trusting God to give what matches the real need deep in our soul or in our world. For Jung, such trust brings its own ambivalence: "Can we address...the good God to the exclusion of the demon....Can we really put on one side the God who is dangerous to us?...Can we ignore the *absconditus?*"[48]

Jung calls us back time and again to our immediate experiences of God. He focuses not on refined formulations, but upon the instinctive gut encounters, primordial ones, mixed with dread as well as thankfulness, bad as well as good. We need to dig down to the primitive in us to reach a new experience of God, he counsels.[49] There we find not just a God whom we must punch and kick back, but one of unspeakable bliss. Our fear is matched by trust: "In his trial of courage God refuses to abide by traditions, no matter how sacred. In his omnipotence he will see to it that nothing really evil comes of such tests of courage. If one fulfills the will of God one can be sure of going the right way."[50]

These opposites, contained in God's radical freedom, and our utter submission connect and come alive in our experience of the mysterious exchanges between ego and Self. On the one hand, Jung speaks of the radical transcendence of God. He says, "I know that my way has been prescribed to me by a hand far above my reach."[51] Or, "I do not for a moment deny that the deep emotion of a true prayer may reach transcendence, but it is above our heads...."[52] Or, "there is only one divine spirit—an immediate presence, often terrifying and in no degree subject to our choice."[53] On the other hand, Jung recognizes that God comes toward us, addresses us, speaks to us in the intimacy of our own psyche. He says, "God has never spoken to man except in and through the psyche, and the psyche understands it and we experience it as something psychic."[54] The unutterably large enters the life of the infinitesimally small. The radically Other addresses us through the images of our own particular psyche, through coinciding events that strike us as full of meaning, as a telling synchronicity that opens a window for us onto an eternal wholeness of being—the *unus mundus*.[55]

From Jung's remarks, we might sketch a structure undergirding the conversation of ego and Self in us. We can think of this structure as the grammar of our conversation, moving from the ground of our being upward to consciousness. At the deepest level, at our core, dwells the radically free God, unfathomable and ever-present. At the next level, the archetypes exist as contents of the collective unconscious; Jung calls them "God's tools."[56] Above the archetypes, so to speak, the soul exists as the function of relation between our conscious ego and the inaccessible depths of the unconscious.[57] Our souls reflect up to consciousness the images of the archetypes and bring to bear down into us the effects of consciousness on those images. The result is the construction of symbols. The soul is thus like a two-way mirror, reflecting unconscious to ego and ego to unconscious. Always, we must remember, above the soul exists the ego, the center of our consciousness.

The energy of the ego-Self conversation constantly circulates between the great unfathomable depths of God acting in us and on us through the instrumentation of the archetypes. Our soul registers all of this action and spontaneously creates symbols that express "something that is little known or completely unknown."[58] A symbol of this kind does not arise in the form of allegory or sign, but as an "image that describes in the best possible way the dimly discerned nature of the spirit. A symbol does not define or explain; it points beyond itself to a meaning that is darkly divined yet still beyond our grasp, and cannot be adequately expressed in the familiar words of our language."[59] Such symbols are "inexhaustible" because they are not "objects of the mind, but categories of the imagination which we can formulate in ten thousand different ways....They are *before* the mind, the basis of everything mental."[60] Jung cites prayer as one such symbolic action and cites a dramatic example from the Elgonyi tribe of Africa. Its members offered "the livingness from the inside of their bodies, held in their hands and presented to the rising sun. To us it would mean 'I offer my soul to thee, O God.'"[61]

Our souls' reception of the archetypes is one way God speaks to us and a way in which we "know" being. We know archetypes in the concrete experiences of our life, not in the abstract. Our soul creates symbols which themselves express both archetypal influence and the life we live with our neighbors in our time in history, in our particular cultures. The symbols act as "transformers," converting libido from a "lower" to a "higher" form.[62] In analysis or the disciplines of religion we try to understand these symbols and thus to absorb and respond to "the unconscious, compensatory striving for an attitude that reflects the totality of the psyche."[63]

Religious experience has its own momentum, as if looming out of us, demanding both our awareness and its own communication. It "strives for expression," Jung says, and "can be expressed only 'symbolically' because it transcends understanding. It *must* be expressed one way or another, for therein is revealed its immanent vital force. It wants to step over...into visible life, to take concrete shape."[64]

We can see, then, how dangerous it is to pray. For in prayer we stir up the archetypal background through which God touches us, and symbols spontaneously appear that will press us to realize them in action in the world. When contents cross over from unconscious to conscious realms, they impose ethical obligations on us to respond, to realize them, to make them concrete. Otherwise we must lose them, or permit them to let loose something in us too big to contain. It may be even more dangerous not to pray!

THE MASS

Where does this leave us? In Jungian language, we are plunged into the mysterious exchange that occurs between ego and Self. In prayer, our ego and the Self enter into conversation, a mutual exchange that is ultimately mysterious, as anything must be that exists in the realm of primordial and archetypal being, as Jung makes clear in his examination of the Eucharist, the central sacrament in Christianity.

Before coming to the communion table, we collect ourselves in the prayer of confession. Here our ego recognizes all the things it puts in place of God. Confession means admitting into consciousness those things at the center of our being that we have chosen to revolve around in place of God. These may be our problems or our strengths, our faults, our needs, our worst acts, or our best values. Thus it was with the man who wrestled with his drinking: it became the center of his thoughts. When he could, he drank; sometimes he avoided giving into its temptation; at other moments, he felt remorse at having once again succumbed. In each instance the fixation acted in him like a little god, an idol, around which his whole life turned.

In confession we become conscious of just what idols we live in thrall to—getting a job, for example, or trying to understand our neurosis, or working for a better environment, or a political cause, or a determined devotion to our child's welfare. In each case we can identify something that acts as a center for us in place of God; with others we come to recognize that we all do this, all put the best of human values, the most vexing of human problems, everything that besets or gratifies us, in place of the God we are commanded to love first. Thus it is in common that we make our confession.

We collect into consciousness, both in shared and individual confession, what we have identified as our God in place of the true God. Our ego grows bigger this way as it becomes more conscious: in such awareness we gain ourselves. We see where our ego lives and in what it consists, with what or with whom we identify, where we invest our passion. Confession returns a fuller sense of ourselves to us, tells us much more what we are, and who, and what matters to us. It gives us back to ourselves, enlarged in psyche and spirit. We have collected ourselves into one place, so to speak. Our awareness has been made full of just where it is that life blazes for us, where it feels negative, like problems, or compulsions, and where it feels positive, like affection or dedication to something, for someone well outside us, though the feeling is deeply within us.

Having thus possessed our ego, we can bring this as offering and sacrifice to the table of the Eucharist, in the shared human symbols, says Jung, of the bread and wine.[65] The wine represents the best of human spirit, its capacity to soar and create. The bread represents the human body with all its hunger and labor to satisfy its need. Through the bringing of the bread and wine, we offer our ego up to God. We give up and give over what we hold most dear, what we dread most deeply. We sacrifice our identification with whatever we have put in place of God. Because we feel identified with it, we know now that *we* are this problem, this love, this need, this cause. So we feel that we are sacrificing our very selves. This enlarged sense of self that confession returns to us comprises our offering to God. This can be understood as the "broken and contrite heart" that Yahweh asks of Israel—not a burnt offering, but a living, loving spirit that comes home again, to first things put first.

To offer up what we identify with feels as if we are losing it. This is not a kind of magic, says Jung, in which we wheedle with God, secretly believing that what we offer will be returned to us a hundredfold. Such manipulation, such bargaining, we renounce. The mass revolves around sacrifice and open exchange. It is a great wrenching of our being to uncover what we have centered upon and bring it to the real center, the great and true center. It feels like a casting into fire, where we must be burnt up forever with what we most prize, or what has most ruled us.

Why should we bother? Who in their right mind would want to sacrifice their highest hopes and best ideals? What moves us to such acts? The answer is the Self; it is what moves us here. At the same time we possess our egos more fully as we become conscious of all the ego identifications, both good and bad, with things of this world. We feel moved to surrender all our ego concerns to the greater center. We feel relativized. What once we experienced as the center of ourselves—this ego at the center of consciousness—we now experience as being moved by the bigger center. We know ourselves now as object of a greater subject. Out of this inner experience, we surrender all our ego claims. Something mysterious compels us to do so: "The ego must make itself conscious of its claim and the Self must cause the ego to renounce it."[66]

If we just went through the motions of the ritual of confession and its accompanying offering, without feeling any inner compulsion, all we are doing is simply obeying a collective moral code. The Self appears to us, then, identified with the collective superego, that is, with the mores and customs of our religious culture. We want to live in full accord with what our group considers good behavior; we fear the consequences of not doing so. But feeling this new inner compulsion means we have become conscious of the Self that addresses our ego, the Self that moves us to bring our gifts, our sacrifices, and our ego identifications to the altar as symbolized in the bread and wine.[67] We experience the Self moving us from within. It no longer exists in projected form, but now directly engages us. It calls us, as Abraham was called, to renounce our ego and to follow after it. Jung says we know it as a "Yea and Nay" operating within us, like a union of opposites: This "constitutes the most immediate experience of the Divine which is psychologically possible to imagine."[68] As a result, our human ego experiences nothing less than transformation. It moves into direct conversation with the Self and begins to live from there.

The Self matches our sacrifice with its own surrender, yielding its all-powerfulness and infiniteness as it fits into the small confines of space and time in the incarnation of Jesus Christ. The Self, as Jung sees it, calls on the ego to sacrifice its ego centeredness, acting like a father to a son. By making ourselves conscious of our unconscious identifications and then surrendering them to a greater center, we call the Self into being, in human terms. In this way, the ego becomes father to the Self as son. So, for Jung, God becoming man in Christ shows God's transformation. The mass, carried out by God, through the figure of the Christ, and returned through Jesus to God, manifests the Self to humankind, redeeming it from the narrow confines of egocentricity.

We must remember that in offering this psychological interpretation of the mass, Jung does not substitute his terms "ego" and "Self" for "human" and "divine." Instead he hopes to reconnect us to the mass by drawing analogies to our psychological experience.[69] It is useful here, I think, to repeat my own understanding of the Self, not as God within us, but as that which knows about God, through which we know God knows us. For Jung, the Christ manifests the most complete Self-figure; for the Christian, the Self-concept offers a good, an appropriate, symbol for the Christ.[70]

The incarnation of God shows us God's love for us. For God in Christ empties the infinite fullness of being—in the abasement of *kenosis*—to take on the struggles and darknesses of human life. In a sense, the dark side of God meets the dark side of the human, for as Jesus the Christ God takes on and suffers all our shadow bits, submits to all their lethal effects. The two sacrifices meet and converse in the mass. We become one in Christ, where he dwells in us and we in him. A momentous exchange occurs, the darkest mystery of all in the conversation of prayer.

What happens next in the Eucharist occurs to some extent in every prayer: We feel thanksgiving and joy. In Jung's terms, the Self, center of the whole psyche, meets the ego, center of consciousness, and a conversation ensues in the space between the big Subject, the Self, and the little subject, us. An intersubjective space forms. People who pray regularly know this space in themselves and somehow convey it to others. We can even hear a humming sound of their inner conversation if we pay close enough attention. Prayer puts us in an evocative state of mind whereby we receive bulletins from the Self, news from the large to the small self. This becomes a process whereby "new internal objects are created."[71] The core of unconscious psychic life seeks expression; it wants to unfold in relation to others. The process of attending to the core or source point of our being—that level of the unfathomable mystery of God at our center—yields images that feed the soul and prompt us to apposite action in the world. Jung says that the soul is happy when it makes itself a vessel for the unconscious and becomes an image or symbol for it: "The happy state is the creative state."[72] Jung quotes Blake, saying that we feel bliss, ecstasy, "energy as eternal delight."[73] This gives rise to a "feeling of intense vitality, a new potential." For God, "life at its most intense, resides in the soul."[74] Here we feel alive, real, and living creatively.[75] One woman dreamt this state in a short blunt image: "The Grail Cup sings!"

Attention to this sense of being at the core of our being leads us to recognize the uniqueness of what it is that resides in ourselves, and what its presence is in every one of us. Violence is what happens when we foreshorten this inner conversation, interrupting it, forbidding it, even acting to prevent it. We refuse being this way. Conversely, attending to the source and center given each of us feels like joy (Lacan's *jouissance*), wherein our true self can unfold in experience with others and with the world. Being is manifested beyond argument. This is what is meant by the glory of God, as Irenaeus put it so long ago: The glory of God consists of human beings truly alive!

Because we are finite, so must our Self be and the access we have to it. What Jung calls "the dark side" of God is what falls outside what our Self knows, or what we as ego have learned from Self. But still the Self persists, acting in us as link between the God we know and the "unimaginable transcendence" beyond, joining inner and outer God.[76] It connects our inner conversation and the God we must first meet outside ourselves so that we recognize and deal with this holy presence when we go back inside ourselves. The one we converse with, and who initiates conversation with us, arranges all this through the Self in our psyche. It is extraordinarily like a little radio set forced to meet frequencies beyond its capacity to receive. If we pay attention, its power will grow and our skills in tuning will match the growth. We will find our equipment better and better suited to pick up the waves of communication of the One addressing us.

We learn from this inner conversation that God does not want to blast into us, but simply wants to be received. The smallest accord with the movement coming toward us acts like the butterfly effect in chaos theory. Chaos theory says that a butterfly lifting its wing in Chicago changes the atmosphere as far away as China because that delicate individual motion affects everything, all of creation, in a sense. As Jung puts it, "I go together with it [God's will], an immensely weighty milligram without which God had made his world in vain."[77] We do not know that we matter unless we engage in such conversation.

In this engagement, a theological revolution occurs. Earlier, we had prayed to God for the things we wanted and needed, for relief from pain and suffering, for forgiveness, health, peace, justice, love. Now we concern ourselves with taking care of the God we have found within us. The old prayer of the alchemists, spoken by the lapis stone, sums it up: "Protect me, I will protect you."[78] Our need now is quite outside our own pain and suffering, our own urge to forgiveness, for health, for love. Now we want to make a little stable in which God can be born, a little hut in which God can live. In this reversal, conscious and unconscious come together in a feeling of oneness of being.[79] Although this approach to wholeness means a great awareness of bearing our own weight, our own cross, we feel held in greater unity than ever before, both within ourselves and with the whole world. Augustine's commentary on the Gospel of John 26:10 sums it up: "He that believes in me goes into me; He that goes into me, has me."[80]

Notes

This chapter was originally given as a talk to the Analytical Psychology Club of New York City in April 1992, and then published in Joel Ryce-Menuhin, ed., *Jung and the Monotheisms* (New York: Routledge, 1994).

1. C. G. Jung, "Commentary on the Secret of the Golden Flower," *Alchemical Studies, Collected Works* 13, trans. R. F. C. Hull (Princeton: Princeton University Press, 1929/1967), par. 74; C. G. Jung, *Psychological Types, Collected Works* 6, trans. R. F. C. Hull (Princeton: Princeton University Press, 1921/1971), pars. 412–13.

2. C. G. Jung, "The Undiscovered Self," *Civilization in Transition, Collected Works* 10, trans. R. F. C. Hull (New York: Pantheon, 1956/1964), pars. 536–37.

3. Hans Urs von Balthasar, *On Prayer* (New York: Sheed and Ward, 1961), 72.

4. C. G. Jung, *Letters*, 2 vols., eds. G. Adler and A. Jaffé, trans. R. F. C. Hull (Princeton: Princeton University Press, 1973 and 1975), I, 26 May 1945, 41.

5. C. G. Jung, *Dream Analysis: Notes of a Seminar Given in 1929–30*, ed. W. McGuire (Princeton: Princeton University Press, 1984), 516.

6. Jung, "The Undiscovered Self," pars. 507, 512, 521.

7. Jung, *Letters*, I, 9 September 1934, 172.

8. C. G. Jung, *Psychology and Alchemy, Collected Works* 12, trans. R. F. C. Hull (New York: Pantheon, 1953/1966), par. 11.

9. Rosemary Gordon, "Masochism: The Shadow Side of the

Archetypal Need to Venerate and Worship," *Journal of Analytical Psychology* 32, 3, 1987: 227–46.

10. Jung, *Psychological Types*, par. 424.

11. Ibid.

12. D. W. Winnicott, *Playing and Reality* (London: Tavistock, 1971), 1–26, 65–72.

13. S. Freud, *An Outline of Psychoanalysis* (New York: Norton, 1949), 33–36, 45, 108–14; see also H. W. Loewald, *Psychoanalysis and the History of the Individual* (New Haven: Yale University Press, 1978), 13–19.

14. H. Kohut, "On Courage," *The Search for the Self: Selected Writings of Heinz Kohut*, ed. P. H. Ornstein, vol. 3 of 4 (Madison: International Universities Press, 1990), 134–35.

15. W. R. Bion, *Attention and Interpretation* (London: Tavistock, 1970), 26.

16. M. Klein, *Envy and Gratitude and Other Works 1946–1963* (New York: Delacorte Press/Seymour Lawrence, 1957), 187–89.

17. C. Bollas, *Forces of Destiny: Psychoanalysis and Human Idiom* (London: Free Association Press, 1991), 202; M. M. R. Khan, "Lying Fallow," *Hidden Selves: Between Theory and Practice in Psychoanalysis* (New York: International Universities Press, 1983), 183–89.

18. A. B. Ulanov, *The Wisdom of the Psyche* (Cambridge, Mass.: Cowley, 1987), 37.

19. C. G. Jung, "Psychotherapists or the Clergy," *Psychology and Religion: West and East, Collected Works* 11, trans. R. F. C. Hull (New York: Pantheon, 1932/1958), par. 520; A. B. Ulanov, "From Image to Imago: Jung and the Study of Religion," ch. 5 in this book.

20. Jung, "The Undiscovered Self," par. 565.

21. Ibid., pars. 565–66; A. B. Ulanov, "From Image to Imago"; A. and B. Ulanov, *Religion and the Unconscious* (Louisville, Ky.: Westminster/John Knox Press, 1975), 35–39.

22. Jung, *Dream Analysis*, 511.

23. C. G. Jung, "Spirit and Life," *The Structure and Dynamics of the Psyche, Collected Works* 8, trans. R. F. C. Hull (New York: Pantheon, 1926/1960).

24. C. G. Jung, *Symbols of Transformation, Collected Works* 5, trans. R. F. C. Hull (Princeton: Princeton University Press, 1912/1967), par. 95.

25. Ibid.

26. Ibid.

27. Ibid.

28. Jung, *Dream Analysis*, 23.

29. Jung, *Symbols of Transformation*, par. 95.

30. Jung, *Dream Analysis*, 506.

31. Jung, "Spirit and Life," par. 525; C. G. Jung, *Two Essays in Analytical Psychology*, *Collected Works* 7, trans. R. F. C. Hull (New York: Pantheon 1943/1966), pars. 68, 132.

32. C. G. Jung, "Letter to Père Lachat," *The Symbolic Life*, *Collected Works* 18, trans. R. F. C. Hull (Princeton: Princeton University Press 1954/1976).

33. Jung, *Psychological Types*, par. 424; Jung, *Letters*, I, 23 May 1950, 558; Jung, *Symbols of Transformation*, par. 178.

34. Jung, *Psychological Types*, par. 422.

35. Jung, *Symbols of Transformation*, par. 259.

36. Jung, "Commentary on the Secret of the Golden Flower," par. 55.

37. Ibid., par. 71.

38. Jung, *Letters*, I, 13 January 1948, 487.

39. Ibid., 10 September 1943, 338.

40. C. G. Jung, *Memories, Dreams, Reflections*, ed. A. Jaffé, trans. Richard and Clara Winston (New York: Pantheon, 1963), 46.

41. Ibid., 47.

42. Jung, *Letters*, I, 30 January 1948, 492.

43. Jung, *Letters*, II, 17 February 1954, 156.

44. C. G. Jung, "Transformation Symbolism in the Mass," *Psychology and Religion*, *Collected Works* 11, trans. R. F. C. Hull (New York: Pantheon, 1954/1958), par. 1536; A. B. Ulanov, *Picturing God* (Cambridge, Mass.: Cowley 1986), 180; A. and B. Ulanov, *The Healing Imagination* (Mahwah, N.J.: Paulist Press, 1991), 61–64.

45. Jung, *Dream Analysis*, 179.

46. Ibid., 513.

47. Ibid., 519.

48. Jung, "Letter to Père Lachat," par. 1537.

49. Jung, *Letters*, I, 26 May 1923, 40.

50. Jung, *Memories, Dreams, Reflections*, 40.

51. Jung, *Letters*, I, 30 January 1948, 492.

52. Jung, "Letter to Père Lachat," par. 1536.

53. Ibid., par. 1538.

54. Jung, *Letters*, I, 15 August 1938, 98.

55. R. Aziz, *C. G. Jung's Psychology of Religion and Synchronicity* (Albany, N.Y.: State University of New York Press, 1990), 192–93.

56. Jung, *Letters*, II, 1 October 1953, 130.

57. Jung, *Psychological Types*, par. 426.

58. Jung, *Symbols of Transformation*, par. 329.

59. Jung, "Spirit and Life," par. 644.

60. Jung, *Dream Analysis*, 330.

61. Ibid., 331.

62. Jung, *Symbols of Transformation*, par. 344; see also par. 99.

63. Ibid., par. 346.

64. Jung, *Letters*, I, 10 January 1929, 59; see also A. B. Ulanov, "The Holding Self: Jung and the Desire for Being," *The Fires of Desire: Erotic Energies and the Spiritual Quest*, eds. F. Halligan and J. Shea (New York: Crossroad, 1992), 37, chapter 4 of this book.

65. Jung, "Transformation Symbolism in the Mass," *Collected Works* 11, pars. 382–84.

66. Ibid., par. 392.

67. Ibid., par. 394.

68. Ibid., par. 396.

69. Jung, *Psychology and Alchemy*, par. 14.

70. C. G. Jung, *Aion: Research into the Phenomenology of the Self, Collected Works* 9:2, trans. R. F. C. Hull (New York: Pantheon, 1959), par. 70.

71. Bollas, *Forces of Destiny*, 13.

72. Jung, *Psychological Types*, par. 426.

73. Ibid., par. 422.

74. Ibid., par. 421.

75. D. W. Winnicott, "Living Creatively," *Home Is Where We Start From* (New York: Norton, 1986).

76. Jung, "Letter to Père Lachat," par. 1536.

77. Jung, *Letters*, I, 10 September 1943, 33.

78. Jung, *Letters*, II, 3 August 1953, 120.

79. Jung, *Psychological Types*, par. 421.

80. B. Ulanov, *The Prayers of St. Augustine* (New York: Seabury, 1983), 13.

Chapter 3

The Double Cross: Scapegoating

Scapegoating and anti-Semitism are not subjects we can speak about objectively. We can only speak of them out of suffering—unconsciousness, abysmal pain and terror, rage and guilt, and a persistent longing to glimpse a way through their thickets of fear, sadism, violence, and despair.

Two crosses are always involved in scapegoating. The first cross represents suffering: we are nailed to cross-purposes, assaulted, brought to helplessness before the brute fact of evil. The opposites we would embrace pull us apart. The consciousness we strive for is opposed by unconsciousness. The help we offer turns out to hurt. The opposites do not just coincide: they clash; they collide. We are caught in a complex of opposites.

The second cross is the double cross, the trick of one we trusted, the betrayal of what we counted on. In scapegoating we say to the other, You carry the suffering and I will punish you for carrying it. Those we expect to help betray instead. Boatloads of Jews seeking refuge from the Holocaust were turned back from the shores of this country. Jung, the friend of many Jews, finally said to Rabbi Leo Baeck, "I slipped up."[1] Christians, who follow One who came to fulfill the law in love, generate prejudice and persecution many times instead. The Jews—chosen by God, elected to be God's bride—seem left behind by God in the camps of Auschwitz and Dachau. The Jews, abandoned by neighbors and nations to profound suffering, appear to refuse to identify their suffering with the suffering of others: the miseries of blacks victimized by whites, of Ukrainians systematically starved by their government, of Cambodians massacred by the Khmer Rouge, of the millions buried alive in Soviet gulags.[2]

We must go further and ask whether we who are concerned

42

to discuss anti-Semitism are prepared now to scapegoat Jung and Freud and other depth psychologists, as a double cross, to evade our own scapegoating. It relieves us to point to the prejudice of others, and especially such esteemed others as Jung and Freud, on whose work many of us have built our own work. Ultimately we double-cross ourselves by betraying our friends and befriending what betrays us.

Finally, the two crosses are one. The redemptive cross and the scapegoat cross are the same—someone or something to draw off the misery. We only scapegoat those who redeem us: Jesus, the Jew on the cross, double-crossed; the Jews, chosen by God, crucified as a people.

In Judaism (Lv 16:1–28), two offerings must always be brought to the Lord—two doves, two turtles, two pigeons, two bulls, two rams, and finally two goats. The first goat is a sin offering. Its blood is sprinkled within the veil of the Holy of Holies before the Mercy Seat upon the Ark, where Yahweh will appear in a cloud. This goat's blood atones at the holy place for the uncleanness and transgressions of the children of Israel. Then the goat's blood is sprinkled outside the Holy of Holies on the altar, and the goat is taken outside the camp and burned—its own holocaust.

The second goat stays alive and is driven into the wilderness after the priest confesses in words delivered over it the iniquities of the children of Israel. This goat, loaded down with these sins, is sent away into a land that is not inhabited, into the desert outside the boundaries of community. These are the precincts of Azazel, the goat deity dwelling in the desert, to whom the sin offering is dispatched. Later, Azazel is called the leader of the fallen angels, the author of all sin (Enoch 6, 8, 10). Like Prometheus, he also instructs humans in essential human crafts. In later Jewish, Gnostic, and Mohammedan traditions, Azazel is called the leader of all demons. He is associated with the chthonic, demonic forces, both generative and destructive, sexual and combative, that prevail outside the boundaries of Israel.[3]

One set of sins is burnt up outside the camp of Israel and the second set of sins is driven away to the place beyond the bounds. We can see how the Jewish people have been identified with both goats, suffering holocaust and being driven outside the human community to the ends of the earth. More than any other people, they have been the archetypal scapegoat, carrying both kinds of crosses.

A PSYCHOLOGICAL ROOT OF SCAPEGOATING

What then is scapegoating, psychologically? This mechanism is well known to us. It forms a distinct chain of reactions that leads from personal repression to social oppression. Its defined sequence begins when we repress contents we dislike and dread. We disown them. We keep consciousness from such contents, and we eject such contents from consciousness. Our ego recoils from connection to contents we feel are destructive to our ego position and from the disordered chaos from which such contents spring. We refuse consciousness to the annihilating forces we call evil. We either throw such contents out of consciousness into unconsciousness, or we leave them blocked in unconsciousness, refusing them admittance to our awareness. Such refusal brings relief to our egos; we get rid, we think, of disturbing contents.

But such contents do not go away. They go unconscious. They remain in us as live bits of being, as volatile forces now out of reach of our ego and its restraining, civilizing effects. These contents regress and achieve still more powerful form, as a hungry dog we lock in a closet becomes a savage beast bent on killing to satisfy its hunger. A repressed content is like a tiny alligator we bring back from a Florida vacation that becomes increasingly inconvenient as it keeps on growing. We flush it down the toilet into our sewers. There it not only continues to grow, but now, out of sight and out of reach, it joins all the other alligators flushed away by our neighbors. What we repress accumulates more life to itself, growing stronger, bigger, contaminating whatever else is in the unconscious. Pressure builds up that demands release into conscious life. Such contents burst out finally in projections onto others—usually those different from us, alien, because of physical appearance or sex or background, or distant from us because we deem them inferior or superior to us. All that our egos judge unacceptable hurls itself in projection onto our alien or distant neighbors. We identify our neighbors with that bit of ourselves we put onto and into them. Thus we inaugurate a relationship of projective identification with our neighbors. We feel we must control them because they carry a feared bit of ourselves, and we fear them because we cannot control them. They carry the package of unconscious contents we dread in ourselves. Rather, we want to see ourselves as identified with the values and ideals we hold most precious. We contrast our good to our alien neighbors' bad. We draw a boundary around the good with which our egos identify, outlawing the bad with which we identify our neighbors.

We can understand that the initial function of such repression and projection is to differentiate good from bad, to become conscious of what we hold as good and to bind our group into a community, distinguished from other groups. Such initial differentiation and group consciousness might be all right, even furthering consciousness, if it did not go further, but it always does. For the repressed material, the howling dogs and snapping alligators, press to get out, press for contact. What begins as differentiation only too soon leads to a wide gap between our conscious ego identification with the good and our projective identification of our alien neighbor with the bad.

The line is drawn, from repression to regression and contamination of unconscious contents, to projection and projective identification onto our alien neighbor, to attitudes of prejudice from which grow acts of oppression, persecution, and finally, scapegoating. Like one or the other of the original scapegoats, the alien neighbor is seen as the carrier of the sins we must get rid of to keep intact our commitment to the good. In the ironies of opposing consciousness and unconsciousness, we can indulge, even act out in frenzy, all the badness we disown in the name of defending the good. The disease attacks those who attack the disease. In the name of our ideal we attack, violate, persecute, and kill those on whom we have projected our badness. We are infiltrated by the very qualities we tried to control, depositing them in our neighbor. What begins as initial differentiation of opposites ends by making a wide split between us and them, a split which soon becomes a yawning chasm filled with violence, misery, and suffering. That happens because we are unable to hold in consciousness the opposing values of good and bad. If we identify ourselves with the victims of such actions, we become the first goat; we become the victims who are burnt up. In psychological terms, we fall into masochism. If we identify with the ones who accuse their neighbors, we see them as the second kind of scapegoat and ourselves fall into sadism, attempting to purge the community of their presence.

The temptations in scapegoating are double, and each brings its own cross. To get out of the coincidence of opposites—of the good and bad in each of us—we split them. To elude the cross of accepting and suffering the bad and good mixed in us, we double-cross our neighbor. Either way we avoid the real issues: what to do in the face of evil, where to put the alligators, how to hold the opposites within ourselves and our own community. In Jung's vocabulary, scapegoating introduces us to the shadow in ourselves, to the collective shadow in our society, and to the archetypal core that underlies the shadow.[4]

A RELIGIOUS ROOT OF ANTI-SEMITISM

This connection between repression and scapegoating is true of all prejudices that are acted out in social oppression. What is specific to anti-Semitism? What do we repress and project and then identify with Jews? What is the specific archetypal core that informs and inflames the mechanism of scapegoating in anti-Semitism? The answer, in a word, is *religion.*

Although not at the center of debate about anti-Semitism, often obscured by economic, political, and historical circumstances, and often put aside or denied by Jews in their self-appraisals, the religious issue rests in the background of anti-Semitism. It forms the distinct core of the package repressed by and projected onto the Jews.

Even to those who associate Judaism with ethnicity rather than faith, who see it as a culture rather than a religion, religion remains the inescapable fact, for this is a culture shaped by religion, whether it declares for or against the faith. The notorious resentment against Jews for their reputed intellectual superiority, for example, can be traced back to a religious origin. Judaism is the first of the three great monotheisms in human history, and the other two were clearly shaped by it. Islam itself traces its origins to Abraham. Jesus was a Jew.

Anti-Semitism is religious scapegoating, not one of color, class, or sex. And religious scapegoating is the most violent of all, because religion arranges the order of being. On the surface, anti-Semitism seems to follow the mechanisms of all prejudice—repression, regression, contamination, projection, projective identification, prejudice, oppression, persecution, scapegoating.

At the core of anti-Semitism lies the specific archetype that ignites people against Jews. It is unmistakably religious. For the Jews are a people chosen by God, a people who have said Yes to God's choosing, who have engaged in lifelong dramas in yea-saying and nay-saying, turning to God, turning away. They complain that it is God who turns away and abandons them. And yet they know at the same time God is steadfast in demands upon them and in love of them.

It is almost a commonplace to say that what has happened to Jews is what happens to God on earth. Jews have been hunted, hounded, excluded, trivialized, caricatured, mocked, betrayed, double-crossed. We persecute Jews because we persecute the addressing ultimate, the calling to us to be Abraham or to be the bride, to be the feminine receiver and container who will make the transcendent manifest in this life.

Jung knew this addressing, this receiving womanliness. He described Yahweh as one whom we punch and kick back at for dislocating our hip, as with Jacob, or who plagues us as with Job. Jung knew what a fearful thing it was to fall into the hands of the living God, to encounter the archetype of God in our own psyche. Such an experience is steel on stone, a defeat for the ego, and yet of such indescribable bliss, says Jung, that he will not, cannot breathe a word of it.[5]

The Jews symbolically represent those who want to say Yes to God, a Yes that will include questions, resistance, a simultaneous fighting and running away. In such speech with the divine, our bowels loosen, our stomachs heave, our voices fill up, our flesh trembles. We, like the Jews, dare now to be occupied with the Holy One who hovers over the Mercy Seat in the Holy of Holies, and we are frightened—and fascinated.

It is a miracle the Jews still survive, for they carry the projection of the primordial, not only our nay-saying to the center, which is our sin, which we put on the scapegoat we drive into the desert, but also our yea-saying, that part of us that aches for the center, that wants to look, to see who will come through to us.

Jung crafted his whole psychology around this center. He discovered that we carry within our own psyches such a center, a Self that is not God but that within us which knows about God. It is a large knowing, a taste of that which transcends, not just the ego, but the whole psyche, the whole personal psyche, the whole group psyche.[6]

The deepest place of our dread of being is where the Jewish people stand, and they are persecuted for it. In them we persecute our own desire and fear of the center of being. In them we persecute our attraction to the center and our fear of it. What then happens when we scapegoat the Jews? We avoid, compulsively, not only the mystery of our own shadows, both individual and collective, but the mystery of evil that we seek to eject from consciousness and project out of our communities.[7] That is the scapegoat we send into the desert. We also avoid the mystery of living in relation to the center and the burnt offering it seems to demand. That is the goat whose blood is offered at the altar.

We must look at one further thing that comes with all scapegoating, and particularly with anti-Semitism. Jews carry the necessity of drawing a boundary line when the finite comes in contact with the infinite. In repressing and projecting what we find bad, and thus insupportable, we are setting it off from the good. We are making boundary lines that help us to see evil and help protect us from its infectious nature. Such boundaries enhance consciousness and our sense of community.[8] Sending the goat into the desert sends it beyond the boundaries; taking the goat outside the camp to be burned defines the boundaries of inside and out. The anthropologist Mary Douglas tells us that this making of boundaries, that happens for example in the dietary law of Judaism, is an attempt to impose order on untidy experience.[9] It demarcates inside from outside, order from chaos, community from nameless wandering. Drawing boundaries marks off our belonging, living in relation to the center, from homelessness. God's blessing creates a space where being is always being-in-relation to the center, and distinguished from nonbeing, which is to say from not being-defined-in-relation-to, but choosing self-definition instead. We will make the boundaries. We will determine good and evil. We will know it all. We become know-it-alls. Pulling loose from such boundaries means taking to ourselves, our little selves, the big power to say what is good and what is evil—what was seen so unmistakably clearly in the death camps—the power to save or to kill.

Dietary laws in Judaism are like signs designed to inspire meditation upon what God has set apart as holy. Holiness is unity, integrity, completeness. Marion Milner, writing about painting, says the frame marks off a different kind of reality within the picture from what is outside. Our own psychoanalytical sessions do the same, marking off in time and space a special kind of reality that makes possible "that creative illusion that analysts call the transference."[10]

Drawing these boundaries, saying in effect that this is good and this is bad, this sacred, this profane, is possible only if connection to the transcendent is maintained. The goat's blood must be offered back to the Holy, whether at the altar or in the desert. When the scapegoating ritual pulls loose from the transcendent center it falls into idolatry. Symbolic form becomes literal action, whether through inflation we identify with the chosen ones or through deflation become the literal victims of the double cross. When a ritual is literalized, it falls on real living people. Instead of asking what our relation is to the infinite, we take offense at those who claim a covenant: If we can destroy them, we can evade the whole question.

THE DOUBLE CROSS AND JUNG

Jung mixed up the boundary lines, became caught up in them, and paid for it in his own experience of the double cross of scapegoating, both as accuser—drawing whole peoples into types, which inflamed persecution against them—and as accused—where he suffered, and his name goes on suffering, the label of anti-Semitism. Jung, so sensitive to the complexity of opposites, who never wanted to leave one of them out, was enmeshed in a complex of opposites. His strengths and gifts double-crossed him, in his weaknesses, in his blind spots. Jung shows us through his experience what it means to say scapegoating delivers us into fully acknowledging our shadow in ourselves and in the collective of which we are a part. We do not acknowledge our shadow from a safe perch in an observer's chair. It means to be pitched into the muck, coming up covered with it, stinking of it, smeared in our eyes so we cannot see clearly. That is the shadow. We slip onto it and into it, as Jung said. And we hurt others because of it. Jung also shows us, in his experience of the Self and of the God-image in him, that a cross awaits any of us who struggle to relate to the Ultimate. Jung tried to keep the opposites together, and fell into them and into their splitting apart.

For example, Jung tells us individuation can only occur in relation to tradition, to the collective, to the prevailing *Zeitgeist* from which we must differentiate ourselves and then relate to again, more consciously. We must become aware of the subjective premise from which we see objective truth, and know that our premise is subjective, so that finally, he wrote, we know that our vision of truth is only a "subjective confession."[11] But Jung himself was caught in the texture of his times and its bedeviling anti-Semitism. He was strongly influenced by his personal collectivity—generations of Christian pastors with all the ambiguity and deviousness of Christianity seeing Judaism as both its foundation and its rival. Christ the Jew, killed by Jews. From another perspective, Jung remained embedded in centuries of Swiss traditions of neutrality, product of a country that observed the clashing opposite views of other peoples and chose to stand apart, to preserve neutrality for itself. Thus under his editorship of the *Journal of the International General Medical Society for Psychotherapy,* Jung published both Nazi and Jewish doctors, expecting that scientific insight would be generated out of their opposing views.[12] Jung did not see in any of these collective and ostensibly objective worlds his own subjectivity, that colored not only his view of the Jews, but also his hope of gathering insight from a sharp opposition neutrally observed.

Another example of where Jung was both crossed and double-crossed between opposites is in the realm of symbol. His great insight is into the openness of the symbol. It points to and evokes the living experience of the unknown, but never defines it exactly.[13] Yet Jung himself falls victim to attempts to define whole peoples in restrictive ways, ways that fed not differentiation, reconciliation, or insight but separation and persecution. Jung reminds us again and again to open ourselves to the person before us, not to try to know what a dream means ahead of time, like a recipe, not to apply reasoning to spiritual paradoxes. He even declares his own typology to be suggestive, never prescriptive. Yet here is Jung applying reductive categories to whole races.[14] Jung's great open consciousness, determined always to see the other, can also contribute to obliterating others by applying mass generalizations to them. Jung tells us repeatedly that the archetype is not a formula clapped onto persons, yet he himself falls victim to a fascination with the Wotan archetype and forgets the persons involved with the new invocation of it.[15]

Jung advocates the recovery to consciousness of the feminine mode of being, with his seminal insight into the contrasexual nature of the human, yet he himself suffered a benighted relation to his own anima during the Nazi years, as the "sick cow" dream and his illnesses of the heart show. Yet growth continued in him and true openness as his near-death vision makes clear. He saw himself being fed kosher food by a maternal anima figure, whom he joined in a "mystical marriage," seeing himself cast as "Rabbi ben Jochai, whose wedding in the afterlife was being celebrated."[16] Jay Sherry suggests that the sick-cow side of Jung's anima—the nurturing feminine with "life-promoting milk"—fell ill from Jung's fascination with the Wotan archetype, suddenly alive again in Nazi Germany, and from Jung's bitterness about Freud after the breakup of their relationship.[17]

Jung, noted for bringing insight into the feeling and sensate levels of the unconscious, was tripped up by the limitations of his own feeling and sensate functions.[18] He expressed his dubious views about archetypal factors in Jewish psychology at a time of racial fanaticism in Germany, where even to be a Jew was enough to put one's life in danger. To put forward for scientific discussion the topic of racial differences in such a climate, even to think in such terms, was a grave error. Jung missed on the feeling and sensate levels—in terms of his typology, his own inferior functions—the reality of the evil being visited upon the Jews. He wrote and spoke about racial characteristics, both during and after the war, in a way that was bound to further inflame the persecution of a whole people. Caught in his own emotions about the Wotan archetype, and his own resentments against Freudian analysis, he did not see the harm he himself was causing.

Jung is singular among depth psychologists in his intense interest in evil, in taking up good and evil as moral categories, in probing the mystery of conscience.[19] Yet Jung did not recognize one of the greatest examples of evil in history when it confronted him in its immeasurable brutality. Jung's incessant protests and objections against the Christian understanding of the force of evil, as described in the doctrine of *privatio boni,* can be understood as that excessive protestation we all fall into when we are fascinated by something and cannot really see what so absorbs us.[20] Jung insists that the doctrine misses the fact that evil really exists, that it is really there savaging our lives. To anyone who grasps the doctrine, Jung's reading grossly misses the point. But the point here is that Jung misses the brute facts of Nazi evil.

Perhaps the two missings—of evil in itself and of the Nazi evil—are linked. In the *privatio boni,* evil is indeed understood to exist, but in a very different way from good. Good is simply being in relation to God, related being, created being, being within the circle of dependent connections to the Creator. Evil denies that connection, seeks to destroy it, to defect from it. Evil exists as denial, betrayal, deficiency, a ruthless attempt to put "nothing" in the place of something.[21] Evil exists outside relation to a transcendent center, usurping the center for its own version and vision of reality. Isn't this exactly what the Nazis attempted?

Aniela Jaffé understands Jung's error about the Jews and about Nazism as the product of a one-sided consciousness. She says his "romantic consciousness" got caught in fascination with the objective psyche displayed in National Socialism, particularly through the Wotan archetype. The "classic" type of consciousness, which, Jaffé says, Jung acquired toward National Socialism, was not fooled for a moment.[22]

Jung missed the evil that was so clear to so many others in the rise of the Nazis because of his faith in his own theory of consciousness. He missed it because of his conviction that healing power is released when consciousness can expand to include all the opposites, when a small ego can behold the *complexio oppositorum* of the Self. Jung described the Self as the God-image within us manifest in the psyche. He described the Self—his image of

God—as the *coincidentia oppositorum* and as the *complexio opposito-rum.* Jung faced cross and double cross when he equated his image of God with God. What he relied upon betrayed him, and he betrayed what he relied upon. Like any person who risks encounter with the living God, Jung was stripped of his God-image. When we identify our God-image with what it points to, as in some ways some of the time we must, because our image acts as a bridge between us and that unknown center to which it leads, it will break beneath our feet, for what it leads to is radically differ-ent from our pictures of it.[23] Jung's faith in consciousness was betrayed. It did not work. It double-crossed him. Consciousness of the opposites and writing about them in categories of Aryan and Jew, of the Germanic and the Jewish, harmed instead of helped, brought attack instead of a healing clarity.

THE DOUBLE CROSS AND US

What is to be done? Jung slipped up because of areas in his large personality of incomplete individuation. They resulted, these areas of absence and deprivation, from the collective *Zeit-geist*, from his own tendencies to type instead of to see symboli-cally, from his own underdeveloped feeling and sensate functions, from his own anima problems, from the resulting blindness to the stark reality of Nazi evil, from his overdeter-mined reliance on consciousness of opposites. Do we, then, dis-miss everything Jung has to say? Hardly. That would be for us to fall into the double cross—either accusing or defending Jung or thinking we can stay out of the whole mess with a neutrality only too much like Jung's at its worst. Seeing Jung caught, we should turn to our own enmeshment in scapegoating, for anti-Semitism is still here, still active among us. What is so powerful about this particular brand of scapegoating that it persists still, after all the horrors of the Holocaust?

The specific scapegoating of anti-Semitism introduces us, not only to our own evil, in collective and individual form, in the myth of expelling evil, but also to our own God-image, our own relation or lack of relation to the transcendent. Whether we are

Jewish or not, whether we practice or repudiate religion, the spiritual question is constellated: What is our relation to the center?

One of the reasons anti-Semitism endures is that we all need to take up two issues: how to deal with the shadow and how to relate to the Self. Jung's insights and Jung's cross and double cross will help us enormously here.

The shadow issue poses itself in a series of additional questions. How do we mark off boundaries to consolidate ego-consciousness without discriminating against those who have different boundaries? How do we differentiate without repudiating?[24] Or, to put the same issue in social terms, how do we each set off order from disorder without disowning our neighbors? How do we think in terms of a whole society while at the same time risking commitment to our particular part of society? How do we get rooted firmly in our soil and remain hospitable to those who root differently or in different earth?

Jung's failures and insights point the way. Our consciousness must develop differently. A double intercession matches the double cross. We intercede for shadow and for ego both. Consciousness intercedes for the left-out bits of shadow in our personality and in our society, while at the same time respecting our need for boundaries. Consciousness also intercedes on behalf of our ego-point-of-view in relation to the opposite points of view that live inside us and around us. The *complexio oppositorum* that Jung sees as essential comes home to us. It becomes our everyday reality. This is living toward the Self. We try to intercede on behalf of what we believe in and on behalf of what others believe in too. For this we urgently need the help of the Hebrew Bible and the feminine mode of being.

To do this work with the shadow means neither expelling evil nor burning it up. It means not identifying with either scapegoat, for both are offerings to the transcendent—the altar deity or the desert deity. It means moving on to the Prophets and the Psalms in the Hebrew Bible, where God says, I do not want burnt offerings, I want a broken and contrite heart; I do not want burnt offerings, I want a faithful and loving spirit. But to make this shift means changing the way we become conscious. The old way was to differentiate opposites—good from bad, us from them, inside boundaries from outside boundaries—by splitting them apart.

But in that way the split widens to a point where we cannot bring the opposites together again, and millions of people perish in the gap left between them. Differentiation then turns into discrimination. Consciousness means repression. The opposites do not belong together as parts of a complex whole, coinciding all at once, but instead proceed serially, sequentially, to a killing exclusivity.

What the texts of the Hebrew Bible are after in the shift from burnt offering to heart offering is inclusion of a feeling, sensate, bodily kind of awareness, where, although different each from the other, we are still all members of the one body. This perception is fostered by the feminine mode of being that goes into the midst of living experience and differentiates aspects of it by a both–and instead of an either–or method of apprehension.[25] The split does not widen to expel opposites nor move to exclude any one of them. The opposites are held in tension to discern and integrate all of them.

The feminine mode of consciousness allows a holding in being of what one is separating in thought. It is a holding in feeling of what we discern differences in, a holding of boundaries to make space for the commitments of the particular persons and groups that together compose the whole. The feminine mode recognizes evil both without sentimentality and without enthusiasm for grand ways of fixing it. Evil is a fact to be reckoned with, and if necessary, to be fought or suffered. The feminine approach helps the ego in its spacemaking function, enlarging awareness so the coinciding opposites can be experienced as complexly related to each other and to the whole of which they are parts.[26] Those coinciding opposites make up different parts of our society, different groups rooted in different commitments, just as much as they make up different segments of each person's personality.

In gaining consciousness of our own scapegoating tendencies, and interceding for another way, we are pushed to become conscious of how we experience the center of existence, of how we experience what it is all for and thus what really matters.

This consciousness of our own images of the center, of what Jung calls our God-images, makes us struggle with mystery as it touches us. If we are in any way to lift from the Jews what history has scapegoated them for—self-conscious relation to the center—

then we must take up that task, their task, ourselves, in our own groups, in our own lives.

This is not to say everyone must become a defined Jew—any more than Muslim or Christian or Buddhist or atheist. It is to say that we must direct our consciousness to the center and decide to struggle with it and about it, to know its great positive qualities, its abiding difficulties, ourselves. That will keep our neighbors safe from the unconscious spiritual burden that we only too easily project onto them.

If we take up this task we will know the cross and double cross, but differently now, as a necessary ritual in relation to the transcendent. We will enter that radical experience that Jung exemplifies, of disidentifying our God-images from God, for relating to the infinite means being stripped of our finite images of it. That which we rely upon will pin us to the cross and will double-cross us. We will be forced to identify what our images of God are, forced to disidentify them from the transcendent itself. This means simultaneously committing ourselves in time and space to belief in whatever our version of the center is and opening to whatever our symbols evoke and point to but never capture or define, let alone prescribe for others. It means drawing boundaries that are both binding and open ended. In religious terms, it means witnessing rather than proselytizing. In psychological terms, we are brought to true consciousness of opposites, rather than coercion. This is a paradoxical knowing and unknowing simultaneously. It is a seeing into the dark ground of the God who presides over both goats, both crosses, within boundary and beyond, the world of deity and of desert.

Notes

This chapter is written from notes for a lecture originally delivered as part of a series entitled "Lingering Shadows: Freud, Jung and Anti-Semitism," sponsored by the C. G. Jung Foundation of New York City, given in April 1989 and published in *Lingering Shadows: Freud, Jung and Antisemitism*, ed. A. Maidenbaum (Boston: Shambhala, 1990).

1. A. Jaffé, "C. G. Jung and National Socialism," in *From the Life and Work of Jung*, trans. R. F. C. Hull (New York: Harper, 1971), 97–98.

2. See R. L. Rubenstein, *Auschwitz: Radical Theology and Contem-*

porary Judaism (Indianapolis: Bobbs-Merrill, 1966); see also R. L. Rubenstein and J. K. Roth, *Approaches to Auschwitz: The Holocaust and Its Legacy* (Atlanta: John Knox, 1987); see also J. G. Gager, *The Origins of Anti-Semitism* (New York: Oxford University Press, 1983); see also R. Reuther, *Faith and Fratricide: The Theological Roots of Anti-Semitism* (New York: Seabury, 1974); see also R. M. Lowenstein, *Christians and Jews: A Psycholanalytic Study* (New York: International Universities Press, 1952).

    3. *The Oxford Dictionary of the Christian Church* (London: Oxford University Press, 1974); see also S. B. Perera, *The Scapegoat Complex: Toward a Mythology of Shadow and Guilt* (Toronto: Inner City Books, 1986), 18–19, 89.

    4. See E. Neuman, *Depth Psychology and the New Ethic,* trans. Eugene Rolfe (New York: Putnam's, 1969), passim, for discussion of the many facets of repression and their effects on society. See also C. G. Jung, "Shadow," in *Aion, Collected Works* 9:2, trans. R. F. C. Hull (New York: Pantheon, 1959), pars. 13–19.

    5. C. G. Jung, *Letters,* 2 vols., eds. G. Adler and A. Jaffé, trans. R. F. C. Hull (Princeton: Princeton University Press, 1973 and 1975), II, 17 February 1954, 156; see also C. G. Jung, *Mysterium Coniunctionis, Collected Works* 14, trans. R. F. C. Hull (New York: Pantheon, 1963), par. 778.

    6. See C. G. Jung, *Psychological Types, Collected Works* 6, trans. R. F. C. Hull (Princeton: Princeton University Press, 1971), pars. 789–90. See also C. G. Jung, *The Archetypes and the Collective Unconscious, Collected Works* 9:1, trans. R. F. C. Hull (New York: Pantheon, 1959), pars. 5, 442, 572, 626.

    7. See C. G. Jung, *Two Essays in Analytical Psychology, Collected Works* 7, trans. R. F. C. Hull (New York: Pantheon, 1966), pars. 27, 35, 41–42, 70–78, 152–54, 185. See also C. G. Jung, *Psychology and Religion: West and East, Collected Works* 11, trans. R. F. C. Hull (New York: Pantheon, 1958), pars. 140, 509–13, 738–89.

    8. See Neumann, *Depth Psychology,* 64–66.

    9. M. Douglas, *Purity and Danger* (New York: Frederick A. Praeger, 1966), 1, 4–5, 29, 50, 53–54, 57, 63–64.

    10. M. Milner, "The Role of Illusion in Symbol Formation," *New Directions in Psychoanalysis,* eds. M. Klein, P. Hermann, R. E. Money-Kyrle (New York: Basic Books, 1957), 86; also cited in Douglas, *Purity and Danger,* 63.

    11. See C. G. Jung, "A Rejoinder to Dr. Bally," *Civilization in Transition, Collected Works* 10, trans. R. F. C. Hull (New York: Pantheon, 1934/1964), pars. 1025, 1034. See also C. G. Jung, *Modern Man in*

Search of a Soul, trans. W. S. Dell and C. F. Baynes (New York: Harcourt, Brace & Co., 1933), 220.

12. See Jung, "A Rejoinder to Dr. Bally," pars. 1026–32.

13. See Jung, *Letters,* I, 6 November 1915, 31–32; 10 January 1929, 60–61; see also Jung, *Psychological Types,* pars. 814–29; see also A. B. Ulanov, *The Feminine in Jungian Psychology and Christian Theology* (Evanston: Northwestern University Press, 1971), ch. 5.

14. See Jung, "After the Catastrophe," *Civilization in Transition, Collected Works* 10, trans. R. F. C. Hull (New York: Pantheon, 1945/1964), pars. 400, 487.

15. See ibid., "Wotan," *Civilization in Transition, Collected Works* 10, trans. R. F. C. Hull (New York: Pantheon, 1936/1964), pars. 371–99, and especially 385, 391.

16. C. G. Jung, *Memories, Dreams, Reflections,* ed. A. Jaffé, trans. Richard and Clara Winston (New York: Pantheon, 1963), 294.

17. See J. Sherry, "Jung, the Jews, and Hitler," *Spring* (1986): 170–74 for full presentation of this idea.

18. Jung, *Psychological Types,* pars. 595–609.

19. See Jung, "A Psychological View of Conscience," *Civilization in Transition, Collected Works* 10, trans. R. F. C. Hull (New York: Pantheon, 1958/1964), pars. 825–57.

20. See Jung, *Letters,* II, 9 April 1952, 52–54; 30 April 1952, 58–61; 30 June 1952, 71–73; 29 June 1955, 268; November 1955, 281; 12 February 1959, 484; 5 November 1959, 519. See Jung, "A Psychological Approach to the Trinity," *Psychology and Religion: West and East, Collected Works* 11, trans. R. F. C. Hull (New York: Pantheon 1948/1958), pars. 247ff.; in the same volume, see also "Foreword to White's 'God and the Unconscious,'" 1952, pars. 451f.; "Foreword to Werblowsky's 'Lucifer and Prometheus,'" 1952, par. 470; "Answer to Job," 1952, par. 685.

21. For further discussion of this denying role of evil, see A. B. Ulanov, "The Devil's Trick," in *The Wisdom of the Psyche* (Cambridge, Mass.: Cowley, 1988), ch. 2.

22. Jaffé, "Jung and National Socialism," 96. Jung describes the two kinds of consciousness in his *Psychological Types,* pars. 543ff.

The romantic type tends to be extroverted, swift in his reactions, expressing himself and needing to make his presence felt. His whole nature goes out to the object, and he gives himself easily to the world in a form that is pleasing and acceptable. Enthusiasm flows out of his mouth. He appears interesting, empathetic. He publishes early and wants to make a name for himself.

The classic type is slower and reaches the ripest fruit of his work only late in life. He needs to stand unblemished in the public eye and does not set other minds on fire. He always keeps his personality in the background and tends to be introverted, hiding his personal reactions and suppressing his immediate reactions. He lets his work speak for him and does not take up the cudgels on its behalf. He seals his lips over enthusiasm and appears commonplace.

As usual with any typology, neither of these descriptions fits Jung precisely. But Jaffé's referral to them as helping to explain Jung's trials with the Nazis is most interesting.

23. See A. B. Ulanov, *Picturing God* (Cambridge, Mass.: Cowley, 1986), 164–71, 179–84.

24. See A. B. Ulanov, "When Is Repudiation Differentiation?" (unpublished paper, 1987).

25. See A. B. Ulanov, *The Feminine,* part III; see also "Between Anxiety and Faith: The Role of the Feminine in Paul Tillich's Theological Thought," in *Tillich on Creativity*, ed. G. Kegley (Lanham: University Press of America, 1989), ch. 10 of this book.

26. See A. B. Ulanov, "The Ego as Spacemaker" (unpublished paper, 1981).

Chapter 4

The Holding Self:
Jung and the Desire for Being

LIBIDO

Jung stands out among the depth psychologists in his concern for religious matters and his conviction that religion is what matters. "We need some new foundations," he wrote, "we must dig down to the primitive in us,...we need a new experience of God."[1] In this way we hold onto ourselves and feel held in being. This, for Jung, is the main problem of our time: "the evolution of the religious spirit," though unhappily it has received only "scant attention."[2] The evolving spirit the psyche presses upon us is the great risk and adventure of individuation, the center of Jung's psychological investigations.[3]

The psyche urges on us this task of coming to ourselves, and constantly calls us back to this task through its own passionate desires. Simone Weil was shrewd in saying that it is only our desire that calls God down.[4] For this desire forms a trajectory spanning the whole arc of our life, from our earliest instinctual beginnings to our groping intimations of a spiritual end and purpose. We must respond to this desiring, do something about it, or it will have its way with us, causing disorientation, nervousness, if not absolute collapse.[5] How many of our problems and possibilities arise when this psychic desire falls on a wrong object that may be too small to carry such intensity? Like the rich man of the Gospels we cannot pull the humps of our camel through the needle's eye. Then, instead of entering the kingdom, we find ourselves addicted to chocolate or cocaine, to binges of work or political or sexual activity. We worship false gods. Yet precisely through that misplacement of desire, we may be moved to relocate our most

60

basic approaches to life. We may be thus led to dig down to the primitive in us and find waiting there a new experience of God.

Take the experience of an artist in his forties who squandered his talent and charm on successive women. He coldly rated these women according to their ability to play the scene in which they found themselves—drinking in a bar, dancing at a formal affair, negotiating a business contract.[6] He invested his desire wholly in each scene, but each time he was left feeling bereft, lonely, near despair, howling inside. He saw himself casting seeds in all directions, and decided to pull his hand in. He stayed home, committed to his analysis. His desire began to gather. Dreams came. They showed him wrestling with a series of interior thugs. First, from a foreign culture came one who immolated himself, then from our own world, a street punk who barred the artist's entrance to a restaurant, finally a tough guy in his own profession, a man under whom he worked. Another dream galvanized his desire. He saw himself with a woman in a hotel where he wanted so much to eat. He left the woman in the public room and went in search of food. In the basement worked two cooks, one a fussy Frenchman complaining that his culinary performances were not appreciated, the other a woman who had bested the chef. She served plainer, more substantial fare, nourishing and delicious. As the dreamer was looking for food, she came up from the basement. Here was a strong object for this dreamer's desire. As she gave him the food he needed, she caught his attention because she would not play his game, not at least according to his rules. He could not talk her 'round, either in the dream nor in his imagination. She kept her own counsel, responding or not as she was moved, not allowing herself to be put in a reactive position to him. He was fascinated, hooked.[7]

A second example is less successful, at least on the face of it. A fifty-year-old man sought analysis because he felt dead, near despair. I had no time for a new patient. The situation was urgent. He needed a reliable space to hold him in being while he dug down deep to a new experience of what really mattered to him. I offered a referral. He refused. He had had three previous analyses that had left him feeling disillusioned. He thought himself entitled now to pick and choose what felt right for him. I could not arrange extra hours. But he was persistent, and so we undertook irregular sessions, whenever our schedules allowed. What I intuitively felt would happen in analysis happened instead in his life. The disillusioned and deeply sad part of him that was dissociated from his successfully functioning life pressed for reentry. It still secretly wanted to come alive. Instead of being held in analysis, it exploded into his marriage and landed him in a tumultuous affair. His passionate desires blazoned; he suffered excruciating pain and guilt.

I felt guilt too, because I could not offer the full shelter of analysis in which this passionate desire could be contained, probed, and allowed to evolve. And yet I wondered if my guilt was misplaced, for help might well be coming to this man more directly, in the exercise of his life. In this sense, my ego wish to help was perhaps too small an object for the desire. In Jung's vocabulary, the Self could take its own direct hand. For in his tangle of relationships and emotions, this man clearly saw that he was caught once again making woman the object of his deepest soul desire. Idolatry again, woman in place of God. Whether his mother's original depression that he served with his desire to make her feel better and come alive, or his wife's pain or joy, or the other woman's, he wanted to serve. What he now had to face was what desire asserted in him, what he owed it. Perhaps the three previous analytical experiences had left him disillusioned because the analysts or the analytical work had become the object of the psyche's passionate desires, a mistake I might have made too.

Is it too much to speak of God here? I think not. If we do not find an object commensurate with the incommensurable passion of the psyche's desire, we end up obsessed, addicted, idolatrous of false gods. It was Jung's struggle to say this, to find words to articulate what he experienced when he dug down to the primitive in the dreams and fantasies that began in 1912. That digging, he said, was the foundation of all his creative activity.[8] The same year he lectured at Fordham on his "Theory of Psychoanalysis."

Jung's statement is strong: "My personal view in this matter is that man's vital energy or libido is the divine pneuma all right and it was this conviction which it was my secret purpose to bring into the vicinity of my colleagues' understanding."[9] What an extraordinary thing to say! For Jung is doing much more than distinguishing his view from Freud's when he says that libido is not just sexual desire.[10] It is a wide and varied kind of desire that excites eagerness, longing, pleasing, willing. Gladly it stirs subject to move toward object.

Jung retains a link with Freud in recognizing that libido includes the wish for sexual fulfillment. In fact, as the Russian philosopher Solovyev reminds us, it is only sexual desire that is strong enough to combat egotism.[11] The wish to be fully filled with life is powerful enough to pull the ego across its borders toward the Self that hides in sexual longing, as in the case of the man who sought his soul in women, only to begin to find it coming up from the basement of his being in the dream-figure of the cook, or the man who saw in his stalemate between wife and lover that the primary issue was what desire in him demanded from him.

Jung's widening of our understanding of libido also brings into play ideas about subject and object that some years later were developed by other depth psychologists. As subjects full of libidinal longing, we feel dependent on others to see us, to support us, to hold us in being with their selves. We cannot begin our journey of coming to become ourselves, to achieve individuation, says Jung, without deep and unconditional relation to others. We cannot even dream by ourselves, for dreams always come from what is between the I and the You.[12] Ronald Fairbairn, one of the first of the object-relations school, stated bluntly that our self faces death if we do not see ourself greeted and loved as a uniquely valuable person. Heinz Kohut explores the same region of dependence and interdependence, seeing our need for mirroring from "self-objects" as persisting throughout our lives.[13]

Jung emphasized the reality of the object to which our passionate libidinal desiring takes us, that is, of the other. Differentiation of self and other is as important in the journey of individuation as the integration of the self as a subject. The other, recognized as really there, opens to the ego the unknowable ground of creativeness, a theme D. W. Winnicott explored brilliantly with children. When a child's projections fail and its aggressiveness to fashion a desired world does not succeed, what becomes clear is that objects survive in their otherness, as their own selves and subjects. External reality opens. Creative living unfolds.[14] For thus we are released from endless self-spinning maneuvers, processes of introjection, and projection of adapting and manipulating. Here before us is another strong subject, meeting us from its other side, very much its own side.

Jung went further still: "The vital energy or libido is the divine pneuma all right...." In us as well as in others, otherness unfolds toward us, desiring us perhaps as much as we long for it. Isn't this what Augustine cried out so passionately to God—"Our hearts are restless until they rest in Thee"? The saint's "Thee" is ultimate reality. It is Wilfred Bion's "O," Paul Tillich's "Ground of Being," our coming home in T. S. Eliot's simple words. This is the root of joy, this desire to recognize the reality of self, of other, of the mysterious ground of being between us.

If, as Jung says, our libido, our desiring, is the divine pneuma in us, even as the mystics tell us our desire to pray is God's Spirit moving in us, then our journey toward ourselves and each other is a religious one.[15] In it we can expect to find not only the self we are each given to be, but Otherness, like a great Self holding us in being. Individuation, then, is not an ego project of self-redemption that we elect. It is risk and exposure "to all the powers of the non-ego, of heaven and hell, of grace and destruction, in order to reach that point where...[we have] become simple enough to accept those influences, or whatever it is we call 'God's will,' which come from the Unfathomable...."[16]

This understanding of Jung's did not spring from his theoretical musings but straight from the bowels of his own being: "The knowledge I was...seeking, still could not be found in the science of those days. I myself had to undergo the original experience, and, moreover, try to plant the results of my experience in the soil of reality;...It was then I dedicated myself to the service of the psyche. I loved it and hated it....My delivering myself over to it...was the only way by which I could endure my existence and live it as fully as possible."[17]

In the individuation process we find desire working both ways, not only in our desire for the unfathomable Other, but in its desire for us. When desire in its full colors breaks through to our consciousness, it brings with it conviction of the reality of the unseen world and its passionate interest in us. The symbolizing of our meeting seems to be pressed from its side as much as our own, a "terrifying discovery" for everyone who opens that door. For, as Jung saw, "a religious experience one way or another, for therein is revealed its immanental life force. It wants to step over...into visible life, to take concrete shape."[18]

We can appreciate what a relief it is to many to see Freud dismissing such religious experience as mere illusion, little more than childish wishes for a heavenly parent to relieve us of our guilt, avenging us and at the same time consoling us for the suffering that makes us feel vindictive. With such denial and reductionism we can remain blissfully ignorant of the door that leads to the terrifying discovery of Being. Rescued into consciousness through the devices of Oedipal explanation, we can avoid the fearful unknown. Jung's greatest separation from Freud was in this experience and the discovery in it "that this door, a highly inconspicuous side-door on an unsuspicious-looking and easily overlooked foot path...leads to the secret of transformation and renewal."[19]

EGO AND THE FIRST DARKNESS

When we open that door, darkness greets us. We are so accustomed to pairing growth with illumination and God with light that we have quite effaced the darkness where God waits, in what Marion Milner's little boy patient called the "lovely black."[20] Not just one but two kinds of darkness confront us here, two kinds of ignorance really, where we are left not seeing or knowing what to do.

The first unknowing surrounds an ego not yet able to claim its own life, to emerge from a state of archaic identity with objects. There our wobbly subjectivity barely sees its differentiation from the object with which it is intertwined in what Jung calls a *participation mystique*. In that mixture with another we fall under "compulsion and impossible responsibility."[21] Joined to another in this way, it is not safety and security we find; we do not feel taken care of. Rather, we become obsessed with taking care of the other in a kind of codepending with our partner in drinking or smoking, or our unceasing compulsive efforts to fix our friend's problems or take on all the burdens of the world. We feel fraught and yet inert. We both depend on the other and feel the other depending on us. Our backs bend under the burden. We simply plod along, yearning for effortless security in the other and feeling our mission to provide care and an end to burdensome problems for others. Our egos are not here yet to house the passionate desire of our psyches. But the energy is—and it rushes out to the objects on which we project all our security and joy. We are living in the dark, ignorant of what is moving us and what it asks of us, but still a mass of bustle and make-do.

Here is an example. A self-employed widower in his late forties saw himself slowly sinking into debt. Expenses far outstripped income. His many responsibilities—children, mortgage, car, all the paraphernalia of a household and a profession—were real and large. He was slipping into a kind of numb inertia, both burdened and helpless, plodding along in his work, feeling he had made every effort to improve his income but with little success. As with Sisyphus, the rock always rolled back to push him down to the bottom of the hill to start over again. He regressed. His debts mounted; so did his depression. The only answer—the one he longed for with heart and soul—that would cure his troubles, make things right, was more money. Money was the object that received all the projections of his passionate desires. Money was the mother who would take care of him. Money was God—all-powerful, all salvation.

I waded in and dared to examine his money complex. In the midst of tumultuous, rough, ragged sessions what slowly emerged from the dark was an ego differentiated from the mother-god, money. He had never felt backed by anyone, but always, since childhood almost, on his own, having to make his own way in the world. His mother's mother-god was money: If you had it you were safe; if you didn't, you lived in constant jeopardy. He began to see that he, like his mother, thought money the only answer and that in his longing for it he was longing for a safe holding self. He wanted finally to be held in being by a mother, herself without anxiety, who would provide shelter for him. His father conveyed the same message, but from the other side. There simply never would be enough money; you just had to plod through the days in backbreaking labor to keep something coming in. No release but death. And his father did die early.

For this man to see what was there in the darkness of his money complex was to leave mother and father, to give up seeing literally and begin seeing symbolically. His ego was alone indeed, not backed up by a Self because he projected what he had of a

Self onto money. Or to put it another way, the Self was hiding in money, trying to get at him but blocked by his identifying it with cash.[22] The Self kept pushing at him but he experienced it only in the dark, in a negative form—not having enough Self to hold him in being. He missed it. He wept for it.

Finally the Self did come. He began to see he had made money his particular Self-symbol, his God-image. He saw through money to what it might convey to him of the transcendent. Like Jesus' parables directed to those who had eyes and would not see and ears and would not hear (Mt 13:13), he knew he had to get new eyes and new ears. And then he felt the faint touchings of the Self coming near.[23] Then, amazingly enough, as he began to free the Self from his projection of it onto matter and saw that it was really what mattered, his income began to go up! Even more astonishing was the fact that when occasionally he fell again into literalizing the Self as money, his income went down. Outer and inner events joined to give him the long-sought backing.

We must remember how many of us know this anguish over money worries, and fall with it into a simple-minded reductionism. Think of how, faced with wandering homeless people, we throw money at them, not really seeing or hearing them, not recognizing them as possessing selves of their own, however covered over and forgotten, individual and unique selves that need to be seen and held in being by other holding selves in order to find and create their own homes.

St. Luke's Hospital, years ago, had in effect a program of seeing selves, in which some of my women students worked. They would be assigned to new mothers who were overwhelmed by money problems and now had to face the responsibility of a child as well. The students were there for the mothers, to see them and hear them, to support and to hold them in being and try to prevent their becoming abusive to their infants out of their lonely terrors and self-loathing. Feeling too tiny to carry such great responsibilities, they would inflict their suffering selves onto their babies.

It takes sacrifice to move into the dark to see where we are caught in inertia, in frustrations of our desires to be taken care of and compulsions to take care of others—utterly, in every thing. We must sacrifice that comforting return to childish dependence on parents and parental substitutes—our bosses, our churches, our beneficial all-providing governments. We must renounce that desire, that incestuous desire, by going forward into the dark of the unconscious to find our own relation to its depths, both perplexing and nourishing.[24]

Here again Jung parts from Freud. Release from regressive pulls to the parents turns out not just to free us to go forward into ego life. We can go now to the unconscious to find our own proper individual place in it, unblocked by parental complexes. This is ego in quest of Self. Here we seek our God-image in the cauldron of immediate experience that Jung sees as the hallmark of religion. Here we do not borrow our relation to God from others, but go to God directly. Dogma, text, and worshiping community support our passionate desire for direct encounter. They do not substitute for it. Jung speaks to the point:

> Shouldn't we let God himself speak in spite of our only too comprehensible fear of the primitive experience? I consider it my task and my duty to educate my patients and pupils to the point where they can accept the direct demand that is made upon them from within. This path is so difficult that I cannot see how the indispensable sufferings along the way could be supplanted by any kind of technical procedure. Through my study of the early Christian writings I have gained a deep and indelible impression of how dreadfully serious an experience of God is. It is no different today.[25]

Our sacrifice of childish dependence leads to a meeting from the other side. It can be a strong and fruitful encounter. A man in his late fifties had avoided conflict assiduously, which meant it ceaselessly attacked him from the outside. He was run out of his job. His wife, near despair over his dodging what he would promise to do, dressed him down. Bright, vigorous, she waded in and he squirmed. He raged inwardly at her tone, her argumentativeness, her always being right when she pointed out that he had lost the tax forms, that he had not written the crucial letter to secure his job future, that he had failed to make a phone call to set up the best deal to sell their house. And on and on. His life, his livelihood, his love for his wife, hers for him—all suffered.

We made little headway analyzing this formidable block. He had the insight that his fear of open conflict and his own aggression stemmed from seeing his father go mad in the midst of a family that denied it. It yielded some relief but only very slow change. Then a dream came that took us further into the concealed depths. An ocean liner is stranded at sea. It is a large ship, full of people, but there it sits, powerless, still, in the waters. The captain takes the dreamer down into the dark engine room. The motors have been sabotaged. The dreamer receives this knowledge, but it does not move him to do anything.

Very gradually, circling round this dream, we learned that the dreamer himself might have sabotaged the engines, preferring inertial stillness to movement. That admission made possible the sacrifice of his tie to his family's way of doing things, denying and living around the father's madness. A second dream confirmed this interpretation. Again, there was a ship, though this time not an ocean liner but a small yacht. It lies idle in the waters, this time off the coast, not far out at sea. The engines are sabotaged again, and this time the dreamer knows he has done the job because he did not want to return to land.

So there we sit in the analysis, idling in the water. The dreams, his wife's desperation as well as his bouts with previous therapists told me not to position myself as mover to his moved, or we, too, would land in a stalemated power struggle. And he has the upper hand, because he can pull out the engines! So I do nothing. I wait on the Self. Over a year later it moved and he responded actively, fearfully.

He was sought for a job in a foreign country that specifically focused on solving conflicts among four groups of people vying for control of a common property. It was as if he was being told, Fine, if you cannot work to use your own aggression in your personal conflicts, then here is conflict in others to work on. He was being sought, not just for a job, but for something greater, from himself or from life. He was being summoned to work on his life-long fear.[26] Appealed to this way, he took his chance; he went at the job with excitement. He turned on his energies. He sacrificed his inertia, gave up his floating in the water, faced into the dark.

EGO AND THE SECOND DARKNESS

If the first kind of darkness comes to us when our ego needs to take hold, to act and emerge from identity with the object, with all our passionate desires locked onto it, the second kind of darkness comes when our ego is established. We have withdrawn our projections and can take all our energies of desire back into our own subjectivity. Our energy returns. We feel invigorated, purposeful, determined. We know what to do. We plan, take risks, bet on our own powers to pull it off. If our first sense of darkness comes from ignorance of the center, our second kind of darkness comes when we have found it and know now that we believe in the transcendent. We have found our images for it, both in tradition and in immediate experience. We have developed our values, taken up our causes, pledged our faith.

At the lowest end of this second stage we may fall into inflation. This is easy to spot. Either we exhibit a general jazzed-up state of being, acting as if we can make anything happen, or an unstable narcissism that always reduces events of worldwide importance to our own dimensions. Remember Saddam Hussein declaring soon after his invasion of Kuwait, "I will not be humiliated..." as if war hung only on his saving face. The inverse is also quickly visible, when in deflation, as in a black hole, our aggrandized depression and anxiety draw everything and everyone and all events into our own orbit: "I and the universe" is the order of being.

At best, something much darker takes over. It is the identifying texture of the developed ego-state. We have withdrawn our libido from projection on others. We have tamed and contained it in images that reflect our own experience of the transcendent and really can devote ourselves to serve those ideals. But how do we find them when darkness covers all? And darkness really does. We are in the dark precisely because we are exercising to the fullest what Jung calls our "religious instinct," the faculty of soul that knows it is related to Deity.[27] In withdrawing our libido from identification with objects and differentiating ourselves from its misdirected passions, we renounce any effort to appropriate unconscious process simply for our power and possession. We sacrifice the idea of the unconscious as a honey pot into which we can fall at any time for sweet pleasures, for beckoning ideas that will attract others, for relationships that simply taste good.

We know the unconscious as other, as the language of the other. We accept its different kind of mentation in conversation with consciousness and accept full responsibility for our thought and our feelings. Let us say that this is the goal of analysis. It is achieved. Then we ask, we must ask: After analysis, what?[28]

If it is really true that the unconscious is another medium through which God touches us, what do we do when the God in hiding there approaches? All our hard-won insight, our enlarged seeing-into falls under the great shadow of the Holy. We are brought into an illuminating darkness. Ignorance, as a cloud of unknowing, overcomes us, for this God is so much bigger than anything we have conceived. Our eye is overwhelmed. It is not eclipsed. Like a cat's pupils, our inner eyes enlarge in the dark. Like the cat, our whiskers twitch, sensing a great presence, there, awaiting us.

Darkness is the necessary way, for the God who draws near lies outside our God-images. It is not so much that our images of God are wrong or our religious practices mistaken. They are simply too small in their finiteness. The dark side of God is a merciful one, effacing useless images, stretching, pushing us beyond even the best of what we have found in our traditions and created in our prayers.[29] We cannot squeeze a big foot into a small shoe. We need new containers. We know it, but still we feel lost, unstable, with nowhere to stand, wandering in the dark. And yet this lonely dark night can be precious, providential. Here is an example.

I speak of a woman, a nun, a generous religious. She has a strong consistent relation with God, fed by daily prayer and a strong steady commitment to do what she can to better the world. She comes to celebrate her jubilee year, a quarter of a century as a nun. Instead of the customary party to celebrate, she looks to nurture a seed of an idea planted when, a year before, she had visited a foreign country. She wants to live among the poor, not as a benevolent patron, but aligning herself with oppressed persons, to learn from them how hope may be kept alive in a seemingly hopeless situation. She understands her choice as a renewal of her vows and an expression of her passionate desire to give herself more completely, to come close to God.

Everything falls apart. The person who had invited her to join in the work abroad abandons her, leaving the country with no indicated date of return, no message. Wherever she tries to find work, for one reason or another, her offer is refused. She must come home, and she does. She is angry, bewildered; her ardent offering of herself has been rejected. Things grow darker. She has no living place and must go to a strange new one. Her old job is gone and she must take a new one that is not, as she sees it, her vocation. Her close friends and family do not understand her anguish. Finally, her health deserts her. The last blow: urgent surgery and a long convalescence take her away from analysis, from the only place she knew where she could examine the anxiety, the tumult, the dejection of this dark moment.

She suffers acutely—anger at the woman who abandoned her, anger at God, for taking everything away just at her moment of renewed devotion, without any indication of where or how to go. She suffers, she is confused, but does not feel abandoned by God. She turns, as always, to God, but wonders if she is using God like an aspirin. In her unsettled condition, her usual ways of praying no longer work. "I'm looking at God, saying do something, be something. But God is deaf and mute." Yet she cannot stop praying. "I'm waiting for something to come; I have to be there. I don't want to be out if I'm waiting for a call." But she finds the silence "terrible"; she knows herself like Jesus hanging on the cross waiting for a response. Her God-image changes. "I feel God as separate, which I experience as a relief." She sees that what she had earlier worshiped was "too trite, too small." What she waits on now, she says, "is not a gentle God. I am afraid of this God, its uncontrollability, its demandingness. What will be asked?" And though she feels that one by one everything that gave her refuge and comfort is being taken from her—her self-offering, her home, friends, job, health, analysis—she feels she must "stay empty. I would not have seen this separate God, different from what we think, if I had been full of my life and ideas." She knows she has been pushed and pulled into this "privileged time of suffering," but fears that even this understanding is arrogant. She lives in her dark night. She says, "If God comes back, it is not going to be because I recreated God; it has to come back of its own."

In this waiting for what comes back on its own, she feels torn by opposing emotions, she says. "I feel God leading me to a place I do not know, but I also feel something being done to me against my will." She wants to surrender completely but feels God is beating her up and angrily she refuses to yield.

She struggles with these opposites for many months, right on into her surgery and convalescence, when she is so helpless she cannot even go to the bathroom unless someone helps her there. In that utter physical dependence, a precious bit of her psychological complex emerges from the dark. She recognizes that once again her projections have obscured God. She has seen God as like her mother, beating the spunk out of her, saying, Do it my way; your reality is not real, does not count! Insight into this projection comes to her with the force of a blow, but through the simplest of incidents. She leaves the hospital to convalesce in a house run by nuns because she cannot get out of bed without assistance. Her mother calls and says, "Let's go out to lunch tomorrow." Even in the extremity of major surgery her mother does not see her reality but unrealistically superimposes her own wishes. When this bit of projection falls away, as God ceases to be her mother, she really sees that surrender to God does not mean self-annihilation. In fact, her utter dependence in her convalescence shows her deeply and fully that God gives us everything we have, makes us what we are. We are utterly dependent on God.

This example shows us much. Nothing, we learn, must stand in the way between us and God. Could we call this God's desire? Once, in praying, she hears God saying, "I want you to love me more than your desire for wholeness and integrity. I want to give you me so you can be a whole passionate woman." We can expect every last problem and bit of projection to be spaded up as God comes to us and our world. The coming of the Holy pushes out whatever lies in the way. All that is dark to us; unconscious projections, like this woman's bit of her mother on to God, will come to light. And conversely, everything that is in the light, like this nun's God-image and her picture of herself among the oppressed and the powerless, will be brought into the dark. Her desire is fulfilled, but not in any expected way. She is powerless, but not with her sharing of others' hunger and poverty, which, though difficult, she could handle. The fulfillment is in her help-

lessness to bring about her dream of service.[30] This powerless-
ness changes her theology. "A whole new model is needed, not to
be a mere provider of services."

Sacrifice at this ego level is our burnt offering. As this
woman says, her "desire is disciplined and educated." We are
brought to offer up all we have found and created as God-images,
both collective and individual. In the mass, which Jung calls a
rite of individuation, we find this self-offering strongly symbolized.[31] We bring as a symbolic part of the bread and wine, in the
sacrifice of the Eucharist, the strongest of our values, the causes
we devote ourselves to, the images that give meaning to our lives.
We do not disparage these values, but recognize them as our centers, and feel moved to offer them up. Our desire is invested in
them; they have become our gods. Our desires become love only
after we offer them up to God. We may even have to offer up our
religion itself, all that we have found as our way to God, in order
to receive God.

And come to us God does, for the sacrifice and self-offering
that goes on in the mass goes both ways. Just as the woman suffers the breaking of her God-images, indeed, the sacrifice of religious certainty, bringing them as gifts to God, so God suffers, we
might say, being seen through the small lens of our projections
in order to come into our focus. That was Job's protest: Why
don't you stay as I know you, as you told me you were, the God of
ethical monotheism? And Yahweh's answer still thunders for us,
Because I am alive and so is my world! The hippo and crocodile
do not fit the rules, nor does the chaos I preside over and hold in
my creative act. Job has an immediate experience of God that
surpasses old words and previous understanding. The new
announces its being, and Job, seeing it, becomes intercessor for
his friends, who still expect God to play by the rules. Job is our
intercessor too, as we are brought into God's vast darkness and
moved to offer up our God-images.

SELF

I have gone back and forth using the words *God* and *Self.* Now I
must try for greater precision. If we understand with Jung that

the Self is our greater personality, the "diamond body" at the center of the whole psyche, which acts like a God within us, what connection can we draw to the God of our religion?[32] For this idea of the Self is simply Jung's God-image, isn't it? Jung constantly dodges this question, protesting that he stopped at the borders of psychology and left metaphysics for the theologians.[33]

There are many ways to argue about that, but one seems to me most persuasive. If we understand the Self not to be God but rather that within us that knows about God, we can ask, with some hope of an answer, What in fact does it know? What happens to us when we experience the Self? Where does it lead? It tells us about our desire for what it leads to, which is the being that holds us in being, God's being. It tells us that our desire can be transformed into a steady, trustworthy, true loving. This is what Saint Bernard knows when he says we move, if we move in this steady loving, from loving God for our own sakes to loving God for God's sake.

What happens to us on our side when we experience the Self and move into living toward it? We know that God is not the invention of consciousness but transcends it.[34] When it touches us we get radically rearranged. We feel pushed off center stage and yet know our presence on stage remains necessary. We feel empty yet vital, a cup that can only receive and yet miraculously always is filled. A woman in her fifties knew this experience and a brief but numinous dream pictured it for her: "The Grail Cup sings!"[35]

We are freed now of the need to know definitively or to control what we know—whether text, person, or event—by reducing things to a formula or simple explanations. We open to the unexpected and irrational.[36] We let things happen. We are surprised. We are alert and actively responsible and take responsibility for our actions. We see that our ego ideas and ideals are partial at best. We become receivers of a new center, as we are moved out of the center, playing our parts.

We engage in a knowing that is a knowing together, joining all that lives in and through us. Consciousness consistently appropriates unconscious levels; we own them as also our responsibility; and unconsciousness constantly refreshes consciousness, dissolving its hard edges and fixed purposes in its endless flow.

Life feels vital to us, exciting. Something addresses us, wants to be housed in us. A middle-aged woman describes such an experience that continued over some weeks at different intervals. She feels, she says, "so much energy, as if burning off dross, just circulating energy down under all my defense....I am not manic. It is just intense energy inside me and emanating through me but it is not me; it 'lives' me." Gradually the intensity gathers into a "column of light, sort of backing me up, originating me. There it is; like an energizing presence manifesting itself as radiant light." It astonished her, for she saw that "it is awake and present eternally, and it is I who need to sleep. It goes on and on, circulating, coming to me, through me to others and through them and back again to its source, in and out like breathing, like the blood to and from the heart." She finds herself daily preoccupied with how to house this energy, how to accommodate it.

That is what makes living with the self an adventure. It is not fixed but gives rise to myriad expressions, and transcendence is part of its nature. We are surprised to discover that we, our egos, as subjects, seem to be its desired objects. Yet we must find ways to house this big objective Other in our subjectivity. This other reality that transcends the borders of subject and object expresses itself in abounding patterns, complexities of relationship that surpass cause and effect sequence. The vitality of presence is not confined to inner experience or outer events but seems to greet us now here, now there, sometimes both at once. Everywhere it is offered and everywhere come opportunities to be related to it. Truly *it* lives us.[37] We feel pulled to the borders of what we know, into that unknowing that is more like contemplating than analyzing, more like loving than understanding.

We get double vision. We see connections between personal and world problems.[38] In facing the thug in ourselves who, in a dream for example, wrecks a roadside café, banging tables, throwing food out on the ground, busting chairs, because he knows no other way to make us see him, we are also facing the throwing of pollution into our cities' rivers, toxic waste into our seas, toxic hostility into our social interchanges. In reaching for the starved child in ourselves, we send food to infants dying of famine in Ethiopia. The woman faced with the task of accommodating energy, dreamt after one of her experiences with it that the basement of her building was being renovated to provide infant day care services to the community.

Tackling the task of housing the energy the Self awakens always means including all parts of the psyche, from the least among us to the most. That double vision means sensitivity to synchronistic happenings, where acausally connected events order our whole lives. Such events confirm something we suspected; or they point a direction we should take; or they knock down a wall between something seen and unseen. These events feel like grace, what scripture calls signs. And we know from scripture these signs are not the end all or be all. It is what they point to that is. They open us to glimpse the whole interconnectedness of life: we are all interdependent, near neighbor and far, this country and the one the other side of the globe, rain forest and city, the spider and the human, matter and spirit, Earth and cosmos.[39]

Living this way we slowly draw to ourselves community that goes far beyond our usual borders of social intercourse. We see that authentic group life turns out not to be based on proximity or expediency but on a deep respectful interest in the "diamond-hard body" in the other. We work to tame the tigers and crocodiles in us and no longer just let loose into society our pouncing hostilities and snapping aggressions. Our desire to align ourselves with transcendence affects the whole social body. It is like a plant; in living true to our own nature we also make oxygen for everyone to breathe. Desiring the center in ourselves, which is in the center of all selves and things, we unclog an artery, making passage from and to the center easier for everyone, and others' efforts make it more accessible to us. Together we build up the spiritual atmosphere. In chaos theory, the butterfly effect means a butterfly lifting its wing can change the course of the whole cosmos. Similarly, one or two of us, desiring to be planted in the center can open a way to it and it to us for all of us. Such a vision of the connection between our desire for personal wholeness and the ultimate wholeness of all of life makes us feel simultaneously that we live in daily life and *sub specie aeternitatis*. A middle-aged woman exclaimed about that double sense on waking from this dream: She sees two pictures of the Buddha, one a huge standing Buddha composed out of parts of everyday life—cars, roads, buildings, lakes, trees, animals, people; the second is an ordinary place in the country, but when she looks again, there facing her is a Buddha in half a cantaloupe melon.

This double vision that sees that inner and outer are the same, one and all are the same, makes our ego very strong in the sense of steady, and very quiet in the sense that it shuts up and we bow our heads before the God the Self knows about. We keep the door open to the other side, and do it daily, full of anguish to remember we still forget the central point, the open secret that what the Self points to is there offering Itself for our taking. We carefully consider it in all we think and do and see our main task, like the woman with the energy, is to house it, in the world. We hold the opposites. This is loving God with our whole heart, soul, mind, might.

Our conflicts do not cease, but our capacity is greater not to get sweated up into a froth. Others can reach us because we are reached by the center. So we look the same, perhaps even a little worse for wear. But we take heart from the story about the one who arrived at the center. He is a ragman who looks anything but unique or special or the saint he may be, but the cherry tree blossoms as he goes by.[40] The poet Juan Ramón Jiménez, winner of the Nobel Prize in Literature in 1956, called the Dean of Hispanic poets, writes of this miraculous arrival in a poem called "Full Consciousness":

> You take me, full consciousness, god desiring
> through the whole world.
> ...
> Your voice of white fire
> Within the totality of water, ship, sky,
> tracing the routes with delicacy,
> tracing with light my certain orbit
> of a black body
> housing the bright diamond inside.[41]

The trajectory of our desire completes its arc receiving the God who desires us, not as human sacrifice but as loving heart. We discover with surprise that our desire, which impels us through our idols to God, is matched by God's bigger desire for us. Our desire is but the pulsing of God's desire bringing us home.

At the end of his life Jung had these words about this mystery: "I falter before the task of finding the language which might adequately express the incalculable paradoxes of love....I sometimes feel that Paul's words—'Though I speak with the tongues of men and of angels, and have not love'—might well be the first condition of all cognition and the quintessence of divinity itself. Whatever the learned interpretation may be of the sentence 'God is love,' the words affirm the *complexio oppositorum* of the Godhead....Here is the greatest and smallest, the remotest and nearest, the highest and lowest, and we cannot discuss one side of it without also discussing the other. No language is adequate to this paradox....No words express the whole....If [we] possess a grain of wisdom,...[let us] lay down [our] arms and name the unknown by the more unknown, *ignotum per ignotius*—that is, by the name of God."[42]

Notes

This chapter was originally delivered to the Fordham University 150th Anniversary Jung Conference in New York City (1991) and published in *The Fires of Desire: Erotic Energies and the Spiritual Quest,* eds. F. R. Halligan and J. J. Shea (New York: Crossroad, 1992).

1. C. G. Jung, *Letters*, 2 vols., eds. G. Adler and A. Jaffé, trans. R. F. C. Hull (Princeton: Princeton University Press, 1973 and 1975), I, 26 May 1923, 40.

2. C. G. Jung, *The Secret of the Golden Flower*, in *Alchemical Studies, Collected Works* 13, trans. R. F. C. Hull (Princeton: Princeton University Press, 1957/1967), par. 80.

3. C. G. Jung, *Memories, Dreams, Reflections,* ed. A. Jaffé, trans. Richard and Clara Winston (New York: Pantheon, 1963), 209.

4. Simone Weil, *Waiting for God,* trans. Emma Craufurd (New York: Putnam's, 1951), 111.

5. Jung, *Secret of the Golden Flower,* par. 15; see also C. G. Jung, *Symbols of Transformation, Collected Works* 5, trans. R. F. C. Hull (Princeton: Princeton University Press, 1956), par. 165.

6. All psychological material is taken from my practice as a psychoanalyst, with gratitude to the persons who allow me to do so.

7. For discussion of the relation of our own counsel and the "Wonderful Counselor," see A. B. Ulanov, "Religious Experience in Pastoral Counseling," in *Picturing God* (Cambridge, Mass.: Cowley, 1986), 106; see also A. B. Ulanov, "The Relation of Religion to Pastoral Counseling," *Journal of Religion and Mental Health* (January 1968).

8. See Jung, *Memories, Dreams, Reflections,* 192; see also C. G. Jung, "The Theory of Psychoanalysis," *Freud and Psychoanalysis, Collected Works* 4, trans. R. F. C. Hull (New York: Pantheon, 1955/1961).

9. Jung, *Letters,* I, 5 October 1945, 384.

10. See ibid., 16 May 1950, 557; see also Jung, *Memories, Dreams, Reflections,* 208; see also Jung, "Theory of Psychoanalysis," pars. 252, 282; see also Jung, *Symbols of Transformation,* pars. 185, 186, 188.

11. Vladimir Solovyev, *The Meaning of Love,* trans. Jane Marshall (London: Geoffrey Bles, 1945), 245; for discussion of this point, see A. B. Ulanov, "Two Sexes," *Men and Women: Sexual Ethics in Turbulent Times,* ed. Philip Turner (Cambridge, Mass.: Cowley, 1989), 22, 23.

12. See Jung, *Letters,* II, 14 September 1960, 592; see also Jung, *Letters,* I, 29 September 1934, 172.

13. See J. Sutherland, *Fairbairn's Journey into the Interior* (London: Free Association Books, 1989), 107; see also H. Kohut, *The Restoration of the Self* (New York: International Universities Press, 1977), 187n, 188n; see also H. Kohut, *How Does Analysis Cure?* (Chicago: University of Chicago, 1984), 48–50; for a discussion of "selfobject" as a function of experiencing, see R. D. Stolorow, B. Brandehaft, and G. E. Atwood, *Psychoanalytic Treatment: An Intersubjective Approach* (Hillsdale: Analytic Press, 1987), ch. 5.

14. See D. W. Winnicott, *Playing and Reality* (London: Tavistock, 1971), ch. 6; see also M. Eigen, "The Area of Faith in Winnicott, Lacan and Bion," *International Journal of Psycho-Analysis* 62 (1981), 413–433; see also A. B. Ulanov, "A Shared Space," *Quadrant* (New York: Jung Foundation, Spring 1985), ch. 8 of this book.

15. For discussion of individuation as a religious journey, see A. Jaffé, *Was C. G. Jung a Mystic?,* trans. Daina Dachler and Fiona Cairns (Einsiedeln, Switzerland: Daimon, 1989), 58, 80, 96, 98.

16. Jung, *Letters,* I, 14 May 1959, 556.

17. Jung, *Memories, Dreams, Reflections,* 192.

18. Jung, *Letters,* I, 10 January 1929, 59.

19. Ibid., I, 30 January 1934, 141; see also Jung, *Letters,* II, 22 November 1954, 196; see also, for discussion of the different methods of Freud and Jung in interpreting the unconscious, A. and B. Ulanov, *Religion and the Unconscious* (Louisville, Ky.: Westminster, 1975), ch. 2.

20. See M. Milner, *The Suppressed Madness of Sane Men* (New York: Tavistock, 1987), 632; see also Jaffé, *Was C. G. Jung a Mystic?,* 87.

21. Jung, *Secret of the Golden Flower,* par. 48.

22. For a fascinating discussion of the Self hiding in money, see *Soul and Money* (Dallas: Spring, 1982). Von Franz also notes that the mythological descriptions of punishments in hell can be understood as

symbols of the "Self constellated in a form which cannot be assimilated." M.-L. Von Franz, *Apuleius' Golden Ass* VIII (New York: Spring, 1970), 6.

23. Louis Dupré discusses the relation of theologies of the soul and the deeper self that Jung writes about. See his *Transcendent Selfhood* (New York: Crossroad, 1976), 95, 99.

24. For discussion of this point of regression into inertia (the theological sin of sloth), childish dependence and their connection to incest, see M. E. Harding, *Psychic Energy: Its Source and Its Transformation* (New York: Pantheon, 1963), 40ff., 142–44; see also Jung, *Symbols of Transformation*, pars. 313, 332, 345, 540; see also E. Humbert, *C. G. Jung: The Fundamentals of Theory and Practice*, trans. R. G. Jalbert (Wilmette: Chiron, 1984), 120–24; see also L. Donn, *Freud and Jung: Years of Friendship, Years of Loss* (New York: Scribner's, 1988), 142, 162; see also C. G. Jung, "Psychology and Religion," in *Psychology and Religion: West and East, Collected Works* 11, trans. R. F. C. Hull (New York: Pantheon, 1938/1958), pars. 8–9.

25. Jung, *Letters*, I, 26 May 1923, 40. Jung wrote almost twenty years later: "The Divine Presence is more than anything else....This is the only thing that really matters....I wanted the proof of a living spirit and I got it. Don't ask me at what price." Ibid., 30 January 1948, 492.

26. An old tale makes the same point. Someone is complaining to God about the assigned cross to be carried. God says, "OK, come with me," and takes the person to a huge cave which is stacked with all kinds of crosses—big heavy ones, little prickly ones, ones with jagged edges, ones with thorns. "Put that one down," says God. "Choose another one!"

27. See C. G. Jung, *Psychology and Alchemy, Collected Works* 12, trans. R. F. C. Hull (New York: Pantheon, 1953), par. 11. For discussion of what Jung calls our religious instinct, see A. B. Ulanov, *The Feminine in Jungian Psychology and in Christian Theology* (Evanston: Northwestern University Press, 1971), ch. 4.

28. This is a title taken from Barry Ulanov's article. For discussion of the unconscious as other and our responsibility for it, see the following theorists: E. Humbert, *C. G. Jung*, 124; H. W. Loewald, *Psychoanalysis and the History of the Individual* (New Haven: Yale University Press, 1978), 12, 21–23, 73; D. W. Winnicott, *Deprivation and Delinquency*, eds. C. Winnicott, R. Shepherd, and M. Davis (London: Tavistock, 1983), 96, 100, 111, 137; see also J. Lacan, *Écrits: A Selection*, trans. A. Sheridan (New York: Norton, 1977), 813, for commentary on Lacan's "essential assertion" that "the unconscious is Other than the subject"; see W. J. Richardson, "Psychoanalysis and the Being-Ques-

tion," in *Interpreting Lacan*, eds. J. S. Smith and W. Kerrigan (New Haven: Yale University Press, 1983), 139–59.

29. For discussion of the finding and breaking of our God-images, see A. B. Ulanov, "Picturing God," in *Picturing God*.

30. Jung writes, "The new thing prepared by fate seldom or never comes up to conscious expectations....It is a strangely appropriate expression of the total personality, an expression which one could not imagine in a more complete form." *Secret of the Golden Flower*, par. 19.

31. C. G. Jung, "Transformation Symbolism in the Mass," *Collected Works* 11, trans. R. F. C. Hull (New York: Pantheon 1954/1958), par. 414.

32. Jung, *Secret of the Golden Flower*, par. 68.

33. See Jung, *Letters*, I, 22 September 1944, 350; 5 October 1945, 384.

34. See Jung, *Memories, Dreams, Reflections*, 348.

35. See C. G. Jung, "The Development of the Personality," in *The Development of the Personality, Collected Works* 17, trans. R. F. C. Hull (New York: Pantheon, 1934/1954), pars. 294–305.

36. Jung writes, "Everything essential happens in the self and the ego functions as a receiver, spectator, and transmitter." Jung, *Letters*, I, 22 December 1942, 326; see also ibid., 8 February 1946, 411; see also Jung, *Secret of the Golden Flower*, par. 23.

37. See Jung, *Secret of the Golden Flower*, par. 117.

38. Jung writes, "A political situation is the manifestation of a parallel psychological problem in millions of individuals. This problem is largely *unconscious* (which makes it a particularly dangerous one!). It consists of a conflict between a conscious (ethical, religious, philosophical, social, political, psychological) standpoint and an unconscious one which is characterized by the same aspects but represented in...more archaic form." Jung, *Letters*, I, 23 September 1949, 535.

39. See C. G. Jung, "Synchronicity: An Acausal Connecting Principle," in *The Structure and Dynamics of the Psyche, Collected Works* 8, trans. R. F. C. Hull (New York: Pantheon, 1952/1960); see also C. G. Jung, *Mysterium Coniunctionis, Collected Works* 14, trans. R. F. C. Hull (New York: Pantheon, 1963), pars. 769–71; see also R. Aziz, *C. G. Jung's Psychology of Religion and Synchronicity* (Albany, N.Y.: State University of New York Press, 1990), 207–10.

40. See M.-L. Von Franz, *Alchemy: An Introduction to the Symbolism and the Psychology* (Toronto: Inner City Books, 1980), 160.

41. Juan Ramón Jiménez, *God Desired and Desiring*, trans. Antonio T. de Nicolás (New York: Paragon House, 1987), 15.

42. Jung, *Memories, Dreams, Reflections*, 354.

Part II

TEACHING JUNG ON RELIGION

Chapter 5

Image and Imago:
Jung and the Study of Religion

Jung's investigation of the human psyche has had an extraordinary and far-reaching impact on the twentieth century. To assess the implications of his work for the study of religion, we must begin where Jung began and ended, with Jung the clinician engaged in psychotherapy with specific persons.[1] Clinical work and clinical focus on the effects of specific psychic images, manifested in the dreams, complexes, symptoms, and defenses of specific persons form the basis of Jung's research and anchor his far-flung speculations about human belief systems and processes of transformation.

A clear example of what I am talking about is Jung's recovery to collective consciousness of alchemy. Here, for him, was a serious endeavor, which had occupied some of the best minds for more than seventeen centuries, but considered mumbo-jumbo, nonsense, in our own century and for several preceding it. He saw there in abstruse chemical operations significant efforts at the transformation of human being and of the world's being. Jung was drawn to alchemy, not as an exotic solipsistic fancy, but as a world of endless parallels to the processes of human individuation. Another example is found in Jung's investigations of Christian dogma as it is reflected in, say, the mass, the doctrine of the Trinity, the problem of theodicy. Again, his understanding here springs directly from his work with patients and with images evinced in his own psychology. Scholars using Jung's insights or methods must always remember the clinical basis of his work. Failure to do so is perilous for any attempt to make use of Jungian theory.

IMAGE AND IMAGO

As a clinician, Jung devised methods that deal with the psyche in its own modes of self-expression—through images. This approach strongly emphasizes the objective existence of the psyche as real, as *there*. The psyche addresses us. It has something to say and a language with which to say it. Jung conceptualized this experience of the psyche as living and autonomous—as other than consciousness though inclusive of it—in his term the "objective psyche."[2] What he means by that is a presence of unconscious mental processes intimately bound up with a life of the instincts antecedent to the growth of the conscious ego. This life of autonomous and spontaneous instinct is the primordial stuff out of which the human ego emerges. Jung saw the objective psyche as existing in all persons, regardless of cultural, historical, social, political, sexual, racial, or religious differences. If we really wish to hear what this level of human psychic process addresses to us, we must learn its language and accept it on its own terms. We must not approach it as simply a language to be translated into our own and understood as we understand our own.

A major difference between Freud's and Jung's approaches to the psyche centers on just this point. Freud approaches the unconscious from the point of view of consciousness and translates its free-flowing primary-process thinking into the terms of secondary-process thinking characterized by logic, verbal concepts, laws of contradiction, and so forth. Freud then gives us the helpful concepts of ego, id, and superego that exchange energy according to principles of reality and pleasure. Jung, in contrast, tries to deal directly with the language of the unconscious, and thus gives us such notions as the shadow, the anima, the persona.[3] Such odd, sometimes even comic terms, account in part for the deep suspicion with which Jung is held by some sections of the psychoanalytic community. Remember, for example, radio's Lamont Cranston, whose melodramatic moments were always identified by the announcement, "The Shadow knows what evil lurks in the hearts of men...." It seems sometimes as if Jung has gone over entirely to the other side, the unconscious one, at the expense of reason. These symbols seem to be used, then, only in a detached verbal way and appear to reasonably normal persons as so much jargon, relentlessly typing actual experiences according to some prefabricated and not quite rational scheme.[4]

Jung stands out from other theorists of the psyche by his central emphasis on images, for it is through images we hear what the objective psyche wants to say to us. The language of the psyche is archetypal images that express the felt meaning of the instincts.[5] Through these images we wrestle with the problems that beset us, and through them we glimpse the way to seek healing. Through these images we experience healing, discover sometimes blessed insights, see conflicts end, gather our energies into new forms that become available to us for living in the world around us, in relation to people around us.

By *image* Jung means something specific, what might be called a fantasy image—not a psychic reflection of an external object, but rather an image depending on unconscious fantasy activity, the product of which appears in consciousness, and often with startling abruptness. The image arrives. We receive it into ego-awareness. It appears to us, it enters our consciousness. We do not produce it or conclude with it, though we must work very hard to lay the ground for its appearance. We cannot construct it or manufacture it, though we can participate in its becoming. At higher levels of development this participation is essential, even if never conclusive for our understanding.

Great psychological value clings to fantasy images. They elicit emotional reactions from us. They engage us by enraging us, by disgusting us, moving us to tears, to awe, to reverence, to perplexity, but always with some degree of fascination.[6] The image grips our attention, even invades us, as, for example, in obsessive fantasies. The image is complex yet has a quality of wholeness about it and its own serious autonomous purpose. "The image," Jung says, "is a condensed expression of the psychic situation as a whole."[7] Not only does it reflect the unconscious contents that are momentarily brought together ("constellated" in the Jungian vocabulary), but also the immediate conscious situation that has stimulated the unconscious in response to some contents and inhibited it in response to others. Any grasp of the meaning of the image, therefore, must include the relation of conscious and unconscious, and not leave either of them out. An image, then, cannot just be taken at face value, but must be entered into, wrestled with, linked up with our conscious thoughts, feelings, and values.

A personal image expresses the contents of what Jung calls the personal unconscious and of the personally conditioned conscious situation.[8] The image often conveys private significance to its owner without expressing much meaning for anyone else. A primordial archetypal image will touch a shared level of human experience, common not only in the present but across history.[9] It will give a personal tone to "certain ever-recurring psychic experiences"; it expresses a living process and "gives a co-ordinating and coherent meaning both to the sensuous and to the inner perceptions, which at first appear to be without either order or connection...."[10] The image thus liberates energy for conscious inspection, meditation, and eventual use. It also links energies to a definite meaning, one that serves to guide action along the path that corresponds to the meaning. It loosens dammed-up energies by transforming natural instincts into mental structures. This kind of image is vital and immediate. It can form the dynamic basis of an idea based upon it. In other words, focus on images not only does not exclude the development of ideas, it may hasten and deepen them.

Images that arrest our attention, intrude on our behavior, and shape society take on a role Jung calls that of the "imago." The imago combines personal and archetypal images into one dynamic unity. An imago inhabits an interrealm between subject and object that expresses the subject's experience of the object.[11] For example, a child's experience of a parent is constructed of many elements—perceptions of what is actually there in the parent, subjective reactions of the child to the parent, projections of the child of its own good and bad feelings onto the parent, and archetypal associations to its mother or father. The resulting imago inhabits the space between the actual outer other—the parent—and the inner experience of the subject. The imago is, then, a large gathering place for the many aspects of the object, for the subject's response to the object, for conscious experience and the unconscious projection onto the object, and for archetypal images evoked by the experience of the object. All of these combine to form the rudimentary layers of a symbolic image that represents the meeting and interpenetration of these multiple levels of reality. To recognize the imago-world means having the ability to develop an authentic symbolic life.

The inner and outer levels of our life are bridged by symbolic images that comprise a distinct realm of reality in themselves. They act as the intercessory agents for consciousness, representing the symbolic value to the subject of the interpenetration of spheres of reality. For example, to a child on one level his mother is altogether "his" in that she belongs to himself (or herself) and is directly connected to a host of subjective reactions, needs, impulses, and feelings in the child's emotional and spiritual world. On another level, the mother is herself, moving in her own world objectively, a world that the child perceives as "other," as belonging to the mother alone. On still another level, she stands for the archetypal world of the mother, embodying in her concrete person some several aspects of that primordial brooding presence. The combined parts of these perceptions and images make up the child's mother-imago. An adult conscious of such a mother-imago still operating can discover through it aspects of self, of the woman who is his mother, and of the mother archetype per se. Consciousness of the imago leads to wide awareness of self, of actual other person, and of dimension of otherness.[12]

We can transpose this concept into the world of religious studies, with some excellent results, I think, just as Jung found in his investigation of the God-image or God-imago. Here, too, the image of God we investigate in our own field of religious study, or in our own religious experience, is made up of several layers. On one level it points to all those impulses, needs, fears, longings for protection, and desires for unity that we connect and project to the God-image. Inevitably, at least in part, it must express the subjective contents that we project onto the image— what Freud called our "wish-God."[13] Freud stopped here in his analysis. But the God-image also includes all that other world belonging to God that breaks into our world as truly objective, as addressing us, blessing us, summoning us. Both these levels are contained in scripture and the texts of faith-theologies, of histories of thought and histories of symbol and myth that exist objectively in documents and worshiping communities. This is a whole world of secondary-process thinking that Freud overlooked in his analysis of religion, making a straight and exclusive line as he did from the fantasy of the believer to belief, excluding texts, history, and a whole structure of documented experience.

We go to another level when we examine images of God from the point of view of the primordial, looking to see which archetypes they embody and inspecting their many greatly contrasting aspects. Cassirer's reference to Usener's notion of "momentary gods" is useful here as a corroboration of method and concept.[14]

Focusing on images this way gives a clinician certain advantages that have exact counterparts in the study of religion. For example, I can review my patients' material with a view to the regnant images operative in each one's psychology. Jung's emphasis on images gives me, as a clinician, a distinct approach to diagnosis and prognosis, not necessarily an exclusive approach or one that competes with other systems, but certainly always a supplementing one of high value. The same is true for those who adopt this approach in the study of religions.

For any analytical system or theory ultimately must offer finely made metaphorical nets to throw over the living data, the poignant suffering before one. Whether we speak of the introjected objects of Guntrip and Klein, or the dynamic deployment of energy in the id, ego, and superego systems of Freud, or the bombardment of stimuli upon the narcissistic wound and borderline defense system of Kohut and Kernberg, we are talking in pictures, in images that shine through even the most complicated and abstruse theoretical formulations. The advantage of Jung's approach is to go directly to the images the psyche offers us about its own condition. Thus, for example, instead of diagnostic labels for a person I may be working with, such as borderline, depressive, schizoid, obsessive, I may think of my patient as occupied with a cluster of recurring gun images—guns that do not work because the bullets are the wrong size, or the firing pin is missing, because the trigger is broken, or the marksman's aim is off. A person who feels himself to be split into a right half and a left half may be involved in this set of images, one whose right half is collapsing while his left half is reduced to chaos and is drenched in pain. Images of right and left, which often superimpose themselves on other metaphors, come to be ways of describing perception, or fear, or suffering from different ends of the psychic spectrum.

Images may come in our dreams and remain with us. Recurrent motifs may last sometimes for decades: there we are once again for the hundredth time in that old childhood room; there we are once again being pursued by a mysterious force; there we are looking anxiously for a bathroom and we find one and the toilets do not work, or are occupied, or are overflowing. Or, let us take a dream in the life of a patient. The dreamer is invited to a momentous viewing where he watches a cliff face being blown up, only to reveal an inner city that had been constructed over a long time and can only now be shown. A wondrous sight, but with a flaw, an upsetting, disturbing flaw. Though the dreamer is protected from the blast, some of the workers are not, and there lies before him now the badly mangled and bleeding body of a woman. The dream poses a crucial pair of problems: how to uncover the city without hurting any part of the psyche and how to protect the woman.

Approaching psychic material in this way, through central images of this kind, gives advantage to both analyst and analysand. Judgment is softened. For no matter how skillfully used, other schemes almost always employ developmental theory that inevitably brings judgment with it—for example, that one is only at a beginning level and not yet making much progress. One is borderline, or schizoid, or obsessive. The immediate *I*, alive and here in particular, is judged by an abstract, generalized standard. I am seen only in terms of those stages. I do it to myself, I hear it from the analyst. The temptation to moralize is almost irresistible. The image, on the other hand, does not judge me, but rather engages me. It is personal, particular; it comes out of me. The problem, to recall one dream metaphor, is how to get the gun working, if I like guns, or how to throw it away, if I do not like them.

Focusing on images changes the way we construct the prognosis of a case. Prognosis will include relating to these images in a direct, immediate way. It is not just knowing about a condition and explaining it conceptually, nor, as Rank so ably criticized Freud and Jung for doing, simply reeducating the patient in our own worldview. We must deal with the facts that have been dealt to us; we must accept and face the concrete images that inhabit us.

These images have their own character and unfold accordingly. Different from conscious rules that measure all data by fixed formulations, the psychic image has no such rules. Its world is not to be seen as arbitrary or chaotic, however. It possesses its own structure, and to that we must pay close attention. Jung uses directed rather than free association for dream images, asking, for example, What in particular made your unconscious fetch this image of a tiger into your fantasy, as opposed to a lion or an elephant? Or, to take a patient's dream, why is a pale, wan, and wormy-looking female figure disgusting to you? Why this disgust and not one of many other kinds? Or, to go on to another dreamer, what is it specifically about a particular room that makes you keep dreaming of it, as opposed to all sorts of other rooms?

The image has its own structure and integrity. It may even be a false image or an evil one, such as the psalmist speaks of, but contained there in dreams, in its own vocabulary, is a specific kind of falsity to which we are subject; there is the specific kind of evil which is ours, which we do. For example, a man dreamt he was in a barn, in a box stall. Small fuzzy little animals were sleeping around him, harmless, engagingly furry. "For some reason I take a stone and squash the animals. Why did I do it?" The dream calls his attention to gratuitous aggression in him and makes it possible to deal with it. Or, in another case, an image may correct a questionable sense of self: "I dreamt I was the pope but my crown kept slipping." The dreamer was a person who suffered from low self-esteem. Images of our false selves, our counterfeit selves, are part of our reality, as are images that are false in the sense of not being quite exact because they do not include everything needed to see ourselves. They offer clues, hints, a fullness of detail, but not rational discourse about ourselves.

The image is inclusive, in its own way, of conscious and unconscious purposes and values, of individual and social realities. Occasionally we experience one of those remarkable dreams in which we see directly how an inner lack in ourselves gets translated into social attitudes; in which failing to live all of ourselves, we translate an exclusive emphasis on one part of ourselves into an exclusive emphasis on one part of social reality, with an accompanying prejudice against other parts. In the rebellions of the 1960s a young man dreamt he and others were planning to bomb a college building when some tight establishment types came up for a tour of the building. The dreamer showed them around, waiting only until they left so he could set off the bomb. But before leaving, the establishmentarian pointed out to the dreamer where there were some old bombs under the building's floor boards, bombs left over from the war, and ready to go off and kill him. Another dreamer, a man who emphasized the powers of reason to excess, in his dreams constantly encountered a small retarded boy holding out his arms to him. The image was pointing out to him that his overemphasis on reason might be linked to fear of some part of himself that he experienced as retarded and uncomfortably dependent.

Somewhat differently, the collective social-political situation may evoke in us parts of our being that cannot otherwise come to life. The psyche for Jung, we must remember, is objective, and lives outside ourselves as well as within us. Depending in part on a particular attitude or our temperament, we may be brought more into ourselves by the words of another person, or the shaping influence of culture, by group or family pressure, or through a political movement that causes to come into our awareness new elements of being that we would not have arrived at alone. In the world of religious studies, the parallel would be the power of the text, or the historical moment, or the confluence of social, economic, and political realities with the inner vision of, say, a Luther or a Gandhi. It may be the perception of new religious insights that make us see the birth of new symbols in our world. But always it is our conscious relation to the concrete and particular and lively psychic image that will bring new social forms alive to us and help retire restrictive old stereotypes or abstract formulas that deaden our sense of the concrete person. Take the present-day emphasis on feminist studies, for example. The issue here is inquiry into the concrete works and lives of women, and, at its best, concrete efforts to discover what images of female and feminine inhabit us, whether we are male or female. It is not, we hope, simply to replace old stereotypes about women with new ones.[15] The new ones may reverse the old ones, but they may also act in equally confining and sadistic ways. We must ask ourselves, in this context, What are the imagos that inhabit us, and what images underlie what we read of the female or the male? If we can no longer so easily project the imagos onto the opposite sex, can we see these imagos and what they disclose as parts of ourselves? Will they lead us really to see more of the other, really to *see* the other, female or male?

On the more subjective side, the world of images and imagos offers individuals a space in which to meditate upon their experience of otherness—of self, of reality. In looking at the images which live within us, whether negative or positive, we open up to a space where we can take apart and recombine different aspects of our psyches, of a drive, of a desire, of a fear. By joining these semiconscious levels with the exposed parts of reality, we help civilize our unconscious primitive material, taming its energies into livable forms. In this sense such symbolic images act to transfer energies from crude to more refined forms. We develop the capacity to substitute a number of different kinds of objects for an original crude impulse, bringing the energy into play in a richly amplified form. What we are doing, which religious study must take very seriously into account, is constructing a relationship to the otherness of the symbol in concrete personal terms. These terms always include our actual ego identity, what might be called our worldly presence. We select different parts out of which we build the unities, those clusters of experience and understanding that give us a sense of life's meaning and reconcile us to its hardships and tragedies. Thus working with images constructs a spiritual relation to otherness, to self, to God.

It is precisely this concrete and lively relation to images that brings a person healing insights. It may be useful to know I have a conflict between a tyrannizing superego and a demanding id-life, but that knowledge does not show me how to come to live with the conflict. A dramatic dream image of a son, believing he must cut off his father's leg in order to save his sister's life, only to discover after performing the bloody amputation that it was not necessary and that now he must carry his father on his back, shows all the sides of the anger and anguish involved in the struggle. The concrete images can lead the dreamer to examine and relate to the underlying issues of the dream and to find another less perilous route to deal with them.

We find help in notions of "narcissistic syndrome," "borderline condition," help in tracing present illness to past failures in the analytical structures of Winnicott's "facilitating environment." But we do not always find relief. The image makes the concept come alive, whether we are looking at it for psychoanalytical or religious purposes. The image gives expression to nondiscursive elements of suffering, gives visibility to hate we cannot bring ourselves to express, gives an outlet to the tension that seeks to be lived, and above all offers a way to live in the present a relationship that will fill up the emptiness of a past relationship that has gone wrong or been left unlived.

Doing this sort of reconnecting has social, intellectual, and religious implications, for denial of the archetypal world may effect a denial of humanity. We become contaminated when there is unlived life in us, victims of an ego too frail to house and humanize the energy that flows through us. We then become a contaminant to others—stifling their feelings, cutting off their connections, discouraging their perceptions.

IMPLICATIONS FOR RELIGIOUS STUDIES

Many precise parallels suggest themselves between Jung's clinical approach to the psyche and the task of the religious scholar. Studying the texts of religious faith is a special enterprise in the intellectual and the academic world. It is so as well—or at least should be—for the depth psychologist. We know these texts of faith were alive to people in the past. We do not always see how much they can mean to us in the present time. They speak of configurations of Being and the human apprehension of them. They solicit participation of the reader and hearer of their words. The scholar, to be a scholar, must somehow enter into the meaning of these words and sense that lively faith at least imaginatively, if not with reverence, in order to understand his or her subject matter at all. This aspect of the nature of religious studies poses special problems for the fate of the discipline. For if the scholar is too much detached from this immediate addressing of his or her own person by the text of faith, then what is there will not be grasped at all. And yet if the scholar simply reads into the text his or her own journey of faith, or a parallel despair of ever finding faith, then what the text really does express will also be lost, but from the opposite side.

Like Jung's notion of the psyche as objective, as absolutely there, autonomous and quite other than consciousness, religious texts also speak from another point of departure. They purport to give voice to the word of God, or of Being, speaking to us. We may hear in them a voice from another world beyond the grave, or from the non-ego reality that goes beyond our ego world of self and society. Religious texts are texts of multiple mysteries. They present what is a radical otherness to our own familiar human world. Like Jung's objective psyche, possessing its own language of images with which to communicate to consciousness, the many different kinds of texts of faith speak in their own particular and even peculiar language. All of them draw heavily on image and symbol. Here Jung's work can greatly help scholars of religious texts, with his research into the history of symbols and with the enormous amount of sheer information he collected about the psychic meaning of specific images and symbols.[16]

Jung's hermeneutic is principally a psychological one: he links symbols to the living process of the psyche, emphasizing as no one else did the peculiar psychic meaning of symbols. He saw that they express the conscious and unconscious situation at any given moment, past or present, and convey to consciousness an energy that is otherwise inaccessible. Thus Jung opens to scholars the life current of religious images by focusing on the psychic experience of doctrines, of faith-images, or God-images. These images express the living apprehension of the mystery of being in relation to the mystery of selves-in-development. Jung helps link up the timeless archetypal meaning of religious symbols to the immediate psychological experience of the scholar and the student.

A great problem in teaching, as we all know, is the deadness that so often threatens it. And so we remember with particular joy those times in our own learning when a subject came alive to us, suddenly there for us as a whole world of interconnected meanings. By reaching out to its life, we discovered something had quickened in ourselves. But we also must know after we taught a particular bit of material that glassy stare in students' eyes that communicates to us an unpleasant unuttered question: So what? We can see clearly that the knowledge has not penetrated or come alive for the students. As teachers of religion, it is this we shall have to answer for on Judgment Day: How could we take something so vitally alive as religion and make it so deadly dull in the teaching of it?

We may make our point understandable to our students but fail to connect it to anything alive in them. To bring it alive, we must touch the psyche—our own and our students'—by making a bridge between the image in the text and the images in the interpreter, in us. At the very least, then, students must come to see that faith is a life as well as a text. Though they need not believe in order to understand a text academically, their grasp of the text does depend on discovering how and what the writers and hearers of the text did believe. In the intellectual study of religious texts we do not seek to convert our students, but we must make clear to them that belief in something is possible and, further, that experiencing that possibility is intrinsic to grasping in any depth the meaning of a text of faith. Just as psychoanalytic theory cannot be understood without reference to the patients in relation to whom the theory is fashioned, we cannot understand religious texts without reference to the believers for whom these images conveyed the heart of being in its crucial otherness. The greater the perception of that fact, the more exciting the study of religion. The dimmer the perception, the larger the pitfalls of pedantry loom.

To know that as a scholar you must deal with the psychic meanings that stand behind what you study and teach is to close the escape hatch of schizoid splitting so typical of academics, where heart and soul are left out of professional work. Such omissions contribute to the demise of religious studies and to their politicization as a desperate effort to revive them.

To approach a text of faith as issuing from an otherness and as bespeaking the divine is often rejected by teacher and student alike as too threatening.[17] One fears that the study of religion will degenerate into formless, subjective emotionalism—not, for example, what Augustine said but how I feel about what Augustine said. This need not be the case. Indeed the fear that it will be is like the patient's fear that recognition of the objectivity of the unconscious as other than consciousness will deliver an already fragile ego into chaos. Behind this fear lies the assumption that conscious ordering is the only ordering that exists, just as behind the scholar's fear lies the assumption that a rational and logical ordering of study is the only kind of possible ordering.

Jung's investigations of imagery offer reassuring evidence that images, and hence the unconscious from which they arise, offer their own kind of ordering, no less structured or significant than rationality, just constructed along different lines. An image rising from the unconscious unfolds and includes things not seen before. It proceeds to new insights. The task is to connect its unconscious way with our conscious way so as to have at our disposal both ways of ordering. For example, in a seminary course of study—it could be in homiletics or philosophy of religion or biblical studies—a student may discover that his way toward grasping the image of the Johannine God of love is blocked because he is bypassing some spontaneous personal image of God that resides in him. One of my students dreamt he was worshiping a pig; and really worshiping it, with awe, fear, and trembling. By acknowledging that image, receiving it into his conscious awareness, not identifying with it, but feeling its liveliness, its otherness, and making a space for it, he found more room in himself to apprehend the vitality and inner dynamism of that Johannine image of God as love. The pig does not replace it, nor does a chaos threaten. Instead, a very distinct image appears, a pig that needs investigation, meditation, and response.

In the study of religious texts, most of which are image-laden, images will be touched off in ourselves and our students. We need to make room for them in order to get on with our work. To ignore them is to deny our study a vital energy.

Similar to Jung's focus on images as providing a valuable diagnostic and prognostic tool, focus on the regnant images in a text of faith gives us a way to order our study of the history of a religion. Images unfold and lead to other images that, in conjunction with a literary, social, and contextual situation, build up a history. For example, in studying the Old Testament, certain recurrent clusters of imagery turn up, as is also true, of course, in the New Testament. An interesting question to ask is what made some of the New Testament authors take up those dominant Old

Testament images and christianize them, while omitting others. What was it about the images that determined their selection? This question does not exclude the valuable research into the literary and the contextual sociopolitical-economic situation that also contributed to the selection of certain images. But it adds to that research an inquiry into the images themselves—their archetypal bases and autonomous propensity to undergo transformation to new levels of differentiation in the human psyche under the influence of Christianity. A still more psychological way to ask the same question is, Were those images taken into Christianity images of the "true self," in Winnicott's language, and were those discarded seen as images of a "false self"?[18]

Jung's approach helps in both the subjective and objective tasks of the scholar of religion. On the objective side, new ways open to study texts' images of faith and the ways in which we hear God speak to us there and elsewhere. This emphasis recognizes the autonomy of the psychic image, its inherent vitality, and its power to shape the very structures of society that have apparently shaped it. This perspective supplements our conceptual work in clarifying the social contexts in which religious texts are written, in articulating systematically the truths of theology, philosophy, literature, and so forth. It does not replace those truths; it brings them alive. To find in Tillich's theology, for example, the dominant image of the boundary line gives insight into his whole system and its method of correlation that seeks to bridge the boundaries of pairs of different realities—philosophy and theology, culture and faith, eternal symbols and existential situations. To find in Barth the sovereign image of Christ as mirror that reflects back to us our true image makes immediate sense of the subtleties of his theological method of *analogia fides*.

This emphasis on images in the languages of faith also reminds us that ours is a privileged study, that in the larger world of scholarship we occupy a particular place that others may dismiss as woolly headed, a bit mad, even deluded. But we know it is a privileged study. We read the human records of persons' experiences of truth, of reality, of that which centers everything else, of that which *is*. Focusing on the images in our texts not only gives us an additional way to order those texts, but, parallel to the healing effect of psychological insight, such a focus opens us to the illuminating qualities of truth. In this image or that, we find at least a bit of central truth disclosed, offered, and addressing us directly.

Awareness of such a fact imbues the scholar's day-in, day-out work with unceasing vitality for decades, perhaps for a lifetime. It sustains scholarly work by assuring it of connection to enduring truth. It protects us from becoming burnt-out cases, dried-up relics. Here is the fire, the water, the needed light, the deep darkness. We need such a source to survive the rigors of academic life, in order to do our teaching well in classrooms, and to write with substance. For we perform two functions: We convey information, and we act as a bridge to the inner reality of faith in the texts we study. Jung helps us in both tasks, enlarging our information about images and quickening our ability to convey their psychological meaning for our readers and hearers. We thus reach, in Jung's language, both the ego world of context and society, linguistic form, and political situation in which a religious text is written or an image of God is upheld, and the archetypal world of timeless images conveying permanent truths. To avoid these images is to be detoured into dry abstractions, killing the life, or making the student hunt too hard to find it. We commit our worst sins as teachers in this respect—squashing in our students their love for truth and their hunger to know that a lively durable belief is possible. We bore them to death. As an act of hostility that is bad enough, but in religious studies it is even worse, because we take the central truths of God and cover them over, make them opaque and dull. We set up impossible obstructions.

On the subjective side, Jung helps the scholar of religion by reminding us of the necessity to make more space in our own awareness for the images that inhabit us. Jung's emphasis on the psychic meaning of religious images addresses us as the persons we are—or fear to be—with the meanings we live by or have lost or still seek. This leads us to be aware of our students as persons. Whatever images inhabit us, they must affect our work and what work we are able to make commendable to others. So we need to pay attention to what sorts of images live in us, which ones thwart us, which ones are dead, which alive. Such awareness will increase our understanding of why we cannot finish a thesis or a manuscript. We may be forcing images and hence a specific channel for energy upon ourselves when in fact our energy is already alive and flowing in another riverbed. Knowing what images inform our own lives puts us in conscious touch with them, thus opening ways for them to live in the world. And so zest is added to our teaching, fostering the igniting of imagination in us and all around us.

Coming into awareness of these images within us means just that—awareness, not identification. My student should not say, "Ah ha!" as at last he comes to know he really is a pig-worshiper at heart, throwing over as sham all his old faith in the Christian God of love. That would be identification—now with something from the unconscious side, as before he was too much identified with his conscious image of God. He needs both. *We* need both. Otherwise we fall into that particularly bad practice among religious scholars that gives psychology and Jung a bad name: projection.

We project our personal images onto the texts of faith and reduce its otherness down to our own personal experiences of the otherness of the unconscious. Two crunchy movements then develop: psychological personalism and psychological abstractionism. We put into the text our particular imagos and substitute them for the larger, more encompassing images of faith. My faith becomes all faith. We abstract from the particularity of a text by translating it into the terms of psychological jargon. A parable, for example, becomes nothing more than a joust between ego and shadow. We cease to make a bridge to the psychic meaning of the texts. Instead we replace it with a psychological formula that is too abstract to reach many people where they live. Or we replace the narrative of God's story with our own personal journey, not guessing at the mountainous inflation that act conveys.

At the opposite end of such dangers, we lose the personal dimension altogether. We disappear into the archetypal world, departing from the ego world of the flesh that God entered—the flesh of our bodies, of our time in history, our society and politics and economics and personal relationships. This is comparable to discussing the patient's imagery to the exclusion of the patient's real situation. We take up the images of faith but never find them incarnate in action, attitude, or devotion. We involve ourselves with images without reference to our relation to them, so that we now have many gods, as many as there are separate images. We resist the human task of uniting them. Instead we take our fragmented state, which was once such a problem, as the present solution. But this is identification psychologically, and idolatry theologically. We identify with the psyche's capacity to produce images and make a god out of that.

No, we must have both worlds—the ego world and the archetypal. Only with both are we up to the strains of relating to the otherness that the texts of faith communicate and that our own images and imagos convey to awareness. We need a foot on both sides—an ego firmly enough rooted in its own reality to withstand opening and receiving the beyond-ego world without being swept away, an ego spacious enough to entertain these lively, even threatening images offered in the texts of faith which become tests of faith and demonstrations of faith as they call up images from within our own unconscious.

The scholarship and teaching of religion are not the same as analysis, but then analysis is not the only way to enlarge consciousness and to feed the soul.

Notes

This chapter was originally published in *Jung and the Study of Religion*, eds. L. H. Martin and J. Goss (Washington: University Press of America, 1986).

1. Jung formulated his concepts on the basis of his work with patients, who can be roughly divided into two groups: those suffering from neurosis, and those suffering from psychosis and confined to a psychiatric hospital. The majority of the former group came from the middle and upper strata of society, the latter from the lower strata.

2. For a summary of the meanings of this term, see C. G. Jung, *Two Essays in Analytical Psychology, Collected Works* 7, trans R. F. C. Hull (New York: Pantheon, 1966), pars. 230ff.; see also A. B. Ulanov, *The Feminine in Jungian Psychology and in Christian Theology* (Evanston: Northwestern University Press, 1971), 18–19.

3. For a longer discussion of these differences, see A. and B. Ulanov, *Religion and the Unconscious* (Philadelphia: Westminster, 1975), 65–68; see also 26–32.

4. Particularly vulnerable to this criticism is Jung's notion of a man's anima or a woman's animus. People seem to find it harder to accept that we have a personification of the opposite sex living in us than they do an evil part, symbolized by Jung as the shadow. This may

be due to the fear of sexual discrimination—that men and women will be fixed in stereotypes—or it may result from sexual discrimination, e.g., the attitude that "No other sex part exists in me!" Generally we seem more comfortable with a shadowed part of ourselves that sabotages our actions with motives opposite to our conscious intentions than the more cross-grained textures of contrasexuality. To dream of a dark figure chasing us is not uncommon; hence it is not difficult to take that pursuit seriously as depicting an actual inner conflict. For a woman to dream of a negative animus figure—a contemptuous judging man who berates her—and to accept that that attitude is actually her own, is less acceptable, more easily projected onto actual men in the world around her. For discussion of the anima and animus, see C. G. Jung, *Aion, Collected Works* 9:2, trans. R. F. C. Hull (New York: Pantheon, 1959), pars. 20–42, and A. B. Ulanov, *Receiving Woman: Studies in the Psychology and Theology of the Feminine* (Philadelphia: Westminster, 1981), ch. 6.

5. An example of the way such an image expresses meaning is the following. A woman brought to her analytic session a dream about a big spider—the size of a dog—that appeared at her kitchen door. We worked on her associations to this spider image, which were mainly negative and emotional—fear, revulsion, panic at getting caught in the spider web.

The woman associated to these feelings experiences with her own mother, feeling tangled in a web of her mother's manipulations that were delicate and hard to see but that nonetheless held her fast. She also felt imprisoned in her own negative reactions to her mother, unable to win through to the love that she also felt for her mother. After talking in some detail about these feelings, I ventured that the spider was a symbol associated with the negative mother figure in its ensnaring activity and aggressiveness toward the helpless daughter. The spider can symbolize the deathly womb of the Terrible Mother (see E. Neumann, *The Great Mother*, trans. Ralph Manheim [Princeton: Princeton University Press, 1970], 177, 184–85; C. G. Jung, *Psychology and Alchemy, Collected Works* 12 [New York: Pantheon, 1953], pars. 325f., figure 108 cited by Neumann, 177) and the figure the Indians call "Maya," sitting in the center of her domain, eternally spinning her web of illusion. Yet the spider also symbolizes in a positive way the meeting of death and life, in their ceaseless alternation fundamental to the transformation of life, a sacrifice of the old for the building of the new. The spider who spins its web from out of its own body also symbolizes creative power.

Together, the dreamer and I hazarded an interpretation that ran along the lines of her finding herself in the dream, and there presented with, if not sought out by, an image that referred to her own negative experience of her mother. The interweaving of negative and positive forces in life, though terrifying, was also fundamental to her own transformation.

Fine. Or so we thought. But she came to the next session with the *same* dream image, now dreamt for a second time, except that in this dream she took the spider from her door, down the kitchen steps, across her backyard into a neighboring field, and deposited it at some distance from her house. By the time she got home, barely inside the kitchen again, the spider appeared at the door, in effect knocking to be admitted.

This second dream told both the dreamer and me that the spider image in its personal and archetypal dimensions could not be so easily dealt with by interpretation, even a correct one. The unconscious repeated itself, as if to say, Clearly you did not get the point; so I'll say it again: this spider image wants to come into the kitchen! *Coming in* means more than understanding, however emotionally informed that understanding may be. In this case it means entering into the kitchen space of the woman's psyche and interacting with her there. The kitchen space touched on her own maternal experience as nurturing and feeding her five children, as well as on her ability to transform raw substances into edible and life-building forms. The spider image expresses a meaning yet to be discovered about her maternal instinct, a meaning that would particularly emerge out of admitting negative feelings and the recognition of the inevitable mixture of the negative and the positive in life.

6. Images constantly turn up in people's dreams and fantasies, as we all know but do not always admit. They include persons of all types, from the ordinary to the extraordinary. People known to the dreamer may appear—neighbors, colleagues at work, relatives. People unknown and startling to the dreamer may also appear: a celebrity, a murderer bent on attacking the dreamer with a knife, a child whose helplessness and open love moves the dreamer to tears, a tramp who climbs into the back seat of the dreamer's taxi to grab a ride, a person of another culture, such as a Chinese woman or African warrior or Indian guru. In addition, part-images, human and inhuman, may take over fantasy and dream—such as an ugly wound whose jagged edges will not heal, or a blob of slime on the floor next to one's bed, or an abstract figure of lines and angles, or a vision of intense redness, or a bright yellow sun and deep blue sea. Animals, monsters, scenes of nature, even letters and numbers may come to us in images.

Images also occur spontaneously to people in activities other than dreaming—in prayer, for example. For a discussion of this, see A. and B. Ulanov, *Primary Speech: A Psychology of Prayer* (Atlanta: John Knox Press, 1982, chs. 4 and 5). Images arise in teachers in the midst of presenting material to a class of students, in scientists struggling toward formulation of their findings. Images arrive when persons make love. Images can inhabit our pleasures and suffering. The images that confront us are as numerous and varied as we are ourselves. All examples are taken from my practice as a Jungian analyst with gratitude to the persons who gave me permission to use their material.

7. C. G. Jung, *Psychological Types, Collected Works* 6, trans. R. F. C. Hull (Princeton: Princeton University Press, 1971), par. 743.

8. An unusual example of such a personal image is one presented to a young scientist in a dream the night before she saw her analyst for the first time. After a series of events involving the dreamer and the analyst, the dream concluded with the dreamer beholding with awe a revolving, luminous, white, many-celled structure. This compelling figure reminded the dreamer of the design of cells she was examining in her research and the awe she felt in uncovering nature's secrets, discovering "how things work." Obviously, this image carries a specific personal meaning for the dreamer that derives from her vocation in the natural sciences.

9. An example of an archetypal image can be found in the scientist's dream of note 8. Even though the image of the white, luminous structure in her dream recalled her own specific research, its composition of many cells connected to a center, its central importance to the whole dream, and its numinous effect upon the dreamer, both in the dream and on awakening, connect to the archetypal form of a mandala—that ancient Hindu design that combines the circle and the square, achieving order within diversity, that Jung believed, from its repeated appearance in many patients' dreams, symbolized the center of the psyche.

10. Jung, *Psychological Types*, par. 749.

11. A. and B. Ulanov, *Religion and the Unconscious*, 224ff.

12. Jung gives an example of one of his own imagos in his description of his experience of his mother. For Jung, she possessed two personalities. Number 1 was the conventional, pastor's wife. Number 2 inhabited a pagan land, told strange tales, and uttered unconventional words. At the death of Jung's father she said to Jung, "He died in time for you." (C. G. Jung, *Memories, Dreams, Reflections*, ed. A. Jaffé, trans. Richard and Clara Winston [New York: Pantheon, 1963], 48–49, 96). Jung's imago of his mother included, in addition to his personal

experience of her, the archetypal theme of the dual mother, which he explored in detail in his *Symbols of Transformation, Collected Works* 5, trans. R. F. C. Hull (Princeton: Princeton University Press, 1974), pars. 464–612.

13. Images of God abound in people's lives: ranging from negative ones of God as scolder, scorekeeper, punitive father, to positive ones of God as comforting mother, understanding friend, merciful Lord. Nonhuman images of God also turn up: God as cosmic blur, God as light, God as animal. For discussions of such images of God, see A. M. Rizzuto, *The Birth of the Living God* (Chicago: The University of Chicago Press, 1979), and A. B. Ulanov, "What Do We Think People Are Doing When They Pray?" *Anglican Theological Review* LX, 4 (October 1978).

14. See Ernst Cassirer, *Language and Myth*, trans. S. K. Langer (New York: Dover, 1946), 62ff.

15. For a discussion of the danger of old and new stereotypes, see A. B. Ulanov, *Receiving Woman*, chs. 1 and 2.

16. See A. B. Ulanov, "Religion: Jung's View," in *International Encyclopedia of Psychiatry, Psychology, Psychoanalysis, and Neurology* IX, ed. B. B. Wolman (New York: Human Sciences Press, 1977), 429–32, chapter 1 of this book.

17. See A. B. Ulanov, "The Christian Fear of the Psyche," *Union Seminary Quarterly Review* XXX, 2–4 (Winter–Summer, Summer 1975).

18. See D. W. Winnicott, "Ego Distortion in Terms of True and False Self," in *The Maturational Processes and the Facilitating Environment* (New York: International Universities Press, 1965).

Chapter 6

Teaching Jung in a Theological Seminary and a Graduate School of Religion

I read with great interest David Tacey's article on teaching Jung in the academy and recognized in him a collegial spirit. For years (my own tenure is now thirty) only a few of us have worked, both as clinicians and professors, teaching theories of the unconscious in institutions of higher learning. The amazing fact about the unconscious—that it exists and is unconscious—raises fascinating problems in the teaching-learning context.

PSYCHIC REALITY

The teacher should not, I believe, do therapy in the classroom, for that violates students' psyches. But neither should the teacher talk about the unconscious in a way that leads students into intellectual dissociation from the presence of the psyche right there in people in the classroom. What then can we do with the unconscious in the educational setting?

This problem is not faced only by teachers of depth psychology, but by all teachers of quality, those who teach material that matters. I think of two colleagues as examples. Both are men—one in the crossdisciplinary fields of literature, arts, and religion; the other, in the discipline of speech analysis and training—who exhibit enormous skill, force, and tact. They stick to their material—the texts—and to the students' reception and use of their matter, and they bring their students to the spirit of what matters. As a result, letters from students indicate, these teachers often change their students' lives. These men do not do therapy in the classroom. In the case of one man, his hearing a student's true voice waiting to be liberated from inferiority or grandiosity complexes aids the unique unfolding of the student's personality in the context of a particular spoken text. For some students, this acute listening transforms their lives.

In the other case, the man meets his students in the material they study together. He summons them into this matrix, asking them to open themselves to text, author, and cultural surroundings, that is, to bring and show themselves in response. His own passion for the material ignites theirs. A Jungian analyst I know, on hearing this teacher lecture publicly, said of him, "When I hear most lecturers I am often moved at the moment; when I hear this man, I go home and read and read." The letters this teacher receives from students, often years after the conclusion of the course, express thanks for his opening up the world of the material, in which the student was able to find what a Jungian analyst might call "the living psyche."

For the teacher of theories about the unconscious psyche, the net tightens. We have to ask ourselves, What sort of tiger have we caught here? For we are, students and teachers alike, studying ourselves when we study such material. Unlike our analysts-in-training, our academic classroom students may or may not be in treatment themselves. The classroom gets crowded, filling up with hidden questions, unconscious questions put by our psyches, questions that we often resist hearing. Each of us feeling this resistance is challenged to see if our objections to the psychological theories under discussion amount to a preference to work out our conflicts through generalized issues of social justice or theoretical constructions rather than acknowledging their personal roots. The room palpably fills up with the different levels of psychological development among the students, each registering, through individual confusion and bewilderment, different developmental imperatives.

Hermeneutical questions particularly crowd in on us. If as teachers we make room for different levels of development and a variety of resistances to a given psychological theory, understanding that it may be liberating to one student while judgmental for another, how do we go about the business of assessing the theory's intrinsic truth? Is truth simply relative to various subjective viewpoints? Does a norm of truth still exist? By what criteria can it be determined, demonstrated? Professor Tacey's dramatic examples—of students and teachers either altogether excluding study of Jung's theories or altogether embracing Jung to a point of identification that excludes critical reflection—fit here. In my own teaching and supervising of doctoral work in a graduate school of religion, the hermeneutic question reaches a further point of tension: Can something be psychologically true if it is theologically false (or vice versa)?

SEMINARY CONTEXT

Professor Tacey and I share the labor of teaching, but our contexts differ in significant ways. He teaches in a university setting, which, in common with American universities, prides itself on objectivity and critical inquiry, eschewing belief as countermanding those values. In many American educational institutions, even (or perhaps especially) in departments of religion, where Jung is most apt to be taught, the stance of faith is considered to be a drawback to effective teaching. Faith is somehow not rigorous enough, or might contaminate the learning process with a proselytizing fervor.

Yet, as Tacey also underscores, the whole issue of belief, if thrown out the front door, will sneak in through the back. The clinician will recognize what Melanie Klein calls "the symbolic equation" as the unconscious condition informing any touted "objectivity." Teachers, in other words, tend unconsciously to identify with what grips them as truth, and the resultant equation of themselves with their ideas acts as a coercive agent in the class discussions. Instances can occur of a teacher marking a student down for arguing against the teacher's undeclared but powerfully operating "truth." Tacey sums it up succinctly: "There are theologies inside our theories, and articles of faith underpin most of our intellectual positions" (p. 269). In a religious institution, ironically, when differences of theology are being debated at a conscious intellectual level, beliefs sneak in in the form of political ideologies. Here, the coercive symbolic equation is operating at the juncture of belief and action *in society:* theological doctrine which does not pay off in what is considered to be appropriate social action (praxis) is dismissed as bad theology.

My context—teaching in a theological seminary that is also a graduate school of religion—brings some different protections and strains from Tacey's university setting. In a seminary, belief is not held to be a drawback but a resource, indeed a link to the Source. Belief in God, both personal and communal, acts like a pipeline to the energy and affect that can sustain studies and future careers. Such belief suggests "the point of it all" and answers the discouraged and cynical question we hear all the time: So what? Or, What difference can anyone's piddling efforts make in the face of such suffering in the world? The answer of belief circles around an ego attitude that witnesses to a reality greater than itself, greater in fact than all our selves, which gets expressed in such phrases as "for the sake of love," or "for the greater glory of God."

The traditional religious vocabulary is handy, in that it offers both student and teacher a way to point to a transcendent purposiveness that is present here and now in our actions. Such a transpersonal referent should not be seen as diluting objectivity, but rather as endorsing it. From the perspective of the theological seminary, loss of the transcendent referent exposes us to equally unfortunate opposites: addiction to objectivity (all the while repressing subjective identification with one's theory), and passionate overidentification with one's point of view (disavowing one's actual objective distance from the theory on which one has projected one's personal complexes).

The religious awareness that pervades seminary education, that of a transcendent God that goes well beyond our particular God-images, offers the positive advantage of another perspective. In it we include the opposites, instead of choosing one at the expense of the other and ending up in a ceaseless compensatory seesawing, acted out in the kind of community of opposing groups that Tacey bemoans. Ours is, I find, more of a muddle of conjunction than a tension of opposition.

My particular seminary, in contrast to schools of particular churches (such as the Presbyterian, the Episcopalian, and the Catholic) that operate from a shared symbol system of doctrine, is nondenominational. At the center of a nondenominational seminary a hole exists, an empty space where doctrinal demands might be expected. In any given week at Union, for example, the schedule of daily worship will reflect the different and competing symbol systems of the school's students and faculty. A traditional Presbyterian service one day, consisting of sermon, prayers, and hymns, will be followed the next by a group of Catholics reciting the rosary. Yet another day brings a service articulating protest against the unjust discrimination suffered by gays and lesbians, followed on its morrow by the presentation of the ineffable but tough faith that students working as hospital chaplains must draw upon to survive their ministry to people in the grip of mental and physical illness. Different community groups take turns putting into the empty space at the center the symbols that best capture for them the reality of God. Together, we circle around this center-in-process, which acts like a revolving mandala, reflecting all our perspectives. At our best, we stimulate each other, feed each other, learn from each other.

At worst, the vertigo of this evolving space makes us feel that the center does not hold. Sometimes, we compete to fill it entirely with our particular God-images, seeking to foist them upon each other with all kinds of bullying, even theological sadism, if others do not agree. As in other religious arguments, the struggle over religious perspective keeps increasing the stakes. Those who disagree are accused of unjust attitudes, prejudiced actions, and unfaithful behavior—modern versions of old fashioned "damnation." Once, when asked what community life was like at Union, a colleague of mine (quoting Elijah, 1 Kgs 19:10b) said, "I, I alone am left, and they seek my life."

Nonetheless, the apparently empty space at the center of a school like Union, which includes Christian students of all denominations and degrees of faith, some Jewish students and Greek Orthodox, a few Moslems, and people of all ages, classes, races, cultures, and sexual orientations, does offer always the potential of an extraordinary freedom. The gap in the symbol system at the center works for us because it mirrors the unavoidable gap between the finite and the infinite. Our communal and personal squabbles circle 'round our shared acknowledgment that nothing human can define an unfathomable God.

TEACHING JUNG

It is within this religious setting that our students study Jung, and where I myself feel compelled to emphasize the gap between things finite and infinite. The fact that Jung is taught in conjunction with other major and conflicting theories of depth psychology constantly calls attention to definitive gaps and differences in all of them. The temptation to idolize Jung that Tacey describes is thus depotentiated, because Jung's theories are always looked at in relation to other maps of the psyche and varying intellectual contexts that are expected, like it, to miss the ultimate mark. We see again and again that no theory brings the last word of truth.

Our students in the Program of Psychiatry and Religion range across, in all, five programs leading to degrees, all of which contain large components of interdisciplinary conversations with religion as well as praxis. As a result, much of the attraction to and resistance against Jung's work that Tacey describes shifts over to the dramatic experience of the psyche per se.

The teaching of Jung or any other depth psychologist occurs, then, as a way of dealing with the theoretical and practical issues that surround people learning to work in a parish, a hospital, a prison, a classroom, or a clinical setting with people suffering emotional illness, and it becomes yet another way to aid persons' spiritual development, both in prayer, worship, and practice, to adjust to widely differing cultural contexts both here and abroad. The seminary setting helps to position students to see through theories to the transcendent itself, and conversely to test theory against the practical and intellectual labor of discerning whether a point of view aids or obstructs human efforts to live justly and walk humbly with one's God. For the seminary training ministers, social workers, future religious teachers and publishers, and scholars of religion, all under one roof, the proof is in the pudding. Intellectual learning couples inexorably with professional vocation.

Students who concentrate in psychiatry and religion train for all the professions cited above, and move on, many of them to become chaplain-teachers in medical or mental hospitals, and for clinical ministries such as those of pastoral counselors. A steady number of students seek additional education in the training institute of whatever school of depth psychology draws them to become analysts. A student at the doctoral level may choose the option of training at both Union and a training institute at the same time, in order to be able to teach at the graduate or undergraduate level and also to practice as a clinician. Thus, students studying Jung at Union do so within the context of highly demanding theoretical and professional training, and with the constant experience of an ongoing interdisciplinary conversation that seeks to explore the impact of psychic reality on religious life and thought. For these students, the psyche has become an unmistakable and clearly delineated reality. A recognition that the psyche exists and that a goodly portion of it exists unconsciously distinguishes the particular city of psychiatry and religion within the country of the larger seminary.

CONTROVERSY

Taken as a whole, Union holds a firmly and widely established reputation as a seminary committed to social action, and it is fair to say that it is not a psychologically minded community. The dismissal, scorn, and sheer ignorance of psychic reality that Tacey describes in his world can be found in ours too. It is an attitude applied with equal repressive force to all of depth psychology, not just to Jung. Jung may however be singled out as particularly offensive, as an essentialist who perpetuates sexual stereotypes, as a thinker who ignores historical and political contexts, who is too individualistic at the expense of the community needs, and, not least in offensiveness, who substitutes a psychological universe for the religious one. Neither Jung's nor any other analyst's theories are used in fields outside psychiatry and religion to augment methods of interpretation of scripture, doctrine, historical movements, or the problems of ethical discernment. Preference in the practice of general theology is given to the more extroverted hermeneutics that emphasize the sociopolitical context and the sociology of knowledge.

The rejection of depth psychological theories in even this liberal setting comes down, I find, to the fear of the psyche, with

peculiar accent on what I have called the Christian fear of psychic reality.[1] I have even had the experience of teaching a student
who said she felt she was betraying her other teachers' loyalty to
social justice by taking a course in psychiatry and religion, only to
find out how different the material was from all her expectations, that is, her projections and projective identifications.
Indeed, a particularly fascinating subject to students and even to
some colleagues entering the field for the first time is the role of
the unconscious in social-action causes and concerns.

PSYCHIATRY AND RELIGION

Within the Psychiatry and Religion Program, students study the
primary texts of depth psychology from all the major schools and
perspectives. We read Freud, Jung, Adler, Horney, Rank, Laing,
Odier, Kohut, Kernberg, Klein, Boss, Binswanger, Bion, Frankl,
Erikson, Winnicott, Guntrip, Fairbairn, Bollas, McDougall, Milner, Chasseguet-Smirgel, Lacan, Stern, Khan, Loewald, Bowen,
Minuchin, Weigert, Sullivan, Searles, and others.

My own strong bias toward Jung, which I announce openly in
class, is stated to urge students to pay close attention to those theories that either beckon or repel *them*, for I think that will invariably
indicate their most fruitful path to relate to psychic reality. I stress
that *all* the theories studied possess some truth, for they all have
arisen out of clinical work with the psyche and would not have sur-
vived if they had not proved life-saving to the soul of someone. I
encourage students to lift into explicit conversation that inner dialogue with the depths of the psyche that has been going on their
whole lives. I want them to work to find their own voices in that
conversation, not to aim at duplication of Freud or Jung or Klein
or me, their teacher. In preparing their exams and papers I invite,
prod, and even cajole students to concentrate on material that is
hot for them, for that always fosters meaningful creative work that
captures the imagination of others.

The space provided for such confrontations is constructed by
me, by the students, and by the material. In Christian terms, this tri-
angulation of space calls up images of the Trinity, which comprises
a doctrinal picture of the inner life of God, of, so to speak, God's

inner-object relations, of who and what God is when God is not doing anything. In that space, the students and I contribute our presentations, insights, and questions in relation to the specific material we study. When a synergy gets going, where energy flows out to each other and to the material, and back and forth among the three participants—the teacher, the student, the material—then I know the space is alive. Associations, connections occur. The level of ego tasks—mastering the material, applying, for example, the theory of unconscious projections to preaching to a depressed parishioner, grasping the role unconscious anxiety plays in the positions taken by a far-right or far-left political group, inquiring how sexual issues with an inner-anima figure can both impede and advance spiritual growth—begins to differentiate from archetypal levels at which it is possible to inquire in a living context into what symbols the psyche employs to speak of itself, and in what ways this objective psychic reality relates to the spirit or the divine. Excitement heats up, and the new arrives. We face it—in thought, in new connections, in feelings, in body impulses—right there in class. We know we are alive.

INCLUDING THE UNCONSCIOUS

As I have indicated, fear of the psyche, existing immediately within us, between us, and unfolding our uniqueness in response to its own manifestations, lies behind all opposition to depth psychological material in the curriculum. It is a sad commentary on us as a tribe in higher education to note that we have managed to distance ourselves from the hot coals of poetry, mathematics, the classical languages, history, and all the other disciplines of preparatory study so that we can talk about them without passion, without any fear they will still burn our lips (Is 6:7). Study of the psyche, on the other hand, is still new enough to arouse a primitive awe, fear, and fascination. A student from nearby Columbia University, with which Union has close connection and some joint degree programs, obtained permission to take an introductory course I teach in depth psychology and theology, though his professor warned him it would be "too soft." The student exclaimed at term's end that he had worked "more than twice as hard" as in his Columbia psychology courses, not only to cover the quantity of reading assigned, but to keep up with all that leaped up in response within himself.

Here, I would disagree with what I experience as Professor Tacey's implicit and explicit criticism of religion, though I found very interesting his Oedipally tinged interpretation of students' preferences for either Freud (father) or Jung (mother). Tacey's interpretation of religion and of Jung seem to me to be too reductive—as only a return to the womb, and the all-embracing maternal unconscious that bans critical thought and locates authority only in dreams, fantasies, and intuitions from within, while eschewing external standards of judgment and comparison. I found implied in this description of students' attraction to Jung a notion of religion as uncritical, anti-intellectual, immature, clinging, embarrassing, and, in public behavior, eventually fanatic. What seems to me to be lacking in this interpretation is any notion of the epigenesis of religious feeling, of the fact that it develops and differentiates, that it draws upon intellect, texts, historical communities, and mature presentiments of the divine Other.

If we apply Jung's method of prospective interpretation to Tacey's description of students' attraction to Jung as regression to maternal incest, we will be led to agree with Jung that Oedipal conflict can conceal the hidden purpose of seeking union with oneself and with the Self. From the prospective standpoint, one seeks one's own foundations in the psyche, not to disappear in the maternal womb, but to be born out of it with one's own point of view. One then emerges not as a committed Jungian or any other kind of follower, but as secure and original in one's thought and convictions and altogether free to inquire intellectually and emotionally as one feels moved to do so.

The issue that I think unites us who teach depth psychology in higher education and in seminary training rests upon the need to include the *fact* of the unconscious in the curriculum. Here, Jung's notion of the unconscious offers special benefits, recognizing, as it does, a purposiveness in the unconscious in relation to consciousness. The extreme reactions to Jung's theories of scornful rejection and idolatrous adoption that Professor Tacey describes spring, I believe, not from hollow people, but from hollow studies. When students read Jung, something happens that can frighten as much as fascinate. This strong kind of emotional and intellectual reaction—where the student's ego feels gripped by archetypal energy—may not, sadly, be happening in their other courses.

Perhaps in studying Jung, who himself studied the living psyche, the connections between archetypal and ego levels occur more immediately than in the study of other theorists and theories, where the unconscious is approached from the ego point-of-view, thus to be translated upward into conscious concepts.[2] Jung's great gift was to hit upon easily experienceable symbols that speak for the unconscious directly, symbols like the shadow, the inner woman, the Self, the persona as public mask. As a consequence people flee or embrace Jung because they either fear or long for connection to the living psyche.

Yet whether in the profession of religion, in clinical practice, or in higher education, what people look for, I believe, is precisely such a conjunction of the enduring and the immediate. Professor Tacey evidently has had to face the extremes of repudiation or identification with Jung's theories, in a kind of sequential and compensating either–or. Our besetting questions at Union seem more often to spring from conjunctions. Perhaps it is the religious container that lends weight to the urgent questions our professors commonly hear, of how to live the All in the here and now, how to love the whole while making a concrete choice of one path rather than another, how to serve the psyche and recognize in it and through it the Holy that speaks to each of us in the narratives and dramas of our dreams.

Speaking for myself, I see the study of depth psychology as an essential preparation for the religious professions, and in particular the study of Jung. Jung's vision, in my view, is larger than what others offer. Jung reaches to the psyche that exists objectively in our subjectivity, addressing us, pushing, prodding, luring us to meet its unfolding as we try to construct meaning, individually and collectively. I find that we enter a new zone of communication when we accept the fact of psychic reality. Then we are able to see the processes of unconscious mentation in our social, political, and family life as well as in our inner conversation with ourselves. Surely we see in the psyche an incomparable witnessing to the mystery that invokes us and undergirds our callings. What

Jung inaugurated was not just another treatment modality for emotional distress; it was a new way to perceive reality.

Notes

This chapter was originally written in 1996 in answer to a request to respond to David Tacey's article on teaching Jung in the academy in Australia. Both articles were published in the *Journal of Analytical Psychology* 42, 2 (1997).

1. A. B. Ulanov, "The Christian Fear of the Psyche," *Picturing God* (Cambridge, Mass.: Cowley, 1986).
2. A. and B. Ulanov, *Religion and the Unconscious* (Louisville, Ky.: Westminster/John Knox, 1975), 65–68.

Chapter 7

The Opposing Self: Jung and Religion

WHY JUNG ON RELIGION?

How are we to respond to the twentieth-century phenomenon, which Jung noted with such alarm, that the collective containers of religious symbolism are weak, if not altogether gone? For centuries the symbols, rituals, and dogmas of religions, East and West, gathered the psychic energy of countless individuals, even of entire peoples, into traditions that witnessed to life's meaning and acted as underground springs nourishing different civilizations. Jung saw our century as one no longer in daily touch with the meaning of being that lies at the center of life. We have plumbed the resources of consciousness as best we could in our efforts to fathom and to control the contradictions and paradoxes of spirit that have remained to us, but we have lost touch with our roots and the symbolic life that they support and nourish.

Where are we now? What has happened to all the energy that is no longer channeled into religious containers? According to Jung, it has poured back into the human psyche, with disastrous effect. Deprived of its proper outlet in religious experience, it assumes negative forms. For the individual, this misplaced energy can lead to neurosis or psychosis; in society, it can lead to all kinds of horrors, genocide, holocaust, and gulags. It can give rise to ideologies whose potential good is soured by the bullying of adherents into frightened compliance. Afraid of being swamped, we erect barriers of rigid rules and compartments against the negative barrages of psychic energy, creating religious, political and sexual fundamentalisms that trap us in unyielding certainties. And what happens then? We live high and dry, far away from the life-giving waters of religious experience, confined to routines of a humdrum carrying on, without joy or meaning. In such a society we feel afflicted by a deadening malaise, unable to effect healing measures against rising crime and ecological depredation and mental illness. A sense of hopelessness seeps into all, like a rotting damp. These sufferings, as Jung sees them, can be traced to the failure to secure any reliable connection to the psychic reality that religion once supplied us in its various symbol systems.

There is also, however, a positive effect in the pouring back of all this psychic energy into human beings. It is nothing less than the emergence of a new discipline, that of depth psychology, which is a new collective way to explore and to acknowledge the fact that our access to God has fundamentally changed. Our own psyche, which is part of the collective psyche, is now a medium through which we can experience the divine. Jung saw the purpose of his analytical psychology as helping us reestablish connection to the truths of religious symbols by finding their equivalents in our own psychic experience.[1]

IMMEDIATE EXPERIENCE AND PSYCHIC REALITY

The new discipline of depth psychology enables us to study the importance of our immediate experience of the divine, which comes to us through dream, symptom, autonomous fantasy, all the many moments of primordial communication.[2] People have had, and continue to have, revelatory experiences of God. But in earlier times, such encounters were contained by the mainstream of religious tradition and translated into the terms of familiar and accepted religious ritual and doctrine. In our time, Jung believes, these various systems of belief have lost their power for a great many people.[3] For them, religious symbols no longer function effectively as communicators of divine presence. Individual men and women are left alone, quite on their own, to face the blast of divine otherness in whatever form it takes. How are we to respond to such a summons? How are we to find a way to build relationship to the divine? Jung responds to this challenge by marking the emergence into collective discourse of the new vocabulary of psychic reality.

By psychic reality, Jung means our experience of our own

unconscious, that is to say, of all those processes of instinct, imagery, affect, and energy that go on in us, between us, among us, without our knowledge, all the time, from birth until death, and maybe, he speculates, even after death.[4] Coming into conscious relation with the unconscious, knowing that it is there in us, affecting all that we think and do, alone and together, in small groups and as nations, radically changes every aspect of life.

By observing the effects of unconscious motivations on our thoughts and actions, our ego—the center of our conscious sense of I-ness, of identity—is introduced to another world with different laws that govern its operations. In our dreams, time and space collapse into an ever-present now. We can be our five-year-old self at the same time in the dream that we are our present age, and find ourself in a distant land that is also our familiar backyard. Our slips of tongue, where wrong words jump out of our mouths as if propelled by some secret power, our projections onto people, places, and social causes, where we feel gripped by outsized emotions and compulsions to act, our moments of creative living where we perceive freshly, bring a new attitude into being, craft original projects, attest to the constant presence of unconscious mental processes. Something is there that we did not know was there. Something is happening inside us, and we must come to terms with it.

If we pay attention to this unconscious dimension of mental life, it will gather itself into a presence that will become increasingly familiar. For example, just recording our dreams over a period of time will show us recurrent motifs, personages, and images that seem to demand a response from us, as if to engage us in conversation around central themes or conflicts. These dominant patterns impress us as if they came from an other objectively there inside us. Jung calls this ordering force in the unconscious "the Self."

The Self exists in us as a predisposition to be oriented around a center. It is the archetype of the center, a primordial image similar to images that have fascinated disparate societies throughout history. It is, like all the archetypes, part of the deepest layers of our unconscious that Jung calls "collective" or "objective" to indicate that they exceed our personal experience. We experience the Self existing within our subjectivity, but it is not our property, nor have we originated it; it possesses its own independent life.

For example, some aboriginal tribes in Australia pay homage to Oneness. They know its presence in themselves yet they speak of it not as my Oneness or our Oneness but as the Oneness at the heart of all life. When we respond to the predisposition of the Self, we, each of us, experience it as the center of our own psyche and more, of life itself. Our particular pictures of the Self will draw on images from our personal biography, what in the jargon of depth psychologists we call our relations with "objects"—to parents and all other persons who significantly influence us. And what we do in this theater of relations will depend on how we have been conditioned by collective images of the center dominant in our particular culture and era of history, including especially our religious education or lack thereof. But our images of the Self will not be limited to these personal and cultural influences. They will also include such primordial universal images of the Self as may confront us from the deep layers of our own unconscious life.

The Self is neither wholly conscious nor unconscious but orders our whole psyche, with itself as the midpoint or axis around which everything else revolves. We experience it as the source of life for the whole psyche, which means it comes into relationship with our center of consciousness in the ego as a bigger or more authoritative presence than we have known before.[5] If in our ego life—what we ordinarily call "life," the ideas and feelings and culture of which we are strongly aware—we cooperate with the approaches of the Self, it feels as if we are connecting with a process of a centering, not only for our deepest self but for something that extends well beyond us, beyond our psyche into the center of reality. If we remain unconscious, or actively resist the signs the Self sends us, we experience the process as ego-defeating altogether, crushing our plans and purposes with its large-scale aims.

EGO AND SELF, THE GAP AND GOD-IMAGES

A gap always remains between ego and Self, for they speak different languages. One is known, the other unknown. One is personal, the other impersonal. One uses feelings and words, the other instincts, affects, and images. One offers a sense of belonging to community, the other a sense of belonging to the ages. They never merge completely, except in illness (as in mania or an inflated state, for example), but merely approach each other as if coming from two quite different worlds, but still somehow intimately related. The gap between them can be a place of madness, where the ego falls in and loses its foothold in reality, or where the unconscious can be so invaded by conscious ambition and expediency that it seems to withdraw from contact forever, leaving the ego functioning mechanically but juiceless and joyless.

If we really become aware of and accept the gap between ego and Self, it transforms itself into a space of conversation between the worlds. We experience the connecting going on in us and all aspects of our lives. A sense of engagement follows that leads us into a life at once exciting and reverent. For it is precisely in that gap that we discover our images for God. Such images point in two directions: to the purposiveness hidden in our ego life, and across the gap into the unknown God.[6]

Jung talks about God-images as inseparable from those images of the Self that express its function as center, source, point of origin, and container. Empirically, Self and God-images are indistinguishable.[7] This has led Jung's theological critics to accuse him of reductionism, and of bringing down the transcendent God to become a mere factor in the psyche. But Jung defends himself hotly by attacking the argument as nonsense.[8] Can we ever experience anything except through the medium of the psyche? The psyche exists. We cannot get around it. It subtly influences everything we see or know of "objective" reality with our own individual colorations—of physical constitution, family, culture, history, symbol system. Of course our images of God reflect such conditioning.

But do our God-images tell us something else? Yes, Jung answers. These are the pictures through which we glimpse the Almighty.[9] Who knows what God is objectively? How can we ever tell? Only through our own experience of God addressing us, and through other people's experiences reported throughout history. The unconscious is not itself God, but it is a medium through which God speaks.[10] God addresses us through images from the deep unconscious just as much as through the witness of historical events, other people, scriptures, and worshiping communities.

Jung thus provides another method of interpretation of religious tradition to the familiar ones of historical, literary, and sociological-political criticism. When we acknowledge psychic reality, we must add to all the others a method of psychological interpretation of religious materials. Jung's ideas provide a method for investigating recurrent archetypal symbols that specific religious rituals or doctrines embody and employ, by means of linking them to equivalent experiences in our psyches. He applies this method to Eastern as well as Western religious traditions.[11] This method no more reduces revelation to psychology than other methods of, for example, historical or literary or sociological criticism reduce God to historical event, literary metaphor, or sociological sampling.

The transcendent God speaks to us through our God-images and at the same time smashes them, for no human image can take in the incomprehensible divine except in such words and images as the divine shares with us. The images, when they arrive, may evoke in us a negative feeling of such power that we feel invaded and overrun by an alien force, or a positive feeling of being healed or blessed by a life-changing vision.

Jung speaks about religion, its images and symbols, from both sides of the gap between ego and Self. His contribution to religion focuses on bringing unconscious psychic reality into relation to our conscious avowals of faith. He explicitly states that a major function of his psychology is to make connections between the truths contained in traditional religious symbols and our psychic experience. Religious life involves us in ongoing, scrupulous attention to what makes itself known in those moments of numinous experience that occur when ego and Self address each other. We do not control such primordial moments, but rather place our confidence in their meaning for our life. This kind of trustful observance forms the essence of the attitude Jung calls "religious."[12] Our ego acts as both receiver and transmitter of what the Self reveals,[13] which does not mean that we always simply fall in placidly and passively with what comes to us. The conversation with the divine can grow noisy indeed. Like Jonah we may protest our fate, or like Abraham defending

Sodom, we can try to argue Yahweh out of his pledge of destruction. Our proper ego attitude in the fact of the Self and what it reveals is a willing engagement. A process of sustained communication develops, out of which both ego and Self emerge as more significant and conscious partners. No one else can engage in this process for us. Society cannot give it to us. In immediate confrontation with the mysterious Other who seizes our consciousness grows the root of our personal self and our heartfelt connection to the meaning of reality.

OFFICIAL RELIGION

Religious dogma and creeds, for Jung, stand in vivid contrast to such immediate experiences, and he always values the latter over the former. Jung does see great value in dogma and creed, however, as long as we do not substitute them for direct experience of the divine. Dogma and creed function as shared dreams of humanity and offer us valuable protection against the searing nature of firsthand knowledge of the ultimate. They offer us different ways to house our individual experiences of these puzzling or disturbing numinous events. Like Nicholas von der Flüe, we may find refuge in the doctrine of the Trinity as the means of translating into bearable form a theophany so powerful that the experience was said to have changed his saintly face forever, into a frightening visage.[14]

By connecting our immediate psychic encounters with the numinous to the collective knowledge of God contained in humanity's creeds and dogmas, we fulfill what Jung emphasized as the root meaning of religion.[15] *Religio* and *religere* mean we must bind our individual experience back into the common possession of religious tradition. That protects us from too great a blast of the Almighty by offering us the softening containers of humanity's collective symbols. To the ongoing life of inherited symbols we contribute our own personal instances of what they represent collectively, thus helping to keep tradition from ossifying. If we do not live the tradition in this way, it falls into disuse, becoming a mere relic. We may give it lip service, but it no longer quickens our hearts. In our personal experience of the timeless symbols of tradition, we are lifted beyond ourselves to partake of the ancient mysteries while at the same time living our ordinary ego lives, paying taxes, voting, making meals, cleaning out closets, fetching the children from school, holding down jobs.

Bound up in tradition in such lively ways, we participate in our own special groups and join the whole of humanity. Our secret numinous experience, now shared, brings us into the community upon which we depend to digest whatever the experience represents. Not only are we part of the human family, but by bringing to it our own personal experiences of the transpersonal, our unconscious flows together with everyone else's and we join in the attempts of the unconscious to create a new basis of community. Our immediate experiences of the divine revivify tradition and remind us in fresh ways that our shared life together depends upon a very deep source of what we love in common.

Religion also means that as individuals we must be bound back to the pivotal numinous experiences that mark our lives, because they establish in full consciousness our particular idiosyncratic roots in transcendence. According to Jung, forgetting such experiences, or worse, perjuring them by acting as if they make no difference, exposes us to the risk of insanity. Encounters with the holy are like flames. They must be shared, to keep the light alive, or they will burn us up or burn us out. The religious life is one of increased alertness, of keen watchfulness of what goes on between this mysterious Thee and me.[16]

For Jung, religion is inescapable. We may reject it, revile it, revise it, but we cannot get rid of it. This early discovery by Jung has been reaffirmed recently in the research of Rizzuto.[17] When he was accused of being a mystic, Jung objected that he did not invent this idea of *homo religiosus* but only put into words what everyone knows. His vast clinical experience with people afflicted with neurosis or psychosis impressed upon him the fact that half of his patients fell ill because they had lost hold of the meaning of life.[18] Healing means revivifying connection to the transcendent, which brings with it the ability to get up and walk to our fate instead of being dragged there by a neurosis. Thus Jung saw the numinous even in pathology; it expresses how we have fallen out of the Tao, the center of life. Recovery requires remythologization.[19]

RELIGIOUS INSTINCT AND SOCIETY

Our instinct to religion consists in our being endowed with and conscious of relation to deity.[20] If we repress or suppress this instinct, we can fall ill just as surely as we do when we interfere with our physical appetite for food, or with our sexual instinct.[21] Many of the substance abuse disorders to which we fall prey can be traced, *au fond*, to displacement onto chocolate, cocaine, Valium, liquor, or whatever, of our appetitive need for connection to the power and source of being beyond us. We can understand this displacement operating in all of our addictions—even the ones that surprise us—such as to a lover or to a child, to becoming pregnant, or to health or diet routines, to money or power, to a political cause or a psychological theory, or even to a religious discipline. The energy that our instinct to religion brings must go somewhere. If it is not directed to the ultimate, it will turn manic or make idols out of finite goods. Jung reminds us, "It is not a matter of indifference whether one calls something a 'mania' or a 'god.'....When the god is not acknowledged, ego mania develops and out of this mania comes sickness."[22]

Our religious instinct also possesses a social function. Our connection to transpersonal authority keeps us from being swept away into mass movements.[23] It offers us a point of reference outside family, class conventions, cultural mores, even the long reach into our private lives of totalitarian governments. Because we feel seen and known by God, however dimly and inarticulately we may express this, we can find the power, when necessary, to stand against the pressures of collectivities for the sake of truth, our soul, our faith. This capacity in individuals offers society a bulwark against movements that can dominate it and destroy it like out-of-control brush fires. Having such a reference point beyond personal whims and needs, and beyond dependence on others' approval, makes us sturdy citizens, capable of contributing to group life in fresh and sustained ways. This furthers the health of society and our enjoyment of its community life. Knowing a connection to the author of life, we feel a mysterious binding force in our own authority as persons, which we come to respect in our neighbor as much as in ourselves. The sense of being a person who matters combats at a depth level any loss of confidence and hope in our society to facilitate an environment where we all can thrive.

In clinical situations, acknowledging the force of religious instinct may save us from abysmal humiliation and depression. When the majority of the world's people are starving, it is morally embarrassing to be afflicted with obsession over one's weight. To see the larger context of this suffering—that it stems from misdirection of soul hunger, twisting the hunger for connection to ultimate purpose—can release a person from self-revilement in order to pay trustful attention to what the Self is engineering through vexatious symptoms.

The religious instinct may lurk in any of our disturbances, from the extreme of homicidal urges to get even with those who threaten and hurt us unbearably to the seemingly mild but actually lethal affliction of the chronic boredom that results from the suffocation of our inner life. In every case, an impulse toward the ultimate, toward expression of what really matters, mixes in with early childhood hurt and distorted relations with other people. Our energy to live from and toward the center has lost its way, or we have lost touch with it. We are out of sorts. We need help. Part of the help, in Jung's view, means feeling emboldened enough to risk again immediate experience of the numinous.[24]

INDIVIDUATION

In our experience of the numinous, according to Jung, what we feel is its effects on our ego.[25] We feel summoned by something beyond ourselves to become all of ourselves. We sense the Self, "heavy as lead," calling us out of unconscious identification with social convention (the persona mask we adopt for social functioning), pushing us to recognize even those parts of ourselves that we would rather deny and disown, those that lie in what Jung calls "the shadow."[26] These parts confront us with evil. If we open to awareness of our shadow, we know firsthand the agony of Saint Paul when he says the good I would, I do not, and the evil I would not, that I do. Becoming ourselves also means encompassing what ordinarily we think of as opposite to us, to claim as part of us a departure point so different from our conscious gender identity that it symbolizes itself in our dreams, for example, as figures of the opposite sex. Jung calls these figures the "anima" in men and the "animus" in women. To be wholly who we are means including as part of our ego identity what these contrasexual parts bring into our consciousness.[27] They open us sexually as well as spiritually to conversation with the mysterious center of the whole psyche that Jung calls the Self, and through it to the reality the Self symbolizes. In sum, the call to live and integrate into a vibrant whole all the parts of us greatly enlarges our ego identity, making us much more vividly the unique individuals we are.

This is not individualism. For the Self brings with it the bigger center that exceeds our limited ego needs and aims. Jung says:

> The self is like a crowd...being oneself, one is also like many. One cannot individuate without being with other human beings....Being an individual is always a link in a chain....How little you can exist...without responsibilities and duties and the relation of other people to yourself....The Self...plants us in otherness—of other people, and of the transcendent.[28]

The Self acts as an unconscious source of community. Awareness of the Self shifts our focus from the private to the shared, or to put it more accurately, to the inevitable mixture of the public in the private, of the collective in the individual, of the universal in the idiosyncratic.

The task of individuation makes us appreciate the world around us with renewed interest and gratitude. For we see that we are continually offered objects with which to find and release our own particular personality. We come to understand that we are objects with whom others can create and unfold their lives. Issues of injustice and oppression are thus brought right into our hearts, as we recognize that in addition to all the rest of the deprivations they effect, they can keep the heart from loving and unfolding, whether in ourselves or in our neighbor, and most often in both of us. When that happens we cease to see in each other the mutual opportunities that are there to become our true selves in company with others. Another whole dynamic substitutes for this life-giving one. Now we feel pushed to discover, however sneakily, who has more and who less, who does what to whom, and how we can wreak revenge. "More" for us now seems possible only as a result of someone else's "less." The interest in each other's unique and secret response to the mysterious call of life is eclipsed, as envious combat takes over.

If, however, we are embarked on our own individuation, we see this process going on in others too, and we gain a whole new sense of community. We recognize how much we need each other to accomplish the tasks of facing our shadows as our own, of encountering otherness as embodied in the opposite sex, of gathering the courage to respond wholeheartedly to the summons of the Self. We connect with each other at a new depth, what Jung calls "kinship."

THE ARCHETYPAL AND THE BODY

Awareness of the Self deeply affects the clinical situation. Analyst and analysand are rearranged around the call to answer the Self. In the midst of working with the most vexing problems—urges to suicide and homicide, depression and anxiety, schizoid splitting, narcissistic wounding, and borderline fragmenting, and the ways these psychic conditions complicate our relating with spouse, parent, or child, interfere with our jobs, and can reduce us to despair—analyst and analysand now look directly to see what the Self may be bringing in us through all these difficulties.

Jung defines the personal layer of the unconscious as a gathering of complexes, clusters of energy, affect, and image that reflect the conditioning of our early life. There, drawn well down into us, we find all those who have had formative effects on us, parents, friends, lovers, of whatever age or place in our lives. Our complexes show the influence of our cultural milieu, the colorations of class, race, sex, religion, politics, education. At the heart of each complex an archetypal image dwells. Engaging that image takes us through the personal unconscious into a still deeper layer that Jung calls "the objective psyche." The archetypes compose its contents, and deep analysis means identifying and dealing with the particular sets of primordial images that operate in us.

My mother complex, for instance, will show the influence of my own mother's conscious and unconscious personality, her style of relating to me and making the world available to me. The cultural images of motherhood dominant in my childhood, and the particular archetypal image of The Mother that arises from the objective layer of my psyche will also shape the mother complex in me. If I see my mother as malign and depriving and jump from this judgment to a condemnation of Western society for generating a culture that is antagonistic to all women who do not conform to the stereotype of the sacrificial mother, I may find rising in me from the unconscious, fantasy and dream images of an ideal mother whose abundant goodness compensates for my conscious, negative experience of motherhood. Another person who has suffered at the hands of a negative mother, but who fell into self-blame instead of blaming her parent, may find pictures of a dread witch or a stonemaking gorgon sent by the unconscious in order to convince the ego that the problem is not hers, but rather stems from the witchlike constellation that surrounds her mother.[29]

Breaking through to the archetypal layer of the unconscious, and finding ways to sustain conversation across the gap between ego and Self, relieves us from the ardors of blaming, either of ourselves or others. We are confronted with life right before us and its blunt questions. How are we to bring together conscious suffering and unconscious compensations for it? How are we to make sense of the ancient truth that parents visit their sins on their children? How are we to reconcile our suffering with the understanding that our parents did their best given their own problems and illnesses? We enter a larger space of human discussion and meditation on the hardships of life, but we are not glued to hardship. Life is addressing us here; it wants to be lived in us and through us. We feel this on a deep body level. Our spirit quickens.

Jung talks about the instinctual and spiritual poles that characterize every archetype.[30] His best definition of the archetype is as our instinct's image of itself.[31] Instinct is body-backed, the body originating energy, life energy. The image is its self-portrait that expresses how we experience it. And so every archetype has a spiritual facet which explains the "incorrigibly plural" quality of human beings' numinous experiences, to borrow Louis

MacNiece's wonderful phrase.[32] Some of us feel the spirit touch us through the Great Mother archetype. Others feel it through feminine wisdom figures; still others through a wondrous child, a compelling quest, and so forth. The unconscious is not creedal, but compensatory. It dishes up the images needed to balance our conscious one-sidedness so that we can include all sides of ourselves as we become ourselves.

In investigating our God-images, we must examine their personal and archetypal bases. Personal factors will include details from our special upbringing and culture. Archetypal aspects will show which of the fund of primordial human images have been constellated in us. Our God-image may be communism because our parents were devout revolutionaries, and that image may have collapsed with the fall of communism in the late 1980s. Our image of the divine may be scripture-based—the Yahweh who woos his people, sews garments for them when they are naked, and designs ephods for them to wear when they lead worship. Whatever they are, our God-images show a definiteness, and through their distinct idiosyncratic qualities we feel the God beyond us touching us in the flesh.

The body means specific form, it means boundedness, not generality or shifting shadows. The body is life in the concrete. Our body restricts us to a certain place and time and thus permits us to focus on what is right there, in front of us. We are thus protected from "the elemental quality of cosmic indistinctness." The body with its definitive finiteness is "the guarantee of consciousness, and consciousness is the instrument by which the meaning is created."[33] Without the body, we can easily float off into the timeless quality of the archetypal, lured by no longer having to be ourselves: "You cease to think and are acted upon as though carried by a great river with no end. You are suddenly eternal...liberated from sitting up and paying attention, doubting, and concentrating upon things....You don't want to disturb it by asking foolish questions—it is too nice."[34]

This drifting as if "one with the universe" is not, however, the life of the spirit, for it is no longer life in the body. We need both body and spirit, or we forfeit both. We possess both or neither. For there to be life in the spirit, we need life in the body. For contact with the unconscious, we need consciousness. Otherwise the unconscious, like the waves of the ocean, wells up, comes forward, builds toward a climax, and then pulls downward, retreats, and disintegrates. For something to happen, consciousness must interfere, "grasp the treasure," make something of what is offered.[35] We need the ego as the center of consciousness to know the Self as the center of the whole, the conscious and the unconscious psyche. We need to enter the conversation that fills the gap between them. That process of conversation constructs the Self that claims us, and builds up an ego that becomes decentered. If we fail to engage in that process, our ego can easily be taken over by archetypal contents, as we see to our horror in any religious or political fanaticism. Under such pressures, we rush out against others compelled by the force of the archetypal. Convinced that we alone possess the truth, we know no bounds in dealing with others who may disagree with or even defy us; segregating, maligning, oppressing, imprisoning, murdering others are crimes we can commit in the name of our twisted version of truth and salvation.

If we do engage in ego–Self conversation we come to know archetypal images inhabiting our very own bodies. This feels like energy, sometimes in greater amounts than we think we can handle. Then our bodies stretch, both physically and psychologically, into new postures and new attitudes of acceptance and celebration. We might, for example, finally lay to rest a lifelong addiction to a substance or a drink or a special kind of food. We might find our blood pressure lowering after many years. We might find back pain dispersing, or our power to endure it increasing. We might feel ushered into sexual ecstasy for the first time after many years. We feel we live in our finite form, in touch with something infinite.

GOD-IMAGES AND EVIL

To enter conversation with our God-image is not an easy task. The partial nature of this dialogue, its basis in small individual experience, and its all too limited human perspective soon become only too clear. The conversation begins to crumble. We realize with unerring certainty that we are not reaching God or the transcendent, or whatever we choose to call it, from our side. We cannot cross the gap: we can only receive what comes from the other side, from the mysterious center of reality that our all too human symbols point to. Jung's image of the Self, for example, cannot be taken as God in us, let alone the transcendent God, because it too is a product of a merely human theory. It cannot substitute for the reality to which it points, the reality to which the Self—that is, that within the psyche that knows about the transcendent—is trying to lead us.

Attempting to engage our God-image in serious conversation and meditation is to face its inadequacy to cover the complexity of human life. For example, Jung asks, What about evil? The suffering of the innocent? Jung is distinguished among depth psychologists for his preoccupation with finding answers to these questions.[36] They are not questions we can avoid, for our own shadow natures throw us right into them. Terrible things happen all around us, to ourselves and others. We lose our minds. Human rights disappear. Bodies are born crippled and we are maimed. Storms and floods destroy our world. We murder each other. How can there be a just, powerful, and merciful God when so much suffering exists?

Jung's answer places evil, finally, in God directly. God's nature is complex and bears its own shadow side. It needs human beings, with their focused body-based consciousness, to incarnate these opposites in divine life and thus help in their transformation. In considering the Book of Job, Jung surmises that Yahweh suffers from unconsciousness, himself forgetting to consult his own divine omniscience. Job's protests against his unmerited suffering makes Yahweh aware of his own shadow dealings with Satan, and finally he can answer Job with the figure of Christ, who takes the sufferings of human beings into his own innocent divine life and pays for them himself.

Jung considers the Christ figure the most complete Self symbol we have known in human history, but he is aware that the Christian myth must be lived onward still farther.[37] Christ, unlike the rest of us, is without sin. Evil splits off into the opposing figure of the Devil or the Antichrist. Christianity, Jung says, thus leaves no place for the evil side of the human person.[38] For him, the doctrine of evil as the privation of good fails to recognize the actual existence of evil as a force to be contended with. The doctrine of

God as the *summum bonum* lifts God to impossible heights, while crushing humans under the weight of sin.

Critics of Jung question his reading of the Christ figure as separated from evil. In fact, they say, Christ lives his whole life on the frontiers of evil. Christ is no stranger to evil and sin, from birth as an outcast in poverty, his occasioning Herod's murder of innocent babies, to facing the demons of mental illness, righteous rule-keeping, scapegoating judgments, abandonment by his friends and neighbors, the refusal of the good, not to speak of his own fate, suffering betrayal, abandonment, and death.[39]

Jung works out a solution that is satisfactory to himself. We can read this as the fruit of his engagement with his own God-image. He sees God as both good and evil. Some critics of Jung surmise he projected his own unintegrated aggression onto the Godhead.[40] We serve God, in this reading, by accepting the opposing elements in ourselves—conscious and unconscious, ego and shadow, persona and anima or animus, finally ego and Self. These opposites are best symbolized by masculine and feminine, and thus Jung brings into religious discussion the body-based sexuality and contrasexuality of the human person.[41] This inclusion goes a long way toward recovering the inescapable importance of the feminine mode of being, so long neglected in patriarchal history.[42] By struggling to integrate the opposites, we incarnate God's struggle. The solutions we achieve, however small, contribute to divine life. Thus we participate in Christ's suffering and serve God by becoming the selves God created us to be. We fulfill our vocation, redeeming our own pain from meaninglessness and participating in the life of God.

THE TRANSCENDENT FUNCTION AND SYNCHRONICITY

Jung demonstrates in reaching his own working solution to problems he knew directly what is in some ways his most daring and far-reaching method, that of the transcendent function. He enters the conversation of opposites, lets each side have its say, endures the struggle between the opposing points of view, suffers the anguish of being strung out between them, and greets the resolving symbol, when it appears, with gratitude. The psyche, says Jung, possesses this function to overcome opposition through arriving at a third point of view that includes the essence of each conflicting perspective while at the same time combining them into a symbol of the new.

We must enter this process and cooperate with it if we are to be fully—and ethically—engaged in living, says Jung.[43] It is not enough just to appreciate the transcendent function and marvel at the new symbols that arise with it. We must live them, use them, bind them back into personal and communal life if we are to submit to the religious attitude. The transcendent function is the process through which the new comes about in us. This is a costly undertaking, for we feel our egos losing their grip on secure frames of reference. We float and drift and seem to know nothing. We hover over the gap between ego process and Self process. When the new begins to show itself in image form, we pause, look, contemplate, in order to integrate into a new level of unity parts of ourselves and of life outside us that were hitherto unknown to us.[44] But to reach that precious ego capacity to reflect and respond to the creating of the new, we must renounce the certainties we have so long depended upon.

The religious attitude, therefore, involves sacrifice.[45] We offer up our identification with our ego's point of view as the best and only authority. We surrender what we identify with as "mine" or "ours," sacrificing our ego claims without expectation of payment. We do this because we recognize a higher claim, that of the Self. It offers itself to us, making its own sacrifice of relinquishing its status as the all and the vast, to take up residence in the stuff of our everyday lives. The conversation between ego and Self becomes our daily meditation.

When this happens, reality seems to reform itself. Odd coincidences of events that are not causally related occur, impressing us with their large and immediate meaning, what Jung called "synchronicity."[46] Outer and inner events collide in significant ways that open us to perceive what Jung calls the *unus mundus,* a wholeness where matter and psyche are revealed to be but two aspects of the same reality. Clinically, I have seen striking examples of this. A man struggled in conversation with a childhood terror of being locked in a dark attic as punishment for crying out too often to his parents when he was put to bed at night. Eventually, he reached the key to unlock a compulsive fetish that he now saw had functioned as the symbol to bridge the gap between his adult personality and his abject childhood terror in the locked attic. When this new attitude emerged out of his struggling back and forth with the fascination of the fetish on the one hand and his conscious humiliation and wish to rid himself of this compulsion on the other, an outer event synchronistically occurred. The attic room in the house of his childhood was struck by lightning and destroyed—but only the attic part of the house!

Jung's theory links such outer and inner happenings through his theory of the archetype as psychoid, as possessed of the body and spirit poles.[47] When we engage in the conversation between the ego point of view and the Self's, we touch both poles of the Self archetype, which opens us to what is going on all the time in the interweaving of physical and spiritual events. When our conversation grows deep enough to show us that the Self is not only a center of the psyche but symbolizes the center of all of the life that lies outside our psyche, we become open to the interdependent reality of the whole, not only of all that is human, but of all other animate and inanimate life.[48]

METHOD

Jung gives us a method to approach religious documents of all kinds, which he demonstrates by his attention not only to materials of the Judeo-Christian tradition, but also of alchemy, Zen Buddhism, Tibetan Buddhism, Taoism, Confucianism, Hinduism, elements of African and Native American religions, and the mythologies of many times and cultures.[49] We must ask, How does a given document reflect the conversation of ego and Self? What dogmas and rituals from the ego side collect and contain immediate numinous experiences that give rise to Self symbols? What are the dominant Self symbols that point to a reality beyond the psyche? What are the main archetypal images employed to do such symbol-forming activity? Is the dominant archetype the transformation of father and son, as in the Christian Eucharist, or is it the transformation of mother and daughter, as in the ancient Eleusinian mysteries? Jung saw alchemy, for example, as taking up the problem of the spiritualization of matter which Christianity did not adequately solve.[50] In alchemy, the Self symbol is the lapis or "stone," which unlike the Christ symbol combines good and evil, and matter and spirit; it is the end purpose of all the alchemical operations which symbolize all our attitudes.

Jung leaves us ways that are practical and spiritual, hardheaded and open-hearted, to connect with the archaic roots of our religion, whatever this may be, and with the necessary clinical methods to give full measure to include our experience of the numinous in the enterprise of healing.

Notes

This chapter was originally published in *The Cambridge Companion to Jung*, eds. P. Young-Eisendrath and T. Dawson (Cambridge: Cambridge University Press, 1997).

1. C. G. Jung, *Psychology and Alchemy*, Collected Works 12, trans. R. F. C. Hull (New York: Pantheon, 1953), pars. 13, 14, 15.

2. C. G. Jung, "Psychology and Religion," *Psychology and Religion: West and East*, Collected Works 11, trans. R. F. C. Hull (New York: Pantheon, 1938/1958), pars. 6, 31, 37; A. and B. Ulanov, *Religion and the Unconscious* (Louisville, Ky.: Westminster, 1975), ch. 1.

3. A. B. Ulanov, *The Feminine in Christian Theology and in Jungian Psychology* (Evanston: Northwestern University Press, 1971), ch. 6.

4. C. G. Jung, *Memories, Dreams, Reflections* (New York: Pantheon, 1963), ch. 11; A. Jaffé, *Was C. G. Jung a Mystic?* (Einsiedeln, Switzerland: Daimon), 109–13.

5. C. G. Jung, *Aion: Researches into the Phenomenology of the Self*, Collected Works 9:2, trans. R. F. C. Hull (New York: Pantheon, 1959), pars. 9, 57.

6. A. and B. Ulanov, *The Healing Imagination* (Mahwah, N.J.: Paulist, 1991), ch. 2.

7. C. G. Jung, "A Psychological Approach to the Trinity," *Psychology and Religion: West and East*, Collected Works 11 (New York: Pantheon, 1942/1958).

8. Jung, "Psychology and Religion," pars. 13–21; C. G. Jung, *Letters*, 2 vols., eds. G. Adler and A. Jaffé (Princeton: Princeton University Press, 1973 and 1975), II, June 1957, 377.

9. A. B. Ulanov, *Picturing God* (Cambridge, Mass.: Cowley, 1986), 164–78.

10. C. G. Jung, "The Undiscovered Self," *Civilization in Transition, Collected Works* 10, trans. R. F. C. Hull (New York: Pantheon, 1956/1967), par. 515.

11. Jung, *Psychology and Religion.*

12. Jung, "Psychology and Religion," pars. 2, 6, 8–9.

13. Jung, *Letters*, I, 22 December 1942, 326.

14. C. G. Jung, "Brother Klaus," *Psychology and Religion: West and East, Collected Works* 11, trans. R. F. C. Hull (New York: Pantheon, 1933)/1958); Jung, *Letters,* II, June 1957, 377.

15. Jung, "Psychology and Religion," par. 8; Jung, *Letters*, II, 12 February 1959, 482.

16. Jung, *Letters*, I, 10 September 1943, 338.

17. A. M. Rizzuto, *The Birth of the Living God* (Chicago: University of Chicago Press, 1979).

18. C. G. Jung, "Psychotherapists or Clergy," *Psychology and Religion: West and East, Collected Works* 11, trans. R. F. C. Hull (New York: Pantheon, 1932/1958), pars. 497, 509.

19. A. B. Ulanov, *The Feminine*, 127–36.

20. Jung, *Psychology and Alchemy*, par. 11.

21. A. B. Ulanov, "Jung and Prayer," *Jung and the Monotheisms*, ed. J. Ryce-Menuhin (New York: Routledge, 1994), ch. 2 of this book.

22. C. G. Jung, "Commentary on the Secret of the Golden Flower," *Alchemical Studies, Collected Works* 13, trans. R. F. C. Hull (Princeton: Princeton University Press, 1929/1967), par. 55.

23. Jung, "The Undiscovered Self," pars. 506–8.

24. Jung, *Letters*, I, 26 May 1945, 41.

25. C. G. Jung, "The Development of Personality," *The Development of Personality, Collected Works* 17, trans. R. F. C. Hull (New York: Pantheon, 1934/1954), par. 300.

26. Ibid., par. 303.

27. A. and B. Ulanov, *Transforming Sexuality: The Inner World of Anima and Animus* (Boston: Shambhala, 1994).

28. C. G. Jung, *Nietzsche's Zarathustra*, 2 vols. (Princeton: Princeton University Press, 1988), 102.

29. A. and B. Ulanov, *The Witch and the Clown: Two Archetypes of Human Sexuality* (Wilmette, Ill.: Chiron, 1987), ch. 2.

30. C. G. Jung, "On the Nature of the Psyche," *The Structure and Dynamics of the Psyche, Collected Works* 8, trans. R. F. C. Hull (New York: Pantheon, 1947/1960), par. 277.

31. C. G. Jung, "Instinct and the Unconscious," *The Structure and*

Dynamics of the Psyche, Collected Works 8, trans. R. F. C. Hull (New York: Pantheon 1919/1960), par. 277.

32. B. Ulanov, *Jung and the Outside World* (Wilmette, Ill.: Chiron, 1992), and A. and B. Ulanov, *Transforming Sexuality,* for examples.

33. Jung, *Nietzsche's Zarathustra*, 349–50.

34. Ibid., 240.

35. Ibid., 237.

36. C. G. Jung, "Answer to Job," *Psychology and Religion: West and East, Collected Works* 11, trans. R. F. C. Hull (New York: Pantheon, 1952–1958).

37. Jung, *Memories, Dreams, Reflections*, 337–38.

38. Jung, "A Psychological Approach to the Trinity," par. 232.

39. A. B. Ulanov, *The Wisdom of the Psyche* (Cambridge, Mass.: Cowley, 1987), 46–54; B. Ulanov, *Jung and the Outside World*, ch. 5.

40. J. Redfearn, "The Self and Individuation," *Journal of Analytical Psychology* 22, 2 (1997); D. W. Winnicott, "Review of C. G. Jung, *Memories, Dreams, Reflections,*" *Psychoanalytic Explorations*, eds. C. Winnicott, R. Shepherd, M. Davis (London: Karnac, 1989).

41. Jung, *Psychology and Alchemy*, par. 192.

42. Jung, "Answer to Job," pars. 107, 619–20, 625; A. B. Ulanov, *The Feminine*, 291–92.

43. C. G. Jung, "The Transcendent Function," *The Structure and Dynamics of the Psyche, Collected Works* 8, trans. R. F. C. Hull (New York: Pantheon, 1916/1960), pars. 181–83; C. G. Jung, *Mysterium Coniunctionis, Collected Works* 14, trans. R. F. C. Hull (New York: Pantheon, 1963), pars. 753–55.

44. A. and B. Ulanov, *Healing Imagination*.

45. C. G. Jung, "Transformation Symbolism of the Mass," *Psychology and Religion: West and East, Collected Works* 11, trans. R. F. C. Hull (New York: Pantheon, 1954/1958), par. 390.

46. C. G. Jung, "Synchronicity: An Acausal Connecting Principle," *The Structure and Dynamics of the Psyche, Collected Works* 8, trans. R. F. C. Hull (New York: Pantheon, 1952/1958), par. 840.

47. Jung, "On the Nature of the Psyche," pars. 368ff., 480.

48. R. Aziz, *C. G. Jung's Psychology of Religion and Synchronicity* (Albany, N.Y.: State University of New York Press, 1990), 85, 111, 137, 167.

49. Jung, *Collected Works* 11, 12, 13.

50. Jung, *Letters*, II, 26 October 1957, 401.

Part III

THE RELATIONSHIP OF JUNG TO RELIGIOUS AND PSYCHOLOGICAL ISSUES

Chapter 8

A Shared Space

Jung is the psychologist of numinous space. He stands out among depth psychologists for his insistent emphasis on the space between us and the *mysterium tremendum.* He puts it bluntly in a letter, "You are quite right, the main interest of my work is not concerned with the treatment of neuroses but rather with the approach to the numinous. But the fact is that the approach to the numinous is the real therapy and inasmuch as you attain to the numinous experiences you are released from the curse of pathology. Even the very disease takes on a numinous character."[1]

In this space where we might not expect it, Jung deals with clinical facts and demonstrates a remarkable clinical skill. In this area we can find crucial similarities and differences between Jung and other depth psychologists—I am thinking here of Melanie Klein, D. W. Winnicott, Marion Milner, Harry Guntrip, and Masud Khan. Jung gets at his clinical facts from the departure point of the space between us and the numinous; they begin the other way 'round, with the spaces of neurosis and psychosis and move through them toward the numinous, which they address in human terms and speak of as revealing the quality of human life.

These distinguished British analysts work hard at the concrete, seeking what we in the New York Association for Analytical Psychology like to call "the clinical facts," filling in the spaces of Jung's far-flung vision of the goal and meaning of analysis, through which they strive toward their own views of meaning and truth. Their effect for us is to ground Jung and to keep us from wafting upward into a never-never archetype-land to the neglect of the clinical facts. Jung's approach might be said to pull us out beyond the focus on "early" origins, with its assumption that "early" equals "deep"; or the questionable religiosity of the fix-it approach, with its hidden assumption that with enough analysis, consciousness, and application of theory and experience, everything and anything can be fixed.

From an objective point of view, all these different theories possess some truth and offer useful ways to map the spaces of the psyche. Any of them may work. But from a subjective point of view, it makes all the difference which theory we take, or which one takes us. For it becomes the Ariadne thread into the labyrinth of human experience and the spaces we share. The theory that inhabits us enables us to construct the spaces of relationship that we will inhabit, to understand the areas of madness and to find the spaces where meaning exists. The theory we identify as our own in turn identifies how we own or disown numinous space, how we feel the unconscious, whether we make room for its presence or run away. Jung's remark that the unconscious is not this or that but the Unknown as it immediately touches us greatly matters here.[2] For the unconscious does touch us, socially as well as individually, in our politics as in our prayers, in our wounded places as in our loves.[3]

How then do we live in it? House it? What finally really matters about this work that we are doing, that all those celebrated clinicians are making it easier for us to do? For whose sake do we do this work? What is it that sustains us in our daily analytical work, supports those of us laboring under the rigors of training or those of us who work year after year, decade after decade in these mysterious spaces?

Discipline is surely one answer. Even dedication. But to what, to whom? It is to that question that Jung directs us, to that space between us and the numinous. And it was that question that Jung was after when he wrote near the end of his autobiography:

> The decisive question for [us] is: [Are we] related to something infinite or not? That is the telling question of [our] life. Only if we know that the thing which truly matters is the infinite can we avoid fixing our interest upon futilities, and upon all kinds of goals which are not of real importance....In the final analysis, we count for something only because of the essential we embody, and if we do not embody that, life is wasted. In our relationships to other[s]...too, the crucial

question is whether an element of boundlessness is expressed in the relationship.

The feeling for the infinite, however, can be attained only if we are bounded to the utmost....Only consciousness of our narrow confinement in the self forms the link to the limitlessness of the unconscious. In such awareness we experience ourselves concurrently as limited and eternal, as both one and the other.[4]

THE BODY, THE FEMININE, AND THE DARK: JUNG AND MELANIE KLEIN

Jung says we finally count for something only because of "the essential we embody." If we do not, life is a waste. We owe to Melanie Klein her great turning inward of Freud's libido theory to develop the notion of internal objects and internalized space, made up not of drives pressing for release and defenses against them, but rather of objects interacting with each other and with the ego. What was linear becomes round and enclosed. What was pressing outward and to be measured or stopped or redirected and let loose again is turned around to encompass the circles of interior life. As Adrian Stokes describes it, our interior life is an intense drama, a crowded scene.[5] I think of Klein's achievement as a distinctly feminine one, as in the feminine mode of inward and downward turning toward the dark insides of things and the early beginnings of infancy.

Although Klein makes no direct use of Jung and probably would have rejected his mapping of the psyche, nonetheless, I find her at given points curiously like him. For example, fundamental to her theory is the fact that psychic life is embedded so firmly in the body. Jung did not systematically fill in the steps of the way archetypes are embodied in infancy and childhood, yet he stressed their physicality, their tangibility, and felt presence. No reader of Jung can doubt his conviction of the physical effects of the archetype felt in the body. Witness his word-association tests, and the sad diagnosis of terminal illness in the child who dreamt of a horse screaming and leaping out of a window.[6] No physical evidence of her brain tumor was yet discernible, but the psyche announced its presence through a palpable imagery.

Similarly, for Klein, the psyche is always in the body. All its images and fantasies are bodily based and felt in the body. Thus we can see a correspondence between her notion that we come into this life with a feeble but definite ego capable of fantasying almost from birth and Jung's notion of the potential for archetypal imagery resident in each psyche from birth.[7] Indeed, for Klein, fantasies that are felt in the body and are instinct-backed are literally mental representations of physical instincts. She says almost word for word what Jung does about the archetypes: that they are mental images of our instinct life. Similarly, Jung's archetypes are like Klein's fantasies. Fantasies, says Klein, are the way we experience inner objects residing within us. Fantasies, for Jung, derive from archetypes and are the ways through which we contribute to the objects we introject.

Klein concentrates her investigations of inner space on what Jungians would call "the mother archetype." Her entire work researches this primordial image of the maternal as mother of all life. Klein finds the basis of mental life organized first in relation to the mother, who is experienced in physical terms as a good and bad breast and, at the beginning, as containing within herself the father, who is a good and bad penis. An image for Klein's whole system I find not only useful but entertaining is that of the Goodyear blimp sailing in the sky; I think of it featuring two sets of letters, *breast* on one side, *penis* on the other.

Klein explores, anchors, and makes concrete the vicissitudes of infant mental life in relation to this all-powerful archetype, and again like Jung, rescues actual mothers—we poor women—from being made the villains of their pieces. For Klein, an infant's fantasies about his or her mother have much to do with shaping what kind of parent a mother becomes. For Jung, the mother we get is simply part of the cards dealt us in this life: her influence cannot be reduced to what a particular woman does or fails to do. Both Klein's fantasy space and Jung's archetypal space help shape what sort of mothering will occur. The child's psyche bumps into the mother's, and between them, in their shared space, they work out their adventure of love, with whatever degree of success.

Klein, like Jung, reminds us that the adventure includes hate among its states of being. Both rescue mothering and being mothered from the all-sunny, all-cheery vistas that only make the shadows and dark places more treacherous in their obscurity. Klein writes graphically of the cutting and chewing up, the sucking and spitting out, the burning, devouring scalding of mother and the infant's sense of what mother's actions mean to it. No sunny mother, this! No placid, loving infant, this! Here is lusty love, love with teeth, which any parent or lover will recognize instantly, and any patient, with luck, will reach back to. This is the instinctive, primordial side of loving, the hating part.

Jung also recognizes the shadowy ambiguous side of mother–child love, but unlike Klein, he does not inflate it to become the all-in-all, a surrogate god. Jung takes up this God issue explicitly. He does not at all reject it as Klein does. Jung carries the notion of strong ambivalent emotion into his experience of God: There are times you are punched and kicked and times you hit back. Indeed, Jung found it easier to write about this side of his experience of God than the blissful moments. Those, he claimed, he kept secret.[8] In any case, both he and Klein find space for the dark, the envious, the aggressive, the hateful emotions, the turning away from the good, the dread of it.

Klein's mapping of psychic space is routed around two central positions: the paranoid-schizoid and the depressive. (Guntrip wanted to add a third—the schizoid-withdrawn.) In navigating toward and through the first of these, Klein's notion of the embodied psyche, the psyche in space, carries beyond individuals to the body politic, the social body of the human community. For there are catastrophic social and political results if the us/them mentality of the first position arrests too many citizens in their psychological development. Then whole sectors of our inner and outer populations fall victim to the paranoia of projecting all the bad onto our neighbor, preserving for ourselves all the good—usually a fragile good not tough enough to survive, a good buried deep within ourselves and not taken out and lived with except under the most controlled conditions. The reverse is no better. Projecting all good onto our neighbor and denigrating ourselves as all bad does just as much harm, upsetting a precarious personal and world balance of good and evil forces, as the trashing by so many Americans of their own government illustrates and as Klein's ideas about the reverses of the criminal mind show.[9] Isn't this splitting, in either direction, what Jung is writing about in his *Undiscovered Self*? The problem of the undiscovered and undigested shadow translates into the Iron Curtains and Berlin Walls of Europe and the similarly destructive walling off of our ghettos. Mutual us/them projects carve up the spaces of our world into armed camps.

In reaching to the second position—again a metaphor of space—we struggle to put good and bad together. We discover that we, too, and those we revere and love—which for us in this profession would include these giants of the depths, these great theorymakers who mapped unknown psychic territory—all do harm, all have damage to account for, human wreckage. The sadness we encounter in this second position, its depressiveness, is that we are all mixtures of good and bad. Our theories, constructed to heal, can maim. Our theories, designed to help person relate to person, in a constantly enlarging space, can quickly destroy the space as we substitute theory for love.

These dark spaces, both Klein and Jung tell us, must be included; we must make room for them. If we can abide the negative truths as well as the positive, and the work of mourning over what we have willed to death, we can find our way to another space—Klein's place of reparation and Jung's third area that reconciles the opposing first two. In this space we feel the will to build up again and put pieces back together. Klein's dramas of love and hate illustrate one of those forceful sets of opposites which Jung describes: the iron striking the anvil, the flint on the steel, grinding us to a fine powder, refining the soul—if we survive.[10]

In putting Klein's map of the psyche's spaces alongside Jung's, we also need to see where they diverge and lose all connection. A major difference arises from their initial departure points. Klein's self-space and world-space are constructed out of the interplay of introjection and projection. She and the object-relations school as a whole investigate those inner objects that originate outside the psyche, that we introject and match up with our fantasies and body experiences and emotions and then project outward again. This cycle repeats itself in an almost endless rhythm. Although these objects originate outside the psyche, curiously we never get to see them clearly, in their own right, undominated by our subjective fantasies and projections. We never transcend the web of introjection-projection, the pervasiveness of self, to greet the other as self, separate from our making of him or her, an other existing there, a subject, not only shocking us in its differences from us, but also given us for our own positive experience.

In contrast, Jung primarily investigates inner objects that originate within the psyche, arising and constellating spontaneously, especially in conjunction with outer objects, with the clusters of images and fantasies, emotions, and behavior patterns that we call "the archetype."[11] The inner objectivity of the archetype facilitates our seeing the outer object, taking it beyond our introjections and projections. We recognize the otherness of the object, then, as an independent subject existing in its own right. This point of transcendence, which Jung takes as clinical fact, makes a great clinical difference—for example, in the workings of transference and countertransference. We see there a level of human encounter that transcends the simple dynamics of transference. We see in Jung, too, an emphasis on the intrinsic nature of the image, the symbol in itself, which is not to be immediately absorbed into what one already knows, translated upward, so to speak, into the words and concepts of consciousness. Jung's focus on the autonomy of the symbol yields the odd experience of a reversal of ordinary consciousness. Instead of the symbol being the object of my subjective consciousness, I experience myself as its object! With any luck, the two, the I and the It, will come to greet each other as two subjects, as, for example, in the work of active imagination. This territory of the psyche's space is left uncharted by Klein.

One senses this lack of feeling for the transcendence of self toward the other in Klein's strong insistence on the correctness of her theory. In charting the spaces that open toward the numinous, she identifies with her theory. A brilliant analyst clinically, she strikes me as a formidable one, too, pushing, pressing her interpretations (which are always directed to the unconscious of her patient, not to the ego), interpreting the anxiety they arouse as evidence of their correctness. Though warm in person, she was often thought to be relentless in pressing for her theory. How far this is from Jung, who writes that theory was for him "looking about the world," including the place of the divine, looking at the great myths and religions and even the transcendent God.[12] For Jung, theory is part of what we put in the space between ego and Self, part of any approach to the numinous, but not the numinous itself. He finds in theory a net in which to catch the contents of the far-flung spaces, to gather them with his own fervent participation. He owns and disowns theory simultaneously, as his much-quoted remark about clinical work illustrates: that we learn all we can, but when we are before the living person of the patient, we must throw it all out, set it aside, taking first what the other says to us.[13]

I think of Melanie Klein's overdetermined support of her theory as stemming from some hard bit of animus, something left over, left undigested. She is to me a great example of a woman writing and working from the animus—one that is integrated as her own, even if not perfectly so. Hence her toughness, her clarity, and, above all, her originality in charting new spaces in the psyche. But to the end she maintained she was simply extending Freud's insights into the pre-Oedipal years, merely applying the death instinct to the processes of creativity, filling in small details what the master had sketched in the large. That last bit of animus that a woman must integrate as part of herself, taking all the authority of the Self as addressing her within "the narrow confinement" of her own small ego, did not occur. Instead, it asserted itself as the animus so often can, in the need to be right. Nonetheless, all that was charmingly complemented in her personality by a sustained enjoyment of things feminine. After she had written still another of her original papers for a psychoanalytic congress, her next project was to see that she had a new hat. Her friends thought the two tasks—the paper and the hat—were of equal importance to her.[14]

THE OTHER AND THE FEMININE: JUNG AND OTHERS

Closer to Jung's spirit in recognizing the necessity of the other are D. W. Winnicott and those who cluster around him—Marion Milner, Harry Guntrip, Masud Khan. Winnicott gives evidence of his conviction that even originality is not to be found except in relation to others. They form the tradition on which we depend.

He says of his own writing, "What happens is I gather this and that, here and there, settle down to clinical experience, form my own theories and then, last of all, interest myself in looking to see where I stole what."[15]

His style of writing—so simple, so seminal, so enjoyable to read—gives me the same feeling of talking to another person that Jung's does, someone speaking to where I live and talking about what really matters. That is due, I think, to both not having given too much away. Their selves are still capacious enough to house rage and love and omnipotence. In Jung's language, not too much of the Self has been sacrificed to the ego.[16] These authors are alive, never dull. They are awake, not at all tidied up in a neatly packaged theory. Their liveliness has to do with a sense of another beyond the self and a self that is different from the other. Recognizing the importance of the other confers a tremendous sense of humanity upon the self. The sense of self is big because of the sense of the other.

Even Masud Khan, who strikes me as having more of Winnicott's incommunicable isolated self than even Winnicott, says, as he writes about the "privacy" of the self, "My relation with my patients has taught me the humility and the necessity of the need of *the other* for one to be and become oneself."[17] Guntrip goes further; he makes a completely personal map of the psyche's spaces. What was originally Freud's libido of drives and then the object-seeking libido of Fairbairn, with Guntrip becomes a person-centered ego seeking to be a self in relation to other selves.[18] At the end of his life, Guntrip found even this theory too impersonal: "Theory—this is just a schizoid defense. It doesn't lead to change. This only occurs through an enduring personal relationship."[19]

Reaching to the other can extend to the divine, as is poignantly illustrated by Marion Milner's patient Susan, chronicled in such loving and full detail, Susan so grossly ill and in treatment for twenty-two years, at times so poor she could pay only some 25¢ a session. She cried out, "Dear God, help, please do, for me to see myself as I did once, with...my heart...because without a heart where are you?"[20] That lost heart, which for Guntrip is the lost heart of the ego, is for Jung the lost soul for which modern man is searching. Where can it be found? In a sense of what he calls "the boundless within the bound," in a sense of the eternal within the narrow confinement of one's own self, which Jung came to understand. The similarity between Jung and the others is the recognition that whatever our theoretical bias, we need the other to become a self. The difference that sets Jung apart is that he pulls the self out toward the soul, which is to say toward the numinous. The other we need to become a self is the soul, and we get at that through paradox. It is found in a sense of the infinite within the finite, of the eternal within the narrow confinement of one's own small self. For the ego to experience the Self, with others or alone, it must feel its limits to the utmost, embodied in the physical, psychical, historical boundaries of its own reality. Jung, so tied to his own time, could reach back far into the past to uncover for the world the lost values, for example, of the alchemists as seekers in their own times for connection to the ultimate.

This sense of essential paradox, the infinite through the finite, self through other, is touched vividly in Winnicott's epochal mapping of transitional space. There we find the self we create while creating the self we find. There we play across the gap between self and other, a gap which simultaneously expresses a union, that of self and other. I think here of Marion Milner's discussion of the edges of objects in space, a space where they do not touch and a space which also joins them.[21]

Central to understanding this transitional space, and to any sense of self and other, is the female element of being, as Winnicott put it, and Guntrip after him, a notion close to Jung's recognition of the feminine as a distinct and essential mode of being human, a sadly neglected one that needs to be recovered to consciousness.[22] Milner wrote in her first book, before her Freudian analysis and any exposure to Jung or Winnicott, "Every human personality is two-sided....Every man or woman is potentially both male and female."[23]

Familiar to all of us is Winnicott's emphasis on the good-enough mother. This is the mother who may find herself hating her child when she sings the lullaby, "Rock-a-Bye Baby," with its concluding disaster. But hers is a hate she can hold and not take out on the child too crudely, at too great a distance from her love.[24] Indeed, without such a mother we do not even reach to the transitional space made by exciting and precarious play. This is the space where Winnicott locates religion, art, and culture in an adult's life and where we find happening what I believe was specifically religious in Winnicott himself. This is the "sacred moment" of communication where the child brings together belief in the possibility of being understood and helped by another with the surprise of learning something from his or her own self, something hitherto unknown.[25]

Even the analyst works under the cover of the female element, creating a space where a patient can find what he or she brings into analysis in the self that is already in the making. The analyst must hold the situation securely enough to allow the patient to regress back into the moments of gap, where the person was dropped, discarded, because not seen or cherished as one with the royal authority of a self come into being.

Guntrip makes of this female activity the crux of all therapy. Borrowing Winnicott's term, he says the female element is what gets an ego started into life, and all psychic dissociation that brings people to therapy is a dissociation of the female element in ourselves.[26] In his own search for what he came later to call "the lost heart" of his ego—the regressed and withdrawn part—Guntrip found in his analysis with Winnicott enough female elements of being to produce a fine relaxed naturalness and sharing of the ordinary events of living. An example was Winnicott's saying in mid-session, "Excuse me, Harry. I'll be right back. I have to pee." That atmosphere allowed Guntrip to recall and to resolve the unbearable dread that made him feel paralyzed and empty until his seventies, despite his productive life.[27] How different this is from recent emphasis on the "analytic frame"!

In his last book, *Playing and Reality,* Winnicott discusses this female element directly, not in the obvious role of mother now, but as part of a man's personality. The relevant patient had persevered in analysis for a quarter of a century because no matter how fine the work, something essential remained untouched. Only when Winnicott said to him, "I am listening to a girl. I know perfectly well that you are a man but I am listening to a girl...,"[28] did a profound change begin. What was lost had begun to be found. A split-off part had begun to be seen as integral to the rest of the man's personality. Typical of Winnicott was his remark to his audience in describing this clinical moment: "I decided to surrender myself to whatever this might mean in myself...." The result was his theoretical formulation of "the aspect of the personality that has the opposite sex."[29]

So we see edges touching here, though Winnicott's and Jung's theories begin from vastly different points. Jung finds the feminine element—the anima—as that which pulls a man across the threshold down toward the deeper Self, and the feminine in women as that which urges her toward the Self in her, to take the downward-going way to include all parts of herself. The discovery of the feminine factor required from Winnicott a similar going down, a surrendering to follow where the glimpse of anima might lead. Without contacting this element, analytical work looks good, but is without soul, reminding us of Jung's description of the anima as the archetype of life.[30] With characteristic frankness, Winnicott recognized the truth of Jung's concept when he said in his review of Jung's autobiography, "For me, the anima is the part of any man that could say: I have always known I was a woman."[31] To me, Winnicott himself is an example of a man closely in touch with his anima, illustrating what a man can be when his anima is integrated. He possesses an unmistakable quality of zest, a lightness of touch, and yet he must insistently probe to deep dark places, showing startling originality as he brings new things up from where he has descended.

MADNESS AND ILLUSION: JUNG AND OTHERS

Madness is part of the transitional space, too. It is another place where the edges of different theories touch. Inevitably, there is a gap between ideal and real worlds, between inner dreams and outer objective facts, between what we are and what we would like to be. That gap is what we play across and, with any luck, imaginatively fill in with creative living. In Jung's terms, it is a space where archetypes get constellated, where we dress up as witch, clown, queen, or bear, daring to go outside the ego's lines. That gap may also be the space we fall into, fall into endlessly, as if into an abyss, where we can find ourselves locked into being a witch, where we are taken over by bear or wolf. Winnicott places addiction and fetishism in this space, and Jung warns of our becoming possessed here by archetypes, crudely assimilated into the unconscious.[32] Thus we are tempted to deny the gap by living as false selves, by perjuring our own truth.

Right next door to constructive energies, we must remember, lie the destructive, the alienating, where the splitting of opposites into warring fragments occurs and disintegration awaits. Winnicott and Khan help Jungians here by reminding us always of this kind of next-door-neighbor destructiveness. Thus the Jungian notion of Self must not be idealized as a fixed state, monolithic and static in its inclusiveness. Indeed, Winnicott says of the Self's chief symbol, the mandala, that he finds it "frightening," a dead artifact, a defense against split-off rage and omnipotence that Jung could not house.[33] For Winnicott sees Jung as having suffered madness and recovered, but with the costly defense of splitting himself into Number 1 and Number 2 personalities, Number 2 being the real one but a hidden one. Thus for Winnicott, Jung did not have a "unit self" and put so much weight on the Self as "construct" because he knew he was searching for something with which to assure himself he really did know all that he knew.[34]

From Jung's side, we see Winnicott having to reach for something that was immediately accessible to Jung. As Winnicott puts it, "I was sane and through analysis and self-analysis I achieved a measure of insanity." Again, "We are poor indeed if we are only sane."[35] Once more, "Richness of quality rather than health is at the top of the ladder of human progress."[36] I wonder what split-off bit of madness hides in Winnicott's notion that at the core we are isolated, incommunicable selves.

Jung's mapping of the psyche's spaces, transitional or not, includes a place for wounds that do not heal, bits of madness that do not yield. Our unhealed wounds are part of the space between us and the numinous, the unfailing space where the unconscious as the unknown can always touch us. "One's anxiety always points out our task," Jung writes. "If you escape it you have lost a piece of yourself, and a most problematic piece at that, with which the Creator of things was going to experiment in His unforeseeable ways."[37] The quality of feeling alive and real, so central to Winnicott's mappings of the psyche's spaces, cannot be reached unless all the parts are gathered in—the mad and sane, the fragmented and whole. Thus, if we follow Jung here, we protect ourselves from idealizing our theories of mental health, and allow room for the opposing processes of destruction, alienation, and falling apart as parts of the whole self. We need all the parts to be alive and real.

Masud Khan touches the same place of madness when he explores the obsession fantasy or repetitive compulsion that brings the same tired ending to all our new beginnings. The forbidden spaces of our perversions may also be where bits of the true self may be hiding. A split-off but valuable piece of ourselves, a numinous bit, is exactly what compels alienating behavior.[38]

How refreshing that is, how full of hope! How closely that edge touches Jung's emphasis on the symbolic meaning of trapping actions or attitudes. Jung does not pathologize the psyche. He releases us from the curse of pathology by making us see it as one fragment of the whole self. Our task is to house all the pieces and spaces of the psyche, not to get rid of any one of them.

Housing the psyche reaches beyond our individual spaces into society. Khan says we impinge on social space if we cannot use our dream space. Not being able to use our dream space for the dreaming experience, we exploit social space to act out our dreams.[39] The sniper plays out an internal psychic drama against innocent victims in society. Or we ourselves may become the victims, but in a different way. We get stuck in compulsive dreaming and fantasying. Not being able to do anything with the dream's symbols, not housing them or experiencing them, we get trapped in repeating the same dream or fantasy image over and over again. In Jung's words, the ego gets assimilated to the unconscious. The dream ego and the waking ego collapse into each other, obliterating the space between them, destroying the compensation each normally offers the other.

More serious still in these social and political settings is the dilemma of those persons who are not able to house all the psyche and make provision for all its spaces. Winnicott puts it bluntly: Those who do not feel alive and real resent those who do; the unhappy try to destroy the happiness of others; those caught in the prison of rigid defenses hope to destroy the freedom of others. Those who cannot enjoy their bodies look to interfere with the bodily enjoyment even of their own children, whom they love. Those who cannot love seek to destroy others' love by cynicism. Those who must spend their lives in mental hospitals try to make the sane feel guilty that they are free to move about at will in society and its politics.[40] As Dostoevsky shows in *The Devils,* we need to create outer chaos to mirror our inner torment. Unable to house the big spaces of psychic life, people seek totalitarian governments to do it for them. These harsh truths echo Jung's warnings about the dangers that follow a failure to struggle with archetypal forces, each of us individually and together. We are not safe away from these forces. We must try to make space for them or all of our spaces will be lost to us. The winds of unmediated collective psychic forces sweep through families, even through whole nations, striking down everything before them.

What Winnicott and others call "the space of illusion" suggests the space Jung describes as existing between our God-image and God, which amounts to our "feeling for the infinite." It provides the last set of points where the different theories touch each other. For the inevitable gap across which we play or into which we plunge in madness has opposite sides that can never permanently coincide but can only interact. This interaction comprises the space where we take what Marion Milner calls "the spiritual risk" to face what is really there in us with our own original eye.[41] That is very close to what Jung means by achieving the symbolic attitude, reaching to all of the self—including wolfish appetites and monstrous ragings and mute vulnerabilities, as well as firm insights and anchorings among the possibilities of being. For Jung, this self also includes a space the others do not mention—that of a lively, even burning God-image. We feel this God-image to be the divine itself and yet, paradoxically, we know at the same time it is not.[42]

The paradoxical nature of this transitional space forces us to relinquish the question of whether this image originates in us or from somewhere outside us. We can no more ask such precise answers from our souls than we can ask of our child, "Did you create the personality of this favorite bear of yours or did you find it with the animal in the store or in some book you read?" No, the illusionary nature of this space and of the related space between us and the infinite permits a blurring and mixing of self and other, so that Jung's "third thing" eventually must emerge. Added to the separate me and the separate other is a third symbol that includes and bodies forth some of each, and yet is very much itself and cannot be reduced to either.[43]

In therapy, we often talk about this third reality as "the work," that which holds both analyst and patient. In the space of this work both persons find themselves and each other without being reduced to being a mere instance of a theory. What an extraordinary illusion it is that we all share! We, with our analysands in our ordinary offices, on rainy days, in the hot summer, construct the spaces of the psyche as we discover them. We are finding the point, discovering what really matters about it all.

We try to house this experience in the technical terms of "transference" and "countertransference," but those are just names for another of those illusory spaces where persons are constructed. In Winnicott's terms, we play in therapy. In Jung's terms, we build up the third thing. It is a play of symbols which link conscious and unconscious processes, ego-making and ego-transcending activities, creating a space for contents that cannot just be assigned the categories of inner or outer, of the factual or the imagined, the personal or the collective, past or present, for it clearly includes all of them.[44]

In all this activity, there is a non-activity too, that space of disidentification where we take an image seriously but do not therefore equate it with reality.[45] Khan emphasizes Winnicott's idea of the "period of hesitation," that moment in his games with his infant patients just before the baby reaches for the spatula Winnicott has placed on the corner of his desk. Khan applies the idea to adults.[46] This is the moment of space in time just before the analysand takes up the material to be worked on, just before the analyst reaches an interpretation, or the two together concede to the force of the archetype constellating between them. Here we pause and remain for a moment unknowing and unknowable while trust accumulates in knowing and being known.

That moment of hesitation is a recognition of still another gap, another space that makes room for us really to be at the same time it may threaten us. For in that pause in time we see the gap in the space between ourselves and the infinite, the gap that is never closed, never finished, whose edges are never evenly matched. Yet those illusions of mixing—that our dream interpretation really is what the dream means, that our insight really is the truth about where the patient is living, that my vision of you really corresponds exactly to who you are, that our God-image is, in fact, God's reality—may be, in fact, as Milner says, "the essential root of a high morale and vital enthusiasm for living...,"[47] may be those archetypes which Bachelard calls "reserves of enthusiasm which help us believe in the world, love the world, create our world."[48]

It is by contact with such moments of illusion that we discover what we put into the gap, creatively living it and thus filling it. We come to know, as Milner says, what we love and "what is worth striving for," for "love is going on knowing it is worthwhile."[49] Contact with these illusions, that is, with our experience of the space between us and the numinous, helps us live fully toward death. We are able then to pray as Winnicott did in trying to come to terms with his own imminent death. His journal opens with the words: "Prayer. O God! May I be alive when I die!"[50] There are exact parallels in some words of Jung: "Your life is what you try to live....When you die, nobody else will die for you or instead of you. It will be entirely and exclusively your own affair. That has been expected of you through your whole life, that you live it as if you were dying...."[51]

When Jung pushes us toward the space between the ego and the Self, he is pushing us toward a conscious naming of the illusions, the God-images that make it worth our while to go on with this work, to see the illusions we believe in and yet simultaneously know cannot be equated with reality, the illusions that tell us what we love. So although we cannot identify our theories and images with the numinous, we can allow them to remain arrows that point and fly through the space between ourselves and the numinous. Jung, utterly different from other analysts in this, directs us consciously toward those gaps: "The main interest of my work is with the approach to the numinous." Thus, he says, "The decisive question for us is, 'Are we related to something infinite or not?'"[52] That, I would suggest, is the explicit foundation of the work we do.

Notes

This chapter was originally a paper presented to the National Conference of Jungian Analysts in New York City (May 1984) and then published in *Quadrant* (New York: Jung Foundation, Spring 1985).

1.   C. G. Jung, *Letters*, 2 vols., eds. G. Adler and A. Jaffé, trans. R. F. C. Hull (Princeton: Princeton University Press, 1973 and 1975), I, 20 August 1945, 377.

2.   C. G. Jung, "The Transcendent Function," *The Structure and Dynamics of the Psyche*, *Collected Works* 8, trans R. F. C. Hull (New York: Pantheon, 1916/1960), 68; A. and B. Ulanov, *Primary Speech: A Psychology of Prayer* (Atlanta: John Knox Press, 1982).

3.   Jung cites an old German mystic, "God is a sigh in our souls." Jung, *Letters*, II, 10 October 1952, 87.

4.   C. G. Jung, *Memories, Dreams, Reflections*, ed. A. Jaffé, trans. Richard and Clara Winston (New York: Pantheon, 1963), 325.

5.   See A. Stokes, *The Game That Must Be Lost*, *Collected Papers* (Cheadle: Carcanet Press, 1973), 117.

6.   C. G. Jung, "The Practical Use of Dream Analysis," *The Practice of Psychotherapy*, *Collected Works* 16, trans. R. F. C. Hull (New York: Pantheon, 1934/1954), pars. 343–52.

7.   See M. Klein, *Envy and Gratitude and Other Works 1946–1963* (New York: Delacorte, Seymour Lawrence, 1975), 58, 251. See C. G. Jung, "Instinct and the Unconscious," *The Structure and Dynamics of the Psyche*, *Collected Works* 8, trans. R. F. C. Hull (New York: Pantheon, 1948/1960), par. 277; see also Jung, "On the Nature of the Psyche," pars. 398f.

8.   See Jung, *Letters*, II, 17 February 1954, 156.

9.   See M. Klein, "On Criminality," *Love, Guilt and Reparation and Other Works 1921–1945* (New York: Delacorte, Seymour Lawrence, 1975); see also A. and B. Ulanov, *Cinderella and Her Sisters: The Envied and the Envying* (Philadelphia: Westminster Press, 1983, reissued Einsiedeln, Switzerland: Daimon, 1998), 22, 46, for a discussion of envy in politics.

10.   See Jung, *Memories, Dreams, Reflections*, 345.

11.   See R. Gordon, "Narcissism and the Self," *Journal of Analytical Psychology* 25 (1980), 3:247–65; 255 for discussion of the same contrast.

12.   Jung, *Memories, Dreams, Reflections*, 327n; see also 355.

13.   See Jung, "The Practical Use of Dream Analysis," pars. 163, 174, 198, 318; see also C. G. Jung, "Psychotherapists or Clergy," *Psychol-*

ogy and Religion: West and East, trans. R. F. C. Hull (New York: Pantheon, 1932/1958), par. 537.

14. See H. Segal, *Melanie Klein* (New York: Viking, 1979), 177–78, 181. For discussion of the animus, see A. B. Ulanov, *Receiving Woman: Studies in the Psychology and Theology of the Feminine* (Philadelphia: Westminster Press, 1981), ch. 6.

15. D. W. Winnicott, *Through Paediatrics to Psycho-Analysis* (New York: Basic Books, 1975), 145; see also D. W. Winnicott, *Playing and Reality* (London: Tavistock, 1971), 99; see also D. W. Winnicott, *The Maturational Processes and the Facilitating Environment* (New York: International Universities Press, 1974), 187, 194.

16. See. J. W. T. Redfearn, "The Self and Individuation," *Journal of Analytical Psychology* 22, 2 (April 1977): 125–42; 137–39 for discussion of this same point.

17. M. M. R. Khan, *The Privacy of the Self* (New York: International Universities Press, 1974), 9. See also Winnicott, *Maturational Processes,* 187–92.

18. See H. Guntrip, *Psychoanalytic Theory, Therapy, and the Self* (New York: Basic Books, 1971), xi, 20–21, 46, 64, 119, 124.

19. Quoted in B. Landis, "Discussions with Harry Guntrip," *Contemporary Psychoanalysis* 17, 1 (1981): 112–17, 114.

20. M. Milner, *The Hands of the Living God: An Account of a Psychoanalytic Treatment* (New York: International Universities Press, 1969), 205.

21. M. Milner, "D. W. Winnicott and the Two-Way Journey," *Between Reality and Fantasy,* eds. S. A. Grolnick, L. Barkin, in collaboration with W. Muensterberger (New York: Jason Aronson, 1978), 38. See Winnicott's own comment on this conversation in D. W. Winnicott, *Playing and Reality,* 98.

22. See Winnicott, *Playing and Reality,* 77–82; see also H. Guntrip, *Schizoid Phenomena, Object Relations and the Self* (New York: International Universities Press, 1969), 250ff., 257ff.; see also A. B. Ulanov, *The Feminine in Jungian Psychology and in Christian Theology* (Evanston: Northwestern University Press, 1971), ch. 9.

23. Joanna Field (Marion Milner), *A Life of One's Own* (Los Angeles: J. P. Tarcher, distributed by Houghton-Mifflin, 1981), 13; see also 20.

24. See Winnicott, *Through Paediatrics to Psycho-Analysis,* 202.

25. See. D. W. Winnicott, *Therapeutic Consultations in Child Psychiatry* (New York: Basic Books, 1971), 4, 19; see also Winnicott, *Playing and Reality,* 51.

26.   See Guntrip, *Schizoid Phenomena, Object Relations and the Self*, 253.

27.   Landis, "Discussions with Harry Guntrip," 116.

28.   Winnicott, *Playing and Reality*, 73.

29.   Ibid., 75–76.

30.   See C. G. Jung, "Archetypes of the Collective Conscious," *The Archetypes and the Collective Unconscious, Collected Works* 9:1, trans. R. F. C. Hull (New York: Pantheon, 1954/1959), par. 66; see also C. G. Jung, *Psychology and Alchemy, Collected Works* 12, trans. R. F. C. Hull (New York: Pantheon, 1953), par. 74.

31.   D. W. Winnicott, "Review of *Memories, Dreams, Reflections* by C. G. Jung," *International Journal of Psychoanalysis* 45, 2–3 (1964): 451. Readers may want to compare this favorable remark with the less than favorable one in his paper, "Counter-Transference" (1960) in *The Maturational Processes and the Facilitating Environment*, 159. Readers will note the change of view from the 1960 paper to the 1964 book review, and may want to note further exploration of this issue in the 1966 paper, "The Split-Off Male and Female Elements To Be Found in Men and Women," which is published as the second part of ch. 5 in *Playing and Reality*.

32.   See Winnicott, *Playing and Reality*, 5, 22, 40, 50, 99, 120. See also A. B. Ulanov, "The Witch Archetype," *Quadrant* 10 (Summer 1977): 3–22, and A. and B. Ulanov, "The Clown Archetype," *Quadrant* 13, 1 (Spring 1980): 4–27. See also C. G. Jung, "Two Essays in Analytical Psychology," *Two Essays in Analytical Psychology, Collected Works* 7, trans. R. F. C. Hull (New York: Pantheon, 1917/1953), pars. 390–91.

33.   See Winnicott, "Review of *Memories, Dreams, Reflections* by C. G. Jung," 454.

34.   See ibid., 450, 453, 455.

35.   Ibid., 450.

36.   Winnicott, *Maturational Processes*, 66.

37.   Jung, *Letters*, I, 8 August 1949, 517.

38.   See M. M. Khan, "Reparation to the Idolized Self," *Alienation in Perversions* (New York: International Universities Press, 1979), 16; see also Khan, "The Finding and Becoming of Self," *Privacy of the Self*, 198–299, 301, 303.

39.   See Khan, "The Use and Abuse of Dream in Psychic Experience," *Privacy of the Self*, 314.

40.   See D. W. Winnicott, "The Threat to Freedom," unpublished paper, quoted in M. Davis and D. Wallbridge, *Boundary and Space: An Introduction to the Work of D. W. Winnicott* (New York: Brunner/Mazel, 1981), 165–66.

41. See M. Milner, *On Not Being Able to Paint* (New York: International Universities Press, 1979), 14, 38, 41–42.

42. See C. G. Jung, "Answer to Job," *Psychology and Religion: West and East, Collected Works* 11, trans. R. F. C. Hull (New York: Pantheon, 1952/1958), par. 558.

43. Jung writes, "We are crucified between the opposites and delivered up to the torture until the "reconciling third" takes shape....A life without inner contradiction is either only half a life or else a life in the Beyond, which is destined only for angels. But God loves human beings more than the angels." Jung, *Letters*, I, 20 August 1945, 376.

44. See Rosemary Gordon, "The Symbolic Experience as Bridge Between the Personal and the Collective," *Journal of Analytical Psychology* 22, 4 (October 1977): 331–43.

45. See A. and B. Ulanov, *Religion and the Unconscious* (Philadelphia: Westminster Press, 1975), 188–90, 218–19, 231–32, for discussion of disidentification.

46. See M. M. R. Khan, "Introduction to D. W. Winnicott, *Through Paediatrics to Psycho-Analysis*" (New York: Basic Books, 1975), xvii–xviii; see also Khan, "The Role of Illusion in the Analytic Space and Process," *Privacy of the Self*, 260ff.

47. Milner, *On Not Being Able to Paint*, 29.

48. G. Bachelard, *The Poetics of Reverie*, trans. Daniel Russell (New York: Orion Press, 1969), 124.

49. Milner, *On Not Being Able to Paint*, 30; Milner, *Hands of the Living God*, 83.

50. Clare Winnicott, "D. W. W.: A Reflection," *Between Reality and Fantasy*, 19.

51. Jung, *Letters*, I, 20 April 1946, 423.

52. See nn. 1 and 5.

Chapter 9

The Anxiety of Being

Man's life is abundant life, infinitely complex, inexhaustible
in its possibilities, even in the vitally poorest human beings.
—Paul Tillich, "Heal the Sick; Cast Out
the Demons," in *The Eternal Now*

We hear the voice of that depth; but our ears are closed. We
feel that something radical, total, and unconditioned is
demanded of us; but we rebel against it, try to escape its
urgency, and will not accept its promise.
—Paul Tillich, "You Are Accepted,"
in *The Shaking of the Foundations*

In his willingness to combat the anxiety of nonbeing, Paul Tillich
received and welcomed anything that promised to enlarge his—
and others'—courage to be. As a scholar he was passionately caught
up in the spiritual conditions of his times, trying to create a structure of understanding that would support a life of meaning.

Unlike most theologians, Tillich was deeply receptive to
depth psychology. Its insights engaged his heart as well as his
mind, his visceral reactions as well as his speculative thought, his
own strong anxieties as well as his calm theological mind. He
knew doubts, compulsions, splits within himself, all of which
aroused suffering and uncertainty in him as well as fascination, a
fascination summed up best, perhaps, in his absorbing interest in
the demonic, upon which he shed so much light in his epochal
essay of 1926, "The Demonic: A Contribution to the Interpretation of History."[1] He even suffered anxiety about the future of
his systematic theology, as many of his friends attest in their
memories of his worried questions about whether his ideas
would last beyond the grave.

Yet Tillich knew a serene largeness of being, too, a largeness so evident in the quality of his humanity, his love of life, his high good humor, above all his impatience with narrowness and moralism. His being was ambiguous, ambivalent, flawed, spacious, full of images and insights. He was a man to whom the history of thought was the life of the imagination. He cared about Being and about particular human beings. He always saw the specific person there before him and addressed his remarks to the other person's deepest self. I remember when I first met him as a student at Radcliffe, how generously and with what seriousness he listened to me, as he did to almost all young persons. He was much more than the gossip about his problems with women suggests. He saw women as individual persons, complete in their own right, and he called them forward from the distant background position into which they were so often thrust, to affirm their own being. Tillich's perceptiveness of other persons' deep longings is what so touched his audiences, I believe.[2] And that perception lives on still in the printed words of his sermons.[3] Students and seekers of all types and occupations flocked to his lectures, for they heard in him a friendly call that recognized where they were, and with it a stern call that summoned them to come more fully into their own being. They heard themselves addressed by a man with all the perceptiveness and compassion of one who knew in himself what he called "the anxiety of nonbeing."

Tillich knew something more as well. He knew what I would call, in an extension of his concept, the anxiety of being. I am talking about the anxiety so many of us feel about the being that is there before us, within us, around us, the being that is available to us with its abundance of possibilities, its many complex facets, there to be lived, and, even more anxiety-producing, for us to live and to realize. This anxiety, aroused by the astounding fact of being, came very early to Tillich. He said that at the age of eight he was amazed that there could be something rather than nothing.[4]

In 1936 Tillich wrote about the principal metaphor that summed up his being: He lived on a series of boundary lines among many opposites—Europe and America, Philosophy and Theology, Faith and Doubt, Church and Culture.[5] He found his standpoint there, in that in-between place of inclusion and exclusion, a place he defined as both–and, though his harshest critics were to accuse him of being neither–nor. This boundary place expressed his anxiety of being. It signaled his reaching out to include all manner and forms of disciplines from which to build his theological system, and his worry about the effectiveness of including so much.

A theology that embraced all of human life—that was the task Tillich set himself, and it was often a nasty one. His concept of the "God beyond God," for example, brought down upon him severe rebukes for what seemed to persons of faith a windy abstractionism, and for what seemed to persons of precise and logical thought a cloud of vagueness. Yet for Tillich, his notion proposed an important meeting place for all the many persons who live on opposite sides of the boundary lines, those for example of confessional faith on one hand and those drawn by strong but undefined yearnings toward the divine on the other. Tillich took his stand there, on the perpetual border between strong opposing factions, trying to include the perspectives and experiences of each, despite the double exposure to criticism this occasioned. I believe he stood there between disciplines, because on the other side of his own boundary line of nonbeing, with its special difficulties, rested being with its irresistible anxieties. And where he stood, we may stand again to see and understand the richness of opposing ideas brought to confrontation and rapprochement.

CORRESPONDENCES BETWEEN THEOLOGY AND DEPTH PSYCHOLOGY

In this way, we may point to the many lines of correspondence between Tillich's systematic theology and depth psychology—lines that he used like grappling hooks hurled across the point of intersection of the two disciplines, and that we can continue to use in the same dramatic way. For example, his deep appreciation of the power of the demonic forces that can capture a person is very much like a basic concept of object relations theory. That theory focuses on the psyche's mechanism of splitting away from consciousness impulses that the ego cannot tolerate. If the splitting is too extreme, these impulses will assume a demonic autonomous life that can usurp the ego's control and fragment what Tillich called the "center" of the person. Without that center, a person's humanity will be lost.[6]

A correspondence of matching importance can be found between Tillich's stern insistence on the unavoidable, tragic, but still free, fall of humanity from harmony into estrangement, and Freud's and Melanie Klein's understanding of the death instinct as a force that threatens to destroy human beings from within them. Unlike many of Freud's own followers, Tillich accepted the death instinct as a tough fact about life, as mysterious in its source as life itself.[7] Together, the life and death forces produced for him the inescapable ambiguities of life, a truth expressed by Klein in her epochal formulation of the "depressive position."[8] In early infancy, she saw, a child achieves the capacity to accept ambivalence, to recognize that all goodness is mixed with badness and that motives and emotions are not pure. Tillich agreed with his friend Karen Horney's insistence that the ambivalences in culture, with their far-ranging mixtures of good and bad, also must be seen as crucial determinants of mental health and illness. The theologian's vivid descriptions of our existential predicament—an estranged and disordered freedom—and our flight from it into the restrictions of neurosis or the excesses of psychosis, echo the psychoanalyst's graphic portrayals of mental disturbance.

Tillich found in Jung's distinction between lasting archetypes and changing symbols a solution to an ancient Catholic–Protestant conflict. For Catholic theology, the revealed symbols of faith are known, fixed, and unchangeable. For Protestants, religious symbols emerge spontaneously from the experiences of individuals and groups. Each side of this religious boundary offers something valuable but also poses a serious danger. On the Catholic side, there is a continuity to religious symbols but also there is the constant threat of a lifeless rigidity in fixed doctrines that no longer catch persons with a transformative power. On the Protestant side, there is life to symbols but the danger of their coming and going without clear continuity or objective permanence. Tillich saw a solution to these problems in Jung's distinction between the fixed archetypal potentialities that are all around us and the infinitely variable symbols in which the potentialities present themselves.

The archetypal possibilities are differently realized as they fit different individual and social needs. Thus permanence and change work together in religious symbols and can be made to come together in religious life generally.[9]

Tillich's perception of the truth latent in Freud's criticism of religious faith as nothing but the projection of childish wishes for a protecting and authoritative father leads directly to a very large question for Tillich: What is the "screen" upon which the projection is cast? The answer came for Tillich out of the resources of his theological system: "The screen is our ultimate concern.... [T]here is something that precedes the act of projection....It means that if we use the father image in order to symbolize our ultimate concern, then the ultimate concern is not the father image. Rather the ultimate concern is the screen into which the father image is put."[10] Thus Tillich left open a way for many persons unable to enter the church through confessions of faith. He offered them the possibility of finding their own symbols for life's meaning, a meaning he saw as enclosed within the universal human longing for connection to the divine.

Here Tillich knew a special affinity with the existentialist analysts. They shared a common root in Heidegger's examination of the capacity of *Dasein* to shape being. They shared a common emphasis on the power of symbols to illuminate the character of human existence in its relation to being itself. A less obvious, but vivid connecting point between the analysts and the theologian was Tillich's insistence on the central human resource of what he called "the courage to be" and the notion of the will that the existentialists shared with Otto Rank.

Tillich's formulation of the Yes in God that overcomes the No in God, of the Being that embraces its own nonbeing, and of the nonbeing that "drives being out of its seclusion [and] forces it to affirm itself dynamically,"[11] reaches back to the philosophy of Schelling. It also reaches forward to include Jung's later notions about God's "unconscious side," put forth so controversially in his book *Answer to Job*. Tillich's emphasis on the anxiety-creating and anxiety-allaying functions of words connects with the work of Jacques Lacan. Lacan sees the human capacity for language as a creative bridge across the gap left in every child by the alienating discovery that it is not part of the large being of its mother, nor even a part of an imagined being that it somehow shares with the mother, but is only a solitary *"moi,"* separated and alone. Such a function of words, as creating links between self and other and between self and reality, bridges another gap, as Tillich sees it, that between our essential human nature and our existential estrangement. Words cross the gap, yet at the same time resound with our trembling awareness of the gap's existence.[12] But Tillich goes further: He sees the being of words as rooted in the originating Word of God, "the Word cutting into all words."[13]

Tillich pressed the practitioners of depth psychology to expose to consciousness their own ontological roots, to discover by what buried notions of being their particular systems of psychological theory were fed.[14] He rightly claimed that his own investigations into what it means to be a part of those "structures which are presupposed in any encounter with reality"[15] were directly relevant to the working analyst who each day must deal with the healing of the shattered being of specific persons.

It is precisely here, with these important questions of what it means to be, of how particular persons come into being, and from what sources of being healing can come, that Tillich's work remains useful to the practitioners and theorists of depth psychology. The initial link between Tillich and depth psychology is in this area of nonbeing and anxiety, which announces a threat to every person's life in three kinds of attack (as Tillich describes them): of fate and death, of meaninglessness and emptiness, and of guilt and condemnation. The connection between the disciplines is deepened for us when, as depth psychologists or theologians, we contemplate the anxiety on the opposite side of the boundary line, the anxiety of being. We look now, not at how our being is menaced, but at how it has become being in the first place, and what conditions foster the capacity to be.

In depth psychology a shift of emphasis has occurred in recent years, one that mirrors the crossing of the boundary line from the anxiety of nonbeing to the anxiety of being. As depth psychologists have moved into ever earlier years of human life in their etiologies of psychic disorder, their attention has shifted from latent pathology to the mysterious early beginnings of the human self. Their focus now centers on how a person comes to be at all. Freud began with what he saw as the Oedipal conflict of the four- to six-year-old. Klein pushed the theory into the pre-Oedipal years, as early as a child's first year. D. W. Winnicott investigated the very first months of a child's life—and so on. Can we not say that depth psychology projects in this way onto an earlier and earlier chronology the age-old religious quest to relate to the power and presence of being at the source? Depth-psychological theories have become a new vehicle of relationship to the mystery of life. In what have become passionate metapsychological and metaphysical disputes, we can see new religious wars taking shape in analytical societies. This drawing near to the borders of religion from the psychological side, with no matter what rawness of feeling, gives impetus to another movement of thought that Tillich firmly supported and took as a resource for his own system, the discipline of pastoral counseling. There he saw the resources of God's grace and human skills in healing combined, a boundary line successfully negotiated.

Tillich's great interest in the wondrous event of grace begins his crossing from nonbeing to being. Grace, says Tillich, *happens* to us in those moments when reunion spans separation, recognition conquers estrangement, and reconciliation accepts that which is rejected. Grace *is* our capacity to open to the healing power of faith: We are grasped by that which concerns us ultimately. Grace is given us mysteriously, in an encounter of persons; without it, Tillich sees no hope of anyone becoming a person at all.[16] In this construction of grace, Tillich anticipates some of the major developments of depth psychology since his time.

In the explosion of interest in D. W. Winnicott's formulation of transitional space, the very origin of the capacity "to be" is explored in the early infant–mother relationship. Winnicott states the point radically: "There is no such thing as a baby," but only a "nursing couple."[17] In the new Chicago school of Heinz Kohut and his followers, and in the work of Otto Kernberg, the healing of the radical early narcissistic wound to being is examined methodically, as a result of which Kohut, Kernberg, and the others arrive at the point from which Tillich started: "A person becomes a person in the encounter with other persons, and in no other way."[18] Analysts of several schools direct their attention to the intricacies of such an encounter through developing complicated and enlightening theories about the transference-countertransference interaction, that laboratory in the analyst's office where person-to-person encounters are investigated, lived, and reflected upon all at once. Thus the simultaneous presence of many dimensions of being is achieved.

In trying to heal narcissistic injury, what analysts attempt is the establishment of being at the core of personal identity. In working with those called "borderline personalities," in the language of depth psychology, because they slip and slide back and forth across the borders of sanity and psychosis, analysts attempt to cement together a center for being out of many fragments of their patients' personalities. In working with those persons called "neurotic," analysts attempt to strengthen what Tillich would call the forces of being to embrace the forces of nonbeing. The existentialist analysts investigate the dynamics of "ontological insecurity," as R. D. Laing puts it, and the resources of being available to overcome it.

The shift in depth psychology from a focus on pathology to a focus on the origins of our capacity to be corresponds to the shift from the anxiety of nonbeing to the anxiety of being. One form of anxiety leads to the other. What originally appears as a boundary line separating the dimensions of being and nonbeing turns out, on closer inspection, to mark the point of their junction. Tillich declares that the character of the anxiety of nonbeing depends upon the kind of being it tries to negate. He describes three levels of threat to persons that correspond to our bodily, spiritual, and moral existence. Thus for Tillich our anxiety over the quixotic nature of fate and the approaching final verdict of death threatens our "ontic self-affirmation." The task of our courage to be is to affirm existence in the face of this threat. Our anxiety over the immediate meaninglessness or ultimate emptiness of our lives, or of our time, or of history as a whole, threatens our "spiritual affirmation," both in our personal selves and in our cultural life. Our courage once again is demonstrated in our efforts to take these doubts into ourselves, to claim them without suppressing them or overcompensating for them with fanatical assertions of belief, to carry the doubt and live the meaning we know, even if it is not a final, clear, and altogether positive meaning. Our anxiety and guilt at making wrong choices and the threat of ultimate condemnation of our motives or our actions—of the whole sorry mixture of good and bad—

threatens our "moral self-affirmation." Courageous self-accept-
ance, even though we see very good reasons for finding ourselves
unacceptable, answers this last threat to our being.

It is faith, as Tillich understands it, that finally conquers all
three forms of anxiety of nonbeing. By *faith* he means the state of
being grasped and caught up beyond ourselves, by the "God
beyond God." This being grasped changes the geography of our
being, for faith is "not a state which appears beside other states
of mind....It is the situation on the boundary of man's possibilities. It *is* this boundary."[19] The three forms in which anxiety of
being appears describe what it is like to live at that boundary, a
line we have arrived at when we have discovered the courage to
be, and have learned what it means to experience being as
including nonbeing.[20]

THE THREE FORMS OF THE ANXIETY OF BEING

The first form of anxiety of being, which parallels Tillich's
understanding of the threat of "fate and death" in the anxiety of
nonbeing, confronts us at the ontic level in the form of a terror
of being. It is what is there that frightens, not what is not there.
Something exists antecedent to nonbeing and that something
feels the threat of negation. When we permit ourselves to be conscious of this antecedent being, we feel panic. How shall we hold
it all? How can we live with it? How can we embrace its many
dimensions? We are anxious about having any being at all. We
know what Tillich means when he writes that we close our ears to
our own depths. We know what Jung means when he writes,
"Everybody would pay anything, his whole fortune, to avoid
going into himself."[21]

The work of depth psychologists attests to this primal fear
of being as a resistance—as Freud puts it—to the life of unconscious mental processes flowing through us, night and day, from
birth to death. How to include this different order of being with
its confusion of images, affects, impulses, and drives? Its principles of organization differ frighteningly from the rules of conscious thinking that proceed according to an orderly logic, that
provide us with a shared language, a goal-directed behavior, and

a series of clear separations, between subject and object, self and other, and gratification and delay. Unconscious processes of thinking proceed according to principles of contiguity and association, of expressive behavior and violent intensity of emotion. Imagery is wildly inflated. In the unconscious, there is no separation of self and other, of subject and object, or of time and space. How, then, can we make room for its driving, pulsating life within the demands of daily reality functions?

The anxious threat of being takes a double form. Seemingly chaotic unconscious emotions and drives swamp our consciousness, and at the same time our conscious existence may so aggrandize *its* being that it leaves no portals open to us to receive and assimilate the forces of being that live in the unconscious. The anxiety of being shows itself as a fearful uncertainty in the face of an overwhelming number of life forms. We are anxious that we will be swept away, lost in currents of undifferentiated emotions, needs, and drives, never to be able again to form ourselves into a discrete entity, to become a person who can hold it all. We are also anxious over its opposite, that we can become a person. This last is what Otto Rank calls the "life-fear," the fear that one can indeed become an individual differentiated from the group, yet still somehow remain related to the group. It is the anxiety that inevitably accompanies the bringing of something new into being. The free-floating, unorganized affect that characterizes the anxious state presses on one's consciousness to find its appropriate channels of expression.

Anxiety of being shows itself again in our anxiousness about the unlived life in ourselves. Because we are afraid, we shut off being. We refuse to admit into awareness all the bits of being available to us—in our emotions, images, ambitions, needs, hurts, longings— and so they remain there in the shadows, undeveloped and unrealized.[22] We will not open our attention to new ideas, to new kinds of music, painting, literature. We will not engage in discussions of threatening political issues. We will not expose ourselves to the strippings of prayer. We shut up tight to guard an ego fortress. And so the unlived life, existing there unconsciously around the fortress, stirs in us, surrounds us, threatens us with the possibility of violent eruption. Unlike those passionate words of Stravinsky in a newspaper interview shortly before he died, "I want to be awake! awake!" our cry to ourselves is "Go to sleep"—and we do. We retire before our time because we fear we cannot make room for all the being in us.

The answer to anxiety of being, at what Tillich calls the ontic level of self-affirmation, is not courage, as it is with non-being. It is something that proceeds from that courage: love. Love holds our small being in its own larger reality, making room for us to come to be, not unlike Winnicott's "good-enough" mother who holds a situation together for her child, keeping in readiness new pieces of the world to hand the child when it is open to take them up, to inspect them, to make use of them. Love alone confers the power to be. It is the only way that the anxiety of being can be overcome. Love as a holding, a letting-be, a making-provision for being to come into life, permits the unorganized affect of the anxious state slowly to take shape and emerge in the specific being of an attitude, an emotion, an idea, or an action. Love makes room for us to find our way into being. Tillich's frequent use of the image of an embracing or holding "ground" of being points to the reality of this love, which he sees as imbued with "the feminine element of being." He was one of the first theologians to insist on inclusion of such a feminine element of being in our traditional masculine concepts of God.

ANXIETY OF MEANING

The second form of the anxiety of being parallels Tillich's discussion under the rubric of nonbeing of the anxiety of "meaninglessness and of emptiness," which gnaw at our spiritual affirmation. Here the issue is not the meaning that is absent, but the meaning that is present, there, even in the experience of loss of meaning. We know how deeply we fear facing who we are or what is there around us. We know how quickly we construct false idols to shield us from reality. The destruction of meaning involves the destruction of our idols. It is a frightening process, but one that pries us open, blasts us apart sometimes so that we can find the presence of what there is behind our idols, demanding our unguarded inspection of it.

One of our most successful ways to avoid being is to hide among the pseudo issues of nonbeing. We inflate and generalize what faces us, making grandiose, abstract, and hence unanswerable the most concrete bits of being facing us at any particular moment. For example, we may ask the unanswerable question, What is the meaning of suffering? and thereby cleverly avoid a much more immediate question, What am I to make of this suffering afflicting me now? To what use can it be put? The plight of a person suffering narcissistic disorder gives ample evidence of the nature of this dodge. The aggrandized images of self are so exaggerated that no experience of a real self can come into existence and fill the inner emptiness threatening the person. Everything in oneself and in others falls short and betrays expectations. So a person fills with rage and envy and develops an eloquent *I-told-you-so* rhetoric of justification for endless complaining. The available possibilities—of risking dependence on a lover, a friend, or an analyst, for example; or of permitting grief over not having been valued as a person in one's own right; or of registering a sense of helplessness in not knowing how to do a task one has never been taught to handle—all get swept away in cosmic questions that are really pseudo questions. Why is there evil? we ask. Why are people so false? Why does no one ever understand?

Paul Pruyser questions Tillich's whole distinction between neurotic and existential anxiety, asserting that the latter always disguises a version of the former. I would not go that far. We do know formless anxieties about the meaning of events and the ultimate meaning of human history, I believe. The way to meet those anxieties about the existence of meaning, however, is to face whatever bits of meaning may have presented themselves to us in our lives. The question then shifts from the abstract, Why did this happen? to the concrete, What has happened? We focus on seeing what is there in the small but immediate and concrete chunk of being that is presented to us, in an attitude, a quarrel, a job opportunity, an insult, physical suffering, a dream, a historic event, a cultural moment. The problem is not a lack of meanings, but too many of them. We see multiple meanings, ambivalent meanings, even opposite meanings, especially when we look at large historical currents, political issues, or problems of global dimension. It is the abundance of meanings, small and large, that so confounds us. How do we hold them all in awareness? How do we find a pattern or patterns in them?

Anxiety of being about our spiritual affirmation, lacking or faltering as it may be, shows itself in a threatening multiplicity of possibilities, an abundance that may overwhelm our capacity to make rational order out of them. Our systems of thought turn out to be too small, too tight, and yet we fear the loss of them. We defend ourselves by fanatic insistence upon the small order we see while rejecting the larger order we may be shown. Unlike Paul Ricoeur's Job, who renounces the narcissism of his finite perspective for the sake of the larger whole Yahweh has revealed to him, we flee into a defense of our small and partial view, making it into an idol that inevitably must collapse and be smashed into pieces.[23] It is too small to hold the being given it. We are forced to let go of it because we cannot consent to let it be and see what is there in us and around us.

Anxiety of being about our spiritual affirmation shows itself too in the threat with which specific bits of being face us now, with their own meaning exposed to us, to be seen by us. Their presence frightens us. We may indeed glimpse something profound and essential in such experiences. We may indeed know the conviction in any particular moment that this is it, that this is life addressing us, that here we are met, confronted, handed something of utmost importance. How can we take it in?

The anxiety of being is the opening to the being given us in such little fragments of experience, a piece of the whole, a small perception of reality. The answer to such anxiety is again, not the power of courage, though it may issue from courage; it is a responsive opening, a motion of love, a love tough enough not to pull all into itself, a love that allows us to be ourselves. Tillich says, "In the recent psychotherapeutic literature the relation between power-drive and love is in the foreground of interest. Love has been more and more acknowledged as the answer to the question implied in anxiety and neurosis."[24] The answering love is a love that opens us to itself and makes us receive it.

REFUSAL TO BE

The last form of the anxiety of being corresponds to Tillich's use of "guilt and condemnation" in his categories of the anxiety of nonbeing, and to the level of moral affirmation. Here the issue is our guilt before the fact of being, our refusal "to be" in our failure to live the unlived life in us, our refusal to receive the being in the fragments of experience that are offered to us. We put our anxiety in place of being. We refuse the incarnation of being in concrete pieces of attitude, action, relationship, projects, and especially the way it turns up in the mistakes we make, when we cling instead to our emptiness and our grandiose questions. Being for us means deep suffering—but not true being. Our guilt is not over wrong choices, or even mixed choices, as Tillich describes the anxiety of nonbeing at this level. Our guilt is over the many choices constantly presented to us with which to face being as it is, true being. Our anxiety is challenged by such a fullness of choice. It is an anxiety so serious that we would rather destroy or deny the choices than risk their realization. Viktor Frankl presses this point vividly, and challenges all our notions of being, when he insists from the authority of his own experience that even in the deprivation and degradation of being in a concentration camp, people were confronted with choices of how to react, with what spiritual attitude to choose to meet suffering and death.[25] Even in such a place, in the most savage conditions, being presents itself for the taking, insisting on our responding, summoning us to do so.

Our anxiety of being over our moral self-affirmation shows itself, then, in our awareness of that summons "to be," that command to be our true self. We know that we must discard our counterfeit self, must let being incarnate itself. We know that we are being drawn into a partnership where being itself is at stake, where our continuation of life is in question. In old-fashioned anthropomorphic language, this is what was meant by doing God's will, or not doing it, and making God suffer as a result. Jung writes of the same phenomenon in his language of the ego and the Self. The Self, the center of the whole psyche, wants to come into being. It depends on the ego's consciousness to receive it. The ego is the portal to reality and realization for the Self. The Self is the source and refuge of the ego's efforts.[26]

As the experience deepens, our anxiety of being over the perils of moral self-affirmation shows itself, not as condemnation, as it does in the anxiety of nonbeing, not as suffering the wrath of God in the exclusion from his presence, but as just the opposite. We are made anxious now by the presence of God and the abundance of God's grace. We cannot face a presence that can turn a disastrous blow into a source of renewal, a grace that points to the fact of goodness dwelling there, real, alive, in the midst of terrible evil, a grace that can tenderly expose our much-needed defenses to the stripping action of love. And so we resort to unlived life, and to a flat refusal of the bits of being that have been given us. We sense in those fragments the presence of Being itself. We recognize that we might become all that we could and should be. Like animals on the alert to the presence of an alien, we sense what looks like God's possibility approaching our actuality that is really God's actuality approaching our possibility. We are made anxious by our awareness that if we became all that we could be, the intensity of being would be too much for us. Life is more threatening than death. We really could live fully right up to the end, even in illness, poverty, or degradation. Those blessed disabled persons who have found a vocation in their very illness or deformity give evidence of such a capacity "to be."[27] So do countless unnamed others, as grand in their ways as Mother Teresa in hers, all those who become a source of life in the ministry to the sick, the abandoned, and the dying.

We are anxious about such unimaginably large pieces of being coming to us in such little, unmistakably real and attainable bits and pieces, because though very small, these fragments, when really received, will push us right into God. It is too much for us, with all that life rushing to us and through us, to find Being itself present in us.[28] Worse yet, the anxiety of being, met and lived through here in this life, throws us wide open to the threat of a life resurrected from death, a life where we see God face to face, where there is given to us not fragments of a being, but a large being identifiable by its "abundant life," "infinite complexity," and "inexhaustible possibilities." At that point, we hear the complete words being addressed to us. We feel totally summoned, unconditionally demanded of, made to respond. We are promised a fullness of being.

This radical anxiety of being can be met only by love. Only love is strong as death, the author of the "Song of Songs" tells us. Tillich's notion of "ultimate concern" must be both enlarged and diminished into something more concrete in order to house this anxiety of being. The relationship at the boundary line must evolve with all the specific marks of each person's and each faith group's relationship to God, conditioned by the bits of being given and accepted by them in the conflicts and disjunctions of their particular historical time and social structure. This relationship at the boundary will bear the marks of a concrete communication with God, even if it is in silence. It will mark a presence, even if one is only aware of an absence. It is still being that is addressed concretely, being concretely accepted, being lived, being chosen and responded to in this relationship at the boundary. This is love: present, concrete, real enough to sustain us even though it is not exhausted in all its forms in this experience, however large or transforming.

This is what Tillich meant, I believe, in that moving sermon, "You Are Accepted." Receive being. It comes to us. It seeks us out. It shows itself to us, even when it must do so in a hidden form. We do not need to *know* as much as we need to receive what is given. We do not need to *understand* as much as we need to *live* the relation to being in any way in which it offers itself to us. This is the legacy of Tillich, his way of living being as he knew and felt it address him. This is his grateful way of receiving its fragments and quickly sharing them. For this, we can follow him and be thankful.

Notes

This chapter was originally written for inclusion in *The Thought of Paul Tillich*, eds. L. Adams, W. Pauck, R. L. Shinn (San Francisco: Harper & Row, 1985).

1. P. Tillich, "The Demonic: A Contribution to the Interpretation of History," in idem, *The Interpretation of History*, trans N. A. Rasetski and E. L. Talmey (New York: Charles Scribner's Sons, 1936). Originally published as "Das Dämonische, ein Beitrag zur Sinndeutung

der Geschichte," in *Gesammelte Werke*, vol. 6 (Stuttgart: Evangelisches Verlagswerk, 1963).

2. See P. Tillich, "Heal the Sick; Cast Out the Demons," in *The Eternal Now* (New York: Charles Scribner's Sons, 1963), 58–61, where he asserts that everyone longs for salvation.

3. See P. Tillich, *The Shaking of the Foundations* (New York: Charles Scribner's Sons, 1948); idem, *The New Being* (New York: Charles Scribner's Sons, 1955); and idem, *The Eternal Now*.

4. Personal conversation with Tillich in Hamburg, Germany, 1958. Cf. W. and M. Pauck, *Paul Tillich: His Life and Thought*, vol. 1, *Life* (New York: Harper & Row, 1976), 2.

5. P. Tillich, "On the Boundary: An Autobiographical Sketch," first published in *The Interpretation of History*; later published as a separate volume, *On the Boundary: An Autobiographical Sketch*, in a translation revised by Tillich (New York: Charles Scribner's Sons, 1966).

6. P. Tillich, "The Meaning of Health," an address to the New York Society of Clinical Psychiatry, 14 January 1960, in idem, *The Meaning of Health: Essays in Existentialism, Psychoanalysis, and Religion*, ed. Perry LeFevre (Chicago: Exploration Press, 1984), 165–73.

7. See Tillich, "You Are Accepted," in *The Shaking of the Foundations*, 158.

8. See Tillich, "The Meaning of Health," 166–67.

9. See P. Tillich, "Remarks," in *Carl Gustav Jung, 1875–1961: A Memorial Meeting* (New York: Analytical Psychology Club, 1962), 30; see also A. B. Ulanov, *The Feminine in Christian Theology and in Jungian Psychology* (Evanston: Northwestern University Press, 1971), ch. 5.

10. P. Tillich, "Psychoanalysis, Existentialism, and Theology," *Pastoral Psychology* 9, 87 (October 1958): 16–17.

11. P. Tillich, *The Courage to Be* (New Haven: Yale University Press, 1952), 179.

12. See P. Tillich, "Existentialism, Psychotherapy, and the Nature of Man," in *The Nature of Man in Theological and Psychological Perspectives*, ed. S. Doniger (New York: Harper & Row, 1962), 52; see also idem, "Anxiety Reducing Agencies in Our Culture," in *Anxiety*, ed. P. Hoch and J. Zubin (New York: Grune and Stratton, 1950), 117–26.

13. P. Tillich, *Love, Power, and Justice* (New York and London: Oxford University Press, 1954), 33.

14. See Tillich, "Psychoanalysis, Existentialism, and the Nature of Man," 47.

15. Tillich, *Love, Power, and Justice*, 19, 23.

16. See Tillich, "You Are Accepted," 155; idem, *The Dynamics of*

Faith (New York: Harper & Row, 1957), 111–12; and idem, *The Courage to Be*, 166.

17. D. W. Winnicott, *Through Pediatrics to Psycho-Analysis* (New York: Basic Books, 1975), 99; see also *Between Reality and Fantasy: Transitional Objects and Phenomena*, eds. S. A. Grolnick and L. Barkin in collaboration with W. Muensterberger (New York: Jacob Aronson, 1978).

18. Tillich, "Existentialism, Psychotherapy, and the Nature of Man," 51.

19. Tillich, *Courage to Be*, 188–89.

20. Ibid., 179.

21. C. G. Jung, *The Visions Seminars*, 2 vols. (Dallas: Spring, 1976), 1, 30.

22. I use the phrases *bits of being* and *fragments of being* to refer to the pieces of a whole experience we retain in the form of an image, a feeling, a symbol, a partial insight that can reconstruct the focus of the whole. We may, for example, find an image for a long-range goal in our work that connects us to what we see as the value of the whole of our work even though we have not yet achieved that goal. We may have a feeling about a sexual experience that gives us access to our identity as a whole man or woman, even though we have not yet achieved what Freud would call the complete genital stage of development. We may find a symbol for God that opens to us the meaning of religious faith without our being fully in possession of a whole faith. We may gain partial insight into a long-standing hostility we have felt toward a friend, an insight that conveys to us a sense of resolution for the whole of the problem, even though we have not yet reached such resolution. The value of emphasizing the "fragments" or "bits," as I have put it, is that we are relieved from the pressure of a punitive superego that operates according to an all-or-nothing set of standards. Such a superego says that either we possess the whole of something or we have nothing. Such a superego insists that either we reach a perfect solution to a problem or we accomplish nothing. Because we do not in fact ever achieve perfection under such superego dictates, we feel only that we fail, have nothing to show for our efforts, and as a result fall into hopeless discouragement. To stress the positive value of receiving and using the fragments of the whole that we do possess and can reach changes our discouragement into confidence. We see what we can do, what we can accomplish. This perception encourages in us a fresh, positive general outlook as well as helping us accomplish specific tasks.

23. See P. Ricoeur, *Freud and Philosophy: An Essay on Interpretation* (New Haven: Yale University Press, 1970), 548–49.

24. Tillich, *Love, Power, and Justice*, 22–23.

25.   V. Frankl, *From Death-Camp to Existentialism: A Psychiatrist's Path to a New Therapy* (Boston: Beacon Press, 1959).

26.   See C. G. Jung, *Aion, Collected Works* 9:2, trans R. F. C. Hull (New York: Pantheon, Bollingen Series 20, 1959), pars. 43–67.

27.   See Mother Marie des Douleurs, *Joy Out of Sorrow*, eds. B. Ulanov and F. Tauritz (Westminster, Md.: The Newman Press, 1958).

28.   See A. B. Ulanov, "The Christian Fear of the Psyche," *Union Seminary Quarterly Review* 30, 2–4 (Winter–Summer 1975): 140–52.

Chapter 10

Between Anxiety and Faith: The Role of the Feminine in Tillich's Theological Thought

ON THE BOUNDARY

We are not often given a chance in life to repay debts of the spirit to persons to whom we owe them. It is rare to be able to say, "Thank you," directly to such a person. Usually we express our gratitude by passing along to others what was given us. So we thank our mother by being a faithful friend to an elderly lady, or by mothering our own children or someone else's. We thank our teacher by the way we treat our students. It is great luck for me to be invited to honor Paul Tillich by writing this essay. He was my teacher and my friend. I am grateful to be asked to join in honoring him, and thus to thank him, by writing about his thought and its creative sources.

The boundary metaphor so often used to explore Tillich's thought is one he chose to describe his life as well as his thought: "The man who stands on many boundaries experiences the unrest, insecurity, and inner limitation of existence in many forms. He knows the impossibility of attaining security and perfection. This holds true in life as well as in thought, and may explain why the experiences and ideas which I have recounted are rather fragmentary and tentative. My desire to give definitive form to these thoughts has once again been frustrated by my boundary-fate...."[1]

When one lives on boundary lines, as Tillich did, it means one goes back and forth across them and is constantly vulnerable to attack from both sides. This had much to do, I think, with the criticism of Tillich as a fuzzy thinker, afflicted with inordinate

183

inclusiveness, a man neither fully a philosopher nor a theologian. In one sense, fair enough. When one lives on the borderlands one has no clear home, but only the cusp, smack in the middle of both–and. But Tillich is also known, as he should be, for the large embrace of his thought and a generosity of spirit that took every-thing human with the utmost seriousness and openness.

As we all know, his moving back and forth across the boundaries meant he drew comfortably on pre-Socratic thought, on Kierkegaard, and Heidegger, on much in the history of phi-losophy, especially Schelling, and again on much in the history of theology, particularly Augustine and Luther. He moved at equal ease in the world of intellect and the beloved hymns of his childhood worship. He drew on the arts, especially the visual, on conceptual thought, on both new religious movements and ancient religious doctrines, on Eastern and Western traditions of the life of the spirit, and on contemporary depth psychology. He investigated Jewish and Christian ideas, Protestant, Catholic, whatever came to settle on his boundaries.

All these two-sided boundaries are summed up in the cen-tral one of being, as abyss and as ground. Being comes through in unpredictable demonic forces and in the liberating invasion of divine grace. Being holds in itself anxiety, "the awareness of that element of non-being (of the negation of what one is) which is identical with finitude, the coming from nothing and the going toward nothing."[2] But being also acts as the source of religious symbol, which makes the reality of the ground of being palpable, accessible, livable to us. And so Tillich moved between anxiety and faith, both of which spring from being and its ground.

One thing that stands out about Tillich was his devotion to being. People felt it in him. As his friend and colleague Wilhelm Pauck said, "He was a deeply loyal man who remained faithful to himself throughout his life." He assessed in a critical and con-structive way his cultural heritage, transforming it according to the demands of his destiny. Although he was an abstract thinker and "spoke in a quiet even voice," reading from a manuscript, "he gave the impression of speaking from his innermost self to the personal concerns of his listeners."[3]

He was caught by that most haunting question, the sense he shared with so many, of the void in the midst of being, a vacancy that can grip the human spirit and lead it into a depth of despair and anxiety.[4] He found it necessary to receive that abyss as his fate and to welcome liberation from it as his salvation. He probed the threat he felt directly to his being and was prepared to bear the insecurity it created until something could break through from the other side. Tillich's point was not simply to live perched on the boundary line but to reach toward and respond to the possibility there of self-transcendence and to receive it when it came.[5] Boundary living, as he knew it, was forced upon him by the nature of being itself.

He said of himself that being had caught him up in the "philosophical shock" that there was something—being—rather than nothing.[6] He knew moments of "numinous astonishment" where he was gripped by ecstasy, caught in the most direct feelings of mystery, elation, and awe, where the gap between thought-forms and that which they struggle to grasp is for an instant transcended and overcome.[7] In such moments Tillich knew firsthand that God was, as he put it, "consuming fire," unpredictable and uncapturable in any of our human systems or political plans, but there, definitely there.[8]

Thus the central boundary of being in ground and abyss runs like an undercurrent through all the other boundaries Tillich sketched in his voluminous writings. He felt that current with a shuddering, a tremor, a shaking of the foundations. But what shook him most was what he wrote least about.

THE FEMININE

One set of boundary lines is missing in his book *On the Boundary* and, in fact, in all of his systematic presentations. It could be called the boundary between masculine and feminine, between man and woman. This is one boundary he lived but did not write about. This was an essential way, I would suggest, that Tillich addressed the larger boundaries between anxiety and faith, between the demonic and the divine, in his life and thought.

Tillich was a man who struggled to receive the feminine within himself, which accounted in part for his great appeal to women. They felt received by him. The feminine was his means of receiving being. To the masculine Tillich, the feminine added a particular and important presentation of being. It showed the characteristic marks of being as he knew them or hoped to know them, as he wanted to receive them. He brought us to know this side of being too—of dread before the abyss which threatened entrapment in non-free compulsions and fragmentation—what Hannah Tillich called his "pull toward 10,000 legs in Berlin."[9] Over against that threat woman's power of receiving being brought him liberation from compulsion and a gladness in that abundance of being that seeks to make us whole.

What breaks through from the abyss, from the depth of being, can threaten us with the demonic or bless us with the ecstasy of grace. Tillich felt both, I believe, vis-à-vis the feminine.

I want to leave the term *feminine* both somewhat inclusive and imprecise, for reasons of tact as well as lack of full, documented information, and for two other reasons as well. The feminine mode of being resists and withdraws from the masculine approach to it, from what seeks to abstract and define its essential characteristics and then to apply them to all women or to narrowing specific acts and thoughts of the "feminine."[10] I am after something else in the examination of the feminine in this great theologian's thought. I want through him to touch the larger issue of the role of the feminine in creative thought about the depths of being. It will not be lost to the reader that this focus on the feminine could be equally directed to the theological work of Teilhard de Chardin, to Karl Barth, or to the psychological work of Freud and Jung, to mention only a few other examples where relation to women and to the feminine figures so large in a man's creativity.

This is a fascinating and necessary question to take up: What role has the feminine played in creative thought about the depths of being, in experience of the abyss? How have philosophers, theologians, poets been related to it in their personal lives and how does it affect their work? The same question can be asked about the masculine mode of being, and should be asked, particularly for women in these areas, but that is beyond my task here.

The feminine invariably refers to the relation of these men to the women in their lives. How do they receive being through their "eros life"? It refers especially to what seems to be a pattern of relationship.[11] In each case, I would suggest, a split exists between the constant partner and the one (or ones) outside convention. The constant partner—usually the wife, an institution such as the church—abides steadily, cares, compassionates, even argues, but sticks through it, abiding like the earth, the ground, the *is*-ness of life. The apparently conventional marriage goes on side by side with unconventional linkings, which sometimes is only one other relationship, and may be the real inner marriage, as it is said it was the case for Barth. The unconventional partners present the unbounded, ungrounded, flashing and frightening, sometimes destructive fires of passion, of the erotic imagination, of sudden spiritual excitement.

The feminine also refers to a style of openness, to a dimension of being that involves the flesh of life—the spirit unmistakably caught up in the flesh, not the spirit abstracted into thought forms. The flesh of life means the body and the imagination, means an emphasis upon elements of play, of delight and simple openness to what is there in contrast to what we feel should be or think we need or wish to be. The feminine symbolizes a style of being and doing, of thinking and relating, both actively and passively, that takes the downward-going road into the dark origins of things, into the felt impact of thought and of images out of which we abstract conceptions. Here our knowing acts by being one with and our doing is anchored in and arises out of antecedent being. Such knowing and doing strongly accent immediate participation and make little of great distances that may separate us from people, places, or ideas, an experience in which a sense of nearness may overcome reflection, even to the point of muddle, as one gets all mixed up in things. The sense of self here arises from identity with others, who exist to us as subjective objects, that is, objects alive and real as they relate to and are experienced by us.[12] From this source we receive our capacity to be. At this source, when damaged, we suffer the maiming of our capacity to be at all. The feminine can be called an animating connection, a link that conveys, confers, and connects to being, making us feel alive and real, and for the sake of which we can betray, bear guilt, even die.

Psychoanalytic systems talk about this feminine mode of being in different vocabularies, as for example the feminine

identification in the Oedipal complex of Freud, the anima symbol of Jung, or the feminine "position" of Melanie Klein, the
female element of being of Winnicott. The culturalists talk about
it as the capacity for affiliation.[13] Here I am not so much inter-
ested in analytical theory as in the role of this animating connection to being in creative thought about the depths. Its hallmark is
a capacity and willingness to receive being, to be-with-being.
Freud, for example, was constantly mindful in an ambivalent way,
of another current of being—the rush of libidinal, instinctual life
that he always sensed there beneath the surface. His faithfulness
was to receiving this eros-life, an eros in the flesh that is sexuality
in all its literal, imaginative, and spiritual meanings as a major
constituent of human being. From descriptions of Freud's staid
marriage one feels his passion ran into his work, which in turn
attracted to him many of the intelligent, radical, and sexually
unconventional women of his day, and made for that relation
with his sister-in-law that has raised more than its share of specu-
lation. For all that in his theories and attitudes which may have
acted to the detriment of women, we must remember that it is
Freud who announced with such absolute clarity that women are
different and that our way to understand them must also be different. We must ask women themselves to tell us about their
being, he said, and we must ask the poets as well, thus recognizing not only a differing content but also different methods to use
to gather that content.

Tillich did ask women themselves to tell him about their
experiences, as Freud directed, and did resort to the vocabulary
of the poets, that is, of the imagination. A very good friend of
Tillich in his later life (not the author) told me that he said he felt
women were closer to being itself than men.[14] He wanted to listen
to a woman and to know her reactions, experiences, and
thought. He wanted to know what made women tick. He wanted
to hear from them about their own experiences in ecstasy
(including orgasm) and what their imaginings were like, both
physical and spiritual. Women could tell him about being as they
received it. Hearing women speak about their experiences of
receiving being, both demonic and divine, about the witch element and the moments of exaltation in their lives, excited him
and fed his abstract thought. That is the way he overcame the

threat of the abyss. He went into it, tried to receive it, listened to women talk about it, then called them forth to speak of their lives and their own passions. Then, he felt, he could order his own thinking about the abyss and the void, talk about it, put it into words.

Tillich showed a deep respect and keen interest in everything women had to say, as if the feminine was a necessary ground to him. Hearing women was for him to listen in on what made all being tick. This was a way he turned the threat of the void, the compulsion of the demonic, into a liberating word about the depths of being as they threaten to overwhelm us and grasp each one of us.

Tillich was a man who struggled to receive the feminine within himself, which formed no small part of his appeal. For what he was trying to do was to receive the feminine in his own masculine way, not to identify with it, not to substitute it for his own identity. A man who really has his own feminine mode of being presented to him in a real woman has it both in her and in himself.[15] Tillich's exaggerated need for women showed he did not have enough of this connection, of a secure receiving of being in himself. Yet, in success or failure of the sexual boundary line, he posed the central questions, knowing, I think, that he could not answer them. He stayed at this boundary in order to see how one struggles to receive being in the setting of metaphysics. Hannah Tillich writes, "He dared open 'the doors of the deep' to the monsters of his convulsed wishes and unfulfilled desires. By boldly naming them and showing their faces, he coined a new philosophical-theological language....He said 'yes' to his own being."[16]

Jung also battled with his attraction to women and even wrote about it, though the chapter was excised by his family from his famous autobiography. For a time, women embodied the sheer multiplicity of being with its overwhelming archetypal forces and images, its abounding symbols, its out-of-bound energies that broke in upon him and nearly broke him down. Gradually he channeled this abundant power into a strong rich riverbed through his work and his relationship to one particular woman, Toni Wolff. Jung, Toni, and his wife Emma Jung all suffered and struggled to make sense of this generously split-up situation.

Through play with sandcastles and villages made out of stones from the lake near his house, through imaginative dialogues with inner figures and extensive exploration of his dreams, through containment and struggle with two remarkable strong women, Jung was able to piece together methods of working with the great living power of the psyche. These methods have stood the test of time. Others use them now as the therapeutic procedures of active imagination and active dialogue with living symbols of the psyche. Jung himself put it succinctly: "Concepts are coined and negotiable values: images are life."

That is how Tillich found his way, through imaginative play into and through the overwhelming power of being. It was a way that nearly broke him down at the time of the First World War, through its terrifyingly negative force. Tillich was working as a chaplain. The carnage all around him deeply shook him. The disruptive power of nonbeing over life deeply frightened him. But in the midst of all that, as he later acknowledged, there persisted the power of his gripping concern with the ultimate, with an unmistakable Yes in the midst of No. He faced the good as the ultimate good, "which is not good for something else, but good in itself," the good that grasps us and in which we dwell. Despite all our "weakness and evil," it unites us with "the good of everything." There lay his belief in Providence as a "creative and saving possibility implied in every situation, one which cannot be destroyed by any event. Providence means that the demonic and destructive forces within ourselves and our world can never have an unbreakable grasp upon us, and that the bond which connects us with the fulfilling love can never be disrupted."[17]

Like Jung, Tillich found relief and expansion of his hold on being through the play of imagination. He wrote, "The romantic theory of play, Nietzsche's preference for play as opposed to 'the spirit of gravity,' Kierkegaard's 'esthetic sphere,' and the imaginative element in mythology were always both attractive and dangerous to me."[18] He engaged in erotic imaginings with women and with feminine symbols of being, figures like the witch. Women did not get angry at Tillich over any of this.[19] They felt seen and recognized by him. He was present to them, all of him listening to what they could tell him. We can speculate that women were for him like the abyss out of which comes insight and the ability to take in, to receive being. Women were part of the spirit of play breaking through the too tight, entrapping definitions of a narrow, self-contained reason or a moralistic piety. Tillich felt a horror of constricting prim-lipped judgmental attitudes toward life. I remember a lunch in Hamburg with him when I was a student. He got up and changed his place at the table in order not to have to face throughout the meal two black-garbed, stolid, frowning women who looked as if they were stern moralizers. He said he could not take in any food in that atmosphere.

His terror of getting trapped was always apparent in his relations with women. Perhaps that accounts for the number. He was involved each time but never permanently. He played with being in a joyous and undifferentiated way without getting pinned down in one relationship. He played on and with the boundary. In rituals of discussing and mythologizing, of casting the yes and no, the subject and object aspects of life as eros-tinged imaginative forms, touching demonic and divine energies, areas of domination and submission (sadomasochism), of adoring and obeying, of joining and staying out of reach, he moved between direct openness to primary experiences of the being of faith and the anxiety of being possessed.

He said that the qualities of his father and mother wove in and out of his adult life. His father came from eastern Germany and was strongly caught by a sense of duty, of personal sin and authority, of feudal tradition. He could not be talked to before breakfast, and Tillich was specifically forbidden to hop or jump before him as a boy but had instead to submit to instruction on how to walk down the stairs. Yet this same father spoke with power and eloquence about what really matters in life and often held long conversations with his son. His mother, who came from the western Rhineland, was a woman full of zest, who loved to move around. She had a love of the concrete in life and took strongly democratic attitudes. Her death, when Tillich was seventeen, took the ground right out from under him, leaving him shaken, without ontological security. He said of her, "The character of my mother's world asserted itself only through constant and deep struggle with that of my father. In order for the maternal side of my makeup to express itself, outbreaks, often extreme, were necessary."[20] These outbreaks show in his passionate relationships with women and with the feminine in himself. That was how he received the being which he contained in his own personality.

PROJECTION

This raises an important psychoanalytical issue that must be taken up in any discussion of the feminine: projection and the possibility of abuse it brings with it. Introjection and projection are natural functions of the psyche, as natural to it as breathing is to the body. We take in bits and pieces of persons, both loved and powerful, and we take in pieces of the world too—nature, our beloved pets, images regnant in our culture that capture our imaginations. We take all this inside ourselves and mix with it our own fantasies and primordial images and instinctual experiences. We create a world. We recognize that our self and our world with others are inextricably interdependent. The self is social.

We also project outward into the world of shared existence what we make of what we have taken in, and to which we add bits of our instinctual experiences and the images that accompany them. We put those things into other people and into events. For example, to take a figure dear to Tillich's imagination, we add a bit of the witch to our mother and find and create in her a mixture of demonic and loving forces.[21] If our mother is a tough enough female, she combines these opposites for us, exemplifying the way ruthless instinct dwells together with feminine tenderness, how sexual intensity abides with compassion, how a haglike intellectual frenzy coexists with the power of the wise woman, a wisdom as profound as a sibyl's. If either we or mother are not tough enough, the two halves fall apart into very different kinds of women, two opposing images of the feminine: the safe, containing, holding one and the magnetic, exciting, dangerous one who blazes. This has long been the plight of women, to be split up in this fashion. We must find our way to bring the halves together, or to recognize that the halves have in fact been joined together and that it is we who split them.

Freud, Jung, Tillich, and perhaps Barth and Teilhard as well, struggled with putting together these images of being which are so often projected onto women. We stand now at a time in

the history of consciousness when we can withdraw these projections from women and find new ways of receiving the being that
the feminine conveys, thus relieving women of this often crip-
pling burden. Indeed, women are beginning to insist that this be
done. This change, when it comes, will have a revolutionary
impact on the status of women and on what happens between
men and women in their relation to the depths of being. Women
do not want simply to be pushed into compliance with stereotypes, nor do they like to be forced to efface themselves in prefabricated roles. Men and women will have to work out more
consciously and together the exercises of intimacy, exchanging
back and forth the carrying of the connecting link to the depths.
The depths as a result will come closer, but they will be more
dangerous, more apt to implode on our consciousness if we fail
to open channels of relationship to all that energy.

In any case we must raise the issue of projection onto
women as Tillich knew and practiced it. He was determined to
receive being in some knowing way and to feel received by it. He
projected onto women the unity that comes with receiving being
and then setting fire to it. The physical sexual enactments
revealed spiritual being for him, a living toward the center, a feeling of the ground supporting and carrying him. He was after an
animating connection to being that did not separate sexuality
from spirit. The feminine element is always hard to verbalize but
has in it an aspect which leads men and women to that wordless
source of being which Jakob Boehme called the *Ungrund,* a term,
an experience, a hope central to Tillich. This for him was a direct
receiving of God.

In any situation of projection, both personal and impersonal elements exist. The women he knew were real women to
Tillich, nothing abstract or general, but persons in their own
splendid right. They were never passive creatures for him, but
females of authority, with the power to uncover hidden recesses
of being, to show forth its meaning, as he said, and to make him
"dizzy in my blood."[22] In their own lives, these women were often
persons pushed into the background by social custom, by patriarchal marriage styles, or religious institutions and attitudes which
defined women as helpers only, never prophets or priests.[23]
Tillich tried to bring them out, made them step forward to claim

their own large selfhood. He sought them as partners, not as mothers or daughters, but as persons with clear presence and imagination, with their own authority. They responded with gratitude, and sometimes, we know, with ecstasy. Tillich wanted these women as friends, too, and he succeeded in remaining friends with most of them with whom he was involved erotically. A human bond endured, person meeting person. He found often enough in woman one who spoke of the depths, who tried to receive being and could help him receive it, one who knew both ground and abyss, and could help him bridge the gap between them.

Tillich was clearly fed by the women who carried his own feminine side: their receptions of being fed his abstract thought. He used woman to make explicit his intuitions and attractions to being, as he found in her her own words about the nature of being. His moving of those receptions of being into abstract conceptual formulation was his way of overcoming the power of the abyss and of living with the inevitable anxiety and guilt it aroused in him. As he wrote himself about the bigness of personality, "But where there is abundance there is the danger of conflicts, of disease and demonic bondage."[24]

It is also important to ask about the effect on women of having this man project so much onto them of the feminine mode of being. From what we know, we can say women felt affirmed by Tillich, felt they were taken seriously, sometimes for the first time, too often for the last time. As I said before, they did not get angry at his bold approaches. Rollo May writes that they were not even jealous of each other: "But each spoke out of her conviction that she represented something special to Paulus—some unique insight, revelation or secret kind of relationship which occurred in some particular hour or walk together."[25] He found in woman the dignity of one connected to being who embodied it both in her sexuality and her spirit.

At the end of his life Tillich gave a good friend all the letters from women he had received, telling her to read them and destroy them. She did not read many but was nonetheless struck by the overwhelming gratitude and love these women expressed to him. He said to his friend, with characteristic humor, that the letters must be destroyed, alas, so he could be remembered as a systematic theologian and not just as a lover.

In any situation of demonic energy and compulsion, rage, suffering and despair must also occur. The dark side of Tillich's compulsion was suffered by his wife, the one to whom he dedicated both *On the Boundary* and the last volume of the *Systematic Theology*, calling her "the companion of my life," the one of whom he had said, she kept me on the boundary where I belonged. She writes that he said to her, "You were my bridge across the seasons, my continuity in past, present and future."[26]

She confessed herself often delivered into the grip of rage at betrayal, into frenzies of jealousy, into bouts of outrage and pain, into a veritable gnashing of the teeth at always feeling second best, unseen, unprotected. After much suffering, she finally found her way through this abyss, this engulfing maelstrom through the means of meditation and yoga exercises. She carried as heavy a shadow as her husband did. He pitied her suffering and asked her forgiveness before his death. But he could not sever the feminine from his life; he felt his life would end if he did. He was profoundly grateful to his wife for her forgiveness. He knew intimately splits, guilt, anxiety; these experiences lit up his writings for others. He wrote from his innermost self to those who took up the Christian vocation: "And there will be no period in your life, as long as it remains creative and has healing power, in which the demons will not split your souls, producing doubts about your faith, about your vocation, about your whole being. Rejoice in your vocation."[27]

ONE WOMAN'S RESPONSE

Tillich's struggle with being addresses questions to each of us as theologians, teachers, healers, scholars, and students. What connects us to the ground of being? What pulls us toward the "consuming fire"? What allows us or compels us to go up to and into the abyss of being? What forms the connecting link to the creative source of being? Where do we experience the demonic forces breaking in upon us and how do we experience the good-in-itself that is not overcome? Where are we caught in our own compulsions and how do they influence our work? Is it necessary to be so caught, to go so far down into the frightening places in order to speak an authoritative word in creative work for others? Or is that notion of the journey part of the compulsion? A reader may want to say here that because of my decades of work as a psychoanalyst I am biased toward seeing the conflicts, despair, and enthrallment of people to forces beyond their control. There is some truth in that. Yet in my clinical experience there are also endless examples of the enduring strength of the good, the persistence of grace,[28] the affirming of the true self.

Certainly questions might be raised about the role of the feminine for Tillich in putting him in touch with the ground of being and as a force that overtook him, compelling him to inquire of still another woman and another and another. From a woman's point of view, the question looms: Why so many women? For it is certainly more risky and dangerous, to go down deep into the depths with one person. Then one no longer avoids the dread of mortality, symbolized in the fear of fully exhausting relationship with one person. I think Tillich defended against that threat by sheer multiplication of the number of relationships. In one relationship the partners take up the tasks of relating fantasy to reality, of joining inner exploration to outer limitation, of accepting the conundrum of the many found in the one instead of the one found in the many. The feminine mode recognizes in a particular relationship a singularity through which the universal speaks. The feminine mode of being takes up the task of history making, and does not flee from the role of embodying the eternal in the here and now. The large impersonal energies of sexuality that women know as strongly as men are corralled down and through the womanly imagination, which welcomes the spirits in the multiple exchanges of just the two persons, not a multitude. This is being as abyss and as ground held together, not split apart. This is passion and permanence, spirit lived in the flesh, not just dreamed about or cast into unrealizable disguises.

However split, Tillich nonetheless went courageously into his fear of being and his accompanying fear of the devouring feminine. He risked. He went with openness. He suffered his demons and the breaking of conventions. He did not just withdraw into

the safety of the superficial certainties, nor did he escape by pre-
tending that men and women were all alike. The feminine was *the*
link to receiving being for Tillich. He spoke a terrible truth to that
good friend to whom he said that he feared his life would end if
this access was cut off. Both caught in compulsion and loaded
with anxiety, he admitted the one and consented to the other,
going into what pulled him, struggling to articulate the depth of
response aroused in him, which each time held the promise of
taking him further into the recesses of being.

The issue I am after is what Tillich opens in the rest of us
through his own experiences of the metaphysical boundary of
abyss and ground as it is personified in his relation to the feminine. In examining this one man's relation to the feminine as it
influenced his theology in its crossings and recrossings of the
boundary of anxiety and faith, the questions put to us are three:
What is our relation to the feminine? What is our relation to the
opposite sex in person and as mode of being? How does that
affect and inform our work?

Those questions involve everyone's relations to the depths.
For the feminine is not just something found in women, and carried by them in projection. Nor is it some abstract principle floating in the intellectual sky. It is a mode of being human that a man
as much as a woman must reckon with in his own personality, one
that shapes his psyche and his relations with both the world he
finds and the one he creates with others. Women too must take
up this question more fully and face the matching questions
about the role of the masculine mode of being in their work.

It is clear that Tillich wanted to know about being from
women above all. It is equally clear, I think, that he wanted to
know from each woman something of the woman in himself and
that internal feminine was what made him anxious. Thus in his
relation to a specific woman, in demanding information from
her about being, he was also getting and giving information to
his inner woman. Between the two lay the demonic genius of the
mixture of masculine and feminine.

The point here is not to condemn nor to condone another
person in this examination of the role of the feminine in reaching
into the metaphysical depths. The point is to ask ourselves about
our own connections and ruptures of connection with being, to ask

what risks our faith forces us to take, to ask the risky questions about our own devotions and compulsions. Tillich's negative dilemma poses the positive questions for us. He lived his questions and did not just talk about them abstractly. That is what faith does, for it is lived reality, not something distant from life. If we fail to take up these questions as posed for us, each in our own way, fail to face the flaws and dilemmas of our own reality, we fail in faith, may even lose our faith, and with it a precious center of our being.

THE FEMININE IN TILLICH'S WORK

How then did Tillich deal with the Yes and No of his own being? How did he navigate across the boundaries of anxiety and faith? How and where did he find the answer to the question of the demonic that arose, not only in the world around him, with its wars, its economic depressions, its holocausts and hordes of homeless, but also in the splits and compulsions of his own psyche?

We know the answer when we look at his work from the point of view suggested here, but it is worth repeating again with more particular focus on the feminine, because it is in this mode that he received being and that it was made available to him in such abundant measure. I want to point to the specific recognition of the feminine mode of being in Tillich's work. One could argue that Tillich should have written much more explicitly about the feminine. But that is like saying to an author, Why didn't you write a different book? Or arguing that he should have known more than he did, or been more aware than he was, or announced connections he was still groping for in the dark.

Tillich found answers to his questions in timeless archetypal symbols contained in Christian doctrine and participated in by the Christian faithful. He found answers in the symbols he insisted on deliberately plowing back into the ground of being, deliteralizing them, unshackling them from the encrustations of years of repetition that had rendered them remote and meaningless to so many.[29]

We can find traces of the feminine mode of being in Tillich's idea that the religious symbol is the road to transcendent reality. Its life grows out of the ground of its culture and its roots in particular psyches and souls. The symbol connects us to the reality to which it points. If we take up the descriptions of the feminine mode of being, elaborated in endless variations through the ages, as the connecting mode, as the urge to-be-in-the-midst-of, as the spirit always in the flesh, never abstracted from it, then we can see how this feminine element, so strong in Tillich's life, also shaped his creative thought.

The symbol is conceived of in terms of connection above all else. If that connection fails, says Tillich, then the symbol dies. The symbol makes perceptible what is invisible, makes figurative what is beyond sight and touch. It carries into the flesh of historical, communal, and personal experience the power and reality of the transcendent being to which it points. It plants that Other, that transcendent reality, in the human social situation.[30] The symbol earths the consuming fire. It receives being and penetrates us to open us to the power and thrust of being. Through the symbolism of the feminine the spiritual is touched for Tillich. It is a transitive experience; it leads somewhere. It cannot be intransitive; it will not suffer disconnection. The feminine is being-in-the-flesh for Tillich, a hold on the abyss; it is the ground in the midst of it. Latent in Tillich's doctrine of symbols is the meeting, mixing and exchanging of masculine and feminine modes of being.

In Tillich's crossing of boundaries between disciplines he showed an all-inclusiveness, a both–and quality characteristic of the feminine mode of being, where ambiguities are not only tolerated but recognized as intrinsic to any living grasp of reality. The Yes and No always coinhere and cannot be separated in the feminine mode of being-and-doing. This recognition is akin to what has since been called "the matriarchal superego," in contrast to the patriarchal.[31]

Tillich's insistence on embracing ambiguity and on the concrete situation bore fruit for workers in other disciplines. He pushed the rest of us to become aware of the ontic assumptions that lay beneath our theories and methods. Tillich showed a great openness to the unconscious and a willingness to be forced specifically to become conscious of the unconscious as it lived in him and as it showed itself in his times. He was willing even to struggle to become conscious of his own unconscious defense of denial, surely one of the more enraging of human defenses. He pressed colleagues in my own discipline of psychoanalysis to examine the ground out of which they work, to make conscious what they might be denying, to look at the ontic assumptions behind their methods of treatment. He pushed us all toward that ground and abyss of being to which he showed such devotion.

Tillich's emphasis on the symbol connecting us to the ground and abyss of being on the one hand and to spiritual formulation and understanding on the other, his simultaneous emphasis on the demonic and the divine, on truth as both ambiguous and clear, reveals another theme associated to the feminine mode of being: the fixing of the concrete in the ultimate.[32] He insists on grounding everything in questions of the human situation, uncovering there the power of eternal symbols which arouse the great questions in us. His method of correlation is a method of connection—the question is always of the particular concrete human situation rooted in the eternal presence of God as it is conveyed in the timeless symbols of Judeo-Christian tradition. Tillich's method lives on today not so much in a new school of theology as in the spirit taken up in all schools of theology.[33] How does God connect to my situation of color? To my political situation? To our group's concern with "sexual orientation"? To our country's traditions? To the North and South American cultures? To mental health? And so on and so on. What it means to be working under the influence of this feminine mode of being is an unshakable emphasis on the particular and concrete. We have today particularized theologies, which, because they are not sufficiently conscious of the feminine mode of being, ironically impose new abstractions of their own while fighting what they find abstract and impersonal in traditional theology. Haven't we been told enough in these last decades that we are not true believers unless we agree God is black, or red, or dead, or female, or gay, or revolutionary, or Marxist, or a psychological force? The need to make connection with the transcendent in the midst of our concrete lived situation is a necessity Tillich wrote about and left as a legacy to future theologians. That concern with connection is of the highest intensity in the feminine mode of being.[34]

Tillich took up the feminine explicitly in his discussion of the doctrine of the Trinity as the symbol for God.[35] There he wrote directly about the purge of feminine symbolism from Protestant

tradition and of the need to transcend the male–female dialectic
and to correct a one-sided male-dominated symbolism. For him,
this task is best described as a going far down into the symbolic
nature of the ground of being. It points to a positive mother-qual-
ity of giving birth, carrying, and on the negative side, of holding
back, engulfing and resisting a separating independence.[36]

One feels echoes here of his experiences with women and
with the feminine in himself—the constriction of boundedness
and not getting free, but also, the feeling, like Goethe's, of being
pulled ever onward into the depths of being itself. From a psychological point of view, one can speculate about whether the
pull toward women and repeated enactments did not show two
opposite tendencies in Tillich. One is the regressive hold of this
mother-ground upon him from which he could not completely
free himself. The second is the courageous effort to differentiate
not just himself (the ego) from the regressive mother-tie but also
the feminine component (the anima) in himself as a feminine figure in her own right.[37] This struggle to differentiate the feminine
from the maternal is central to the late twentieth century, with its
controversies over abortion and ecology and the particularity of
the life of minorities.

Finally, Tillich's vision of the liberating power of grace also
partook of the feminine mode of being.[38] Grace is a pull toward
participation that liberates from demonic compulsion; it recognizes the reality of the person instead of carrying her or him
away into the abyss. Here we read of Tillich's symbols of reunion
of the estranged with its essential nature, of return of the lost
parts to the integrity of the whole, of the ecstasy of standing
forth, able to say and hear the Word of God, while at the same
time being grasped and carried into a larger wholeness that transcends the splits, ambiguities, doubts, flaws, and despairs of the
human. All these are receivings of being that seek not enlightenment but participation, not perfection but completion, not con-
quest but liberation of who and what we essentially are.

Tillich writes of a kind of knowing that operates in these healing experiences, a knowing that is intrinsic to the feminine mode of
being. In contrast to a controlling knowledge, where detachment
and a technical, instrumental reason reigns, one characteristic of
masculine modes, is a "receiving knowledge" which includes the

emotional element of participation that is more tentative, more subject to reconstruction, where understanding includes more union with the object known.[39] True knowledge for Tillich includes both controlling and receiving, both instrumental usage and union. Thus we can see his efforts to transcend masculine and feminine modes of knowing in a larger vision of knowledge that includes both of them, each with its Yes to the other's No. For Tillich it is the Spirit that pushes toward this fuller knowing, the Spirit that transcends male-female alternatives, by rectifying the overemphasis on male doing with emphasis on the feminine ecstatic reuniting with the whole.

The words that sum up Tillich's gestures toward including the feminine mode of being in his abstract thought are receiving acceptance. The symbol connects with us by bearing toward us the grace of our acceptance by the transcendent. The transcendent takes us in and asks us to receive its acceptance gladly. Being seeks us out. It shows itself to us, even if in hidden forms of compulsions. We need to receive what is given.[40] We must accept the ambiguity that springs from particular lived-in human situations. We are helped to do that by the answer of the New Being that is big and gracious enough to include all that we are in our flawed and only too weak state. The ground of being as inexhaustible depth carries everything finite with it. From it flows the No, the judgment on everything finite which claims to be infinite. Yet from it also flows the endless Yes, the affirmation of everything finite as a medium for the infinite.[41] This is being speaking acceptance to us, graciously extending the invitation always and eternally to come, to come now, to take, to partake, to enter, to be caught up in the life that makes whole.

Tillich wrote one poem in his life, when the ground of being was shattered for him at the death of his mother, that first carrier of the feminine mode of being. I end with its last line. It is about being and the abyss.

O Abgrund ohne grund, des Wahnsinns finstere Tiefe!
Ach dass ich nimmer Dich geschaut und kinlich schliefe!

O abyss without ground, dark depth of madness!
Would that I had never gazed upon you and were sleeping like a
child!

But Tillich was awake to the abyss, and he stayed awake and went always across the boundaries between anxiety and faith to give spiritual form and articulation to his experience of the abyss he both loved and feared. It both shook his foundations and symbolized the unconditional reception by a God who graciously loves us while we are yet sinners. Tillich's fallibilities and capacities teach us courage to take the being offered us. We can be thankful to him, and to being itself.

Notes

This chapter is based on a lecture I gave to the North American Tillich Society, at its International Symposium "On the Boundary," In Celebration of the Centennial of Tillich's Birth, November 22, 1986, Atlanta, Georgia. It was later published in *Paul Tillich on Creativity*, ed. J. A. K. Kegley (Bakersfield, Calif.: California State University, University Press of America, 1989).

1. P. Tillich, *On the Boundary: An Autobiographical Sketch* (New York: Scribner's, 1966), 98.

2. P. Tillich, "What Is Basic in Human Nature," *American Journal of Psychoanalysis* 22 (1962): 120.

3. W. Pauck, "To Be or Not to Be: Tillich on the Meaning of Life," in *The Thought of Paul Tillich*, eds. J. L. Adams, W. Pauck, R. L. Shinn (San Francisco: Harper & Row, 1985), 31–32, 35.

4. J. L. Adams, "Introduction: The Storms of Our Times and Starry Night," in *Thought of Paul Tillich*, 14.

5. R. L. Shinn, "Tillich as Interpreter and Disturber of Contemporary Civilization" in *Thought of Paul Tillich*, 51.

6. J. H. Randall, Jr., "The Ontology of Paul Tillich," in *Philosophy After Darwin* (New York: Columbia University Press, 1977), 216.

7. D. Emmet, "Epistemology and the Idea of Revelation," in C. W. Kegley and R. W. Bretall, *The Theology of Paul Tillich* (New York: Macmillan, 1961), 211.

8. J. L. Adams, "Introduction," 3, cites this quote from Paul Tillich, "Religiöse Krisis," *Vivos Voco* 2 (1922): 616–21.

9. H. Tillich, *From Time to Time* (New York: Stein and Day, 1973), 315.

10. I have written and my husband and I have written extensively elsewhere about the necessary slipperiness and inevitable ambiguity of this term, that points to unmistakable qualities of experience which will elude us all the more swiftly when we use a neuterized vocabulary. See

A. B. Ulanov, *The Feminine in Christian Theology and in Jungian Psychology* (Evanston: Northwestern University Press, 2d ed., 1975), chs. 8 and 9; *Receiving Woman: Studies in the Psychology and Theology of the Feminine* (Philadelphia: Westminster Press, 1981), ch. 4; A. and B. Ulanov, *The Witch and the Clown: Two Archetypes of Human Sexuality* (Wilmette, Ill.: Chiron Publications, 1983), ch. 1.

11.   We have understood this pattern to arise out of a split-anima state intrapsychically. See *The Witch and the Clown*, 323; for the split-animus in women, see ibid., 103, 123–34, 315, 323; see also *Receiving Woman*, 123.

12.   For discussion of subjective object, see D. W. Winnicott, *Playing and Reality* (London: Tavistock Press, 1971), 71, 80, 130. See also H. Kohut, who uses the term "self-object," *The Analysis of the Self* (New York: International Universities Press, 1971), 26–27; see also H. Kohut, *The Restoration of the Self* (New York: International Universities Press, 1977), xiii.

13.   See S. Freud, *The Ego and the Id*, trans. Joan Riviere and James Strachey (New York: Norton, 1960), 21, 23; see also S. Freud, *Three Essays on the Theory of Sexuality, Standard Edition* 7, trans. James Strachey (London: Hogarth Press), 220n; see C. G. Jung, "Concerning the Archetypes, with Special Reference to the Anima Concept," in *The Archetypes of the Collective Unconscious, Collected Works* 9:1, trans. R. F. C. Hull (New York: Pantheon, 1954/1959), and "The Syzygy: Anima and Animus" in *Aion: Researches into the Phenomenology of the Self, Collected Works* 9:2, trans. R. F. C. Hull (New York: Pantheon, 1959); see M. Klein, *Envy and Gratitude and Other Works 1946–1963* (New York: Delacorte Press/Seymour Lawrence, 1975), 82, 135, 169, 306, 307; see D. W. Winnicott, *Playing and Reality*, 72–75; 80–84; see J. B. Miller, *Toward a New Psychology of Women* (Boston: Beacon Press, 1976), ch. 8; see D. Bakan, *The Duality of Human Existence* (Chicago: Rand McNally, 1966), ch. 4.

14.   I knew Tillich when I was a student at Radcliffe and he was University Professor at Harvard. He showed me, as he did many students, this same keen interest in what my experiences of being had been, both imaginatively and in life.

15.   One can hazard that he got repeatedly caught in some degree of projective identifications—where women were identified with the animating connection he projected into them. Melanie Klein originated this term of "projective identification." It describes a process whereby we (unconsciously) put into other people parts of ourselves and then identify the persons with these parts. Thus we feel attached to them, compelled toward (or away from) them. See M. Klein, *Envy and Gratitude*, 8, 10n, 11, 22, 68–69, 143, 152–55, 333–34.

16. H. Tillich, *From Time to Time*, 23.

17. P. Tillich, *The Shaking of the Foundation* (New York: Scribners, 1948), 100, 106.

18. Tillich, *On the Boundary*, 25–26.

19. R. May, *Paulus* (San Francisco: Harper & Row, 1973), 51.

20. Tillich, *On the Boundary*, 14.

21. A. and B. Ulanov, *The Witch and the Clown*, ch. 2.

22. Personal communication from a letter to a close friend of Tillich's.

23. For a discussion of the patriarchal style of marriage, see A. B. Ulanov, *The Feminine*, 257–62.

24. P. Tillich, "Heal the Sick," in *The Meaning of Health: Essays in Existentialism, Psychoanalysis, and Religion*, ed. P. LeFevre (Chicago: Exploration Press, 1984), 273.

25. May, *Paulus*, 51.

26. H. Tillich, *From Time to Time*, 18.

27. Tillich, "Heal the Sick," 274.

28. Title of my husband's book, in process.

29. P. Tillich, *Systematic Theology*, Vol. III (Chicago: University of Chicago Press, 1963), 291. Reading this material and the following citations of Tillich's works urgently demands that we understand and respond to the feminine mode of being. It is rewarding to do so. We learn about Tillich, the theological situation and ourselves.

30. P. Tillich, "The Religious Symbol," *Daedalus: Journal of the American Academy of Arts and Sciences* 87, 3 (1958). See also A. B. Ulanov, *The Feminine*, ch. 5, "The Symbol and Theology."

Tillich writes, "Religious symbolism is not an accidental imagery which could be replaced by other images, but is rooted in a real unity of the realm from which the symbols are taken (the bodily sphere) with the realm in which they function (the mental sphere)." Tillich, *The Meaning of Health*, 38.

Tillich writes, "They have their roots in the totality of human experience, including local surroundings in all their ramifications, both political and economic. And these symbols can then be understood partly as in revolt against these surroundings." P. Tillich, "The Significance of the History of Religions for the Systematic Theologian," in *The History of Religions, Essays on the Problem of Understanding*, Vol. I, ed. J. M. Kitagawa with collaboration of M. Eliade and C. Long (Chicago: University of Chicago Press, 1967), 255.

31. P. Tillich, *The Meaning of Health*, 3. See also A. and B. Ulanov, *Religion and the Unconscious* (Philadelphia: Westminster Press, 2d ed., 1985), 150–60.

32. Tillich, *Systematic Theology* III, 283.

33. See D. Tracey, "Tillich and Contemporary Theology," in *Thought of Paul Tillich*, 266.

34. For further discussion of this point, see A. B. Ulanov, "Picturing God," in *Picturing God* (Cambridge, Mass.: Cowley Publications, 1986).

35. Tillich, *Systematic Theology* III, 293–94.

36. God is almost this mother-ground, this fruitive ground, the vast, unfathomable depths of darkness, to cite Ruysbroeck, who greatly influenced Tillich. See Ruysbroeck, *The Spiritual Espousals* (New York: Harper, n.d.), 179–81.

Tillich writes, "When the Protestants gave up many of the Catholic symbols at the Reformation, an empty space was left in Protestantism. There was an *absence of the female element.*...In some aspects of Jesus there is a female element. In the doctrine of the Spirit there is, because of its half-mystical character, something female. But *a direct female image is lacking.* So *there is an empty space in Protestantism.* It is a very masculine religion. Some elements in the concept of *grace* are also lacking. "Grace is moralized in America and intellectualized in Europe. As for the element of the *soul,* even that word is forbidden in America....So we have 'psychology without a soul.' This situation can be traced to a lack of the female element." *Ultimate Concern: Tillich in Dialogue,* D. MacKenzie Brown (New York: Harper & Row, 1965), 148–49; see also 90–92. See also J. Plaskow, *Sex, Sin and Grace: Women's Experience and the Theologies of Reinhold Niebuhr and Paul Tillich* (Washington, D.C.: University Press of America, 1980).

37. Tillich writes, "The divine structure of grace is not possession or compulsion, because it is at the same time liberating; it liberates what we essentially are." Cited by J. Boozer, "Tillich and the New Religious Movements," in *The Thought of Paul Tillich,* 235, from *A History of Christian Thought,* ed. C. E. Braaten (New York: Harper & Row, 1968), 246.

38. See Randall, "Ontology of Paul Tillich," 224. See also P. Tillich, *Systematic Theology,* Vol. I (Chicago: University of Chicago Press, 1951), 102; see also A. Ulanov, *Receiving Woman,* 72–85.

39. See A. B. Ulanov, "The Anxiety of Being," in *The Thought of Paul Tillich,* 127–34, ch. 9 of this book.

40. His good friend lent me her copy. This is also quoted in May, *Paulus,* 41.

41. See *Theology of Paul Tillich,* eds. C. W. Kegley and R. W. Bretall, 76.

Chapter 11

Religious Devotion or Masochism?
A Psychoanalyst Looks at
Thérèse of Lisieux

WHY MASOCHISM?

The questions most often directed by the world of depth psychology to the world of religion, and to Thérèse specifically, are, Why all the suffering? Is it an essential part of religious life? The recent movie *Thérèse* reawakened this question. Why did she refuse medicine? Why refuse relief from pain? Isn't this masochistic?

A second set of questions follows from the first. If masochism is not true of Thérèse, then why do people associate it with her? Why does her kind of religious devotion strike anyone as a masochistic embrace of suffering? These questions will be my focus. What, in sum, are the differences between religious devotion and masochism? And, if Thérèse is not masochistic, then why is she accused of it?

The second question is easier to answer than the first. I will start with that and return to it again at the very end of this chapter. Thérèse is accused of masochistic sentimentality because of the depth of her feelings, her lavish, all-out loving of Jesus. Loving with all one's heart, mind, soul, and body, like Thérèse's, fills most of us with dread. We cancel that dread by accusing the loving one—Thérèse—of groveling sentimentality. But the underside of sentimentality is power. We accuse Thérèse of too much feeling, too much devotion, while keeping for ourselves the power to put her at a safe distance, and to keep her there. We stay in control of our feelings by caricaturing hers. We charge her and her followers with being like a too sweet and sticky icing in order to

207

avoid facing the real achievement—her capacity to love and to feel without any obstacles in the way of her feeling. Thérèse is accused of masochism and of sentimentally seeking suffering because she threatens us with a possibility we fear to make actual.

Thérèse shows us that within our ordinary lives—going to work in our cars or on the subway, doing our taxes, getting our children ready for school, fixing meals—we can find the mysterious exchanges between ourselves and God in prayer and meditation, no matter how brief or hurried. She reveals the hidden works of love that go on daily, not in some special precious time, but in ordinary everyday time. Thérèse poses a tremendous threat because she brings hidden mystic life out into the open and says, in effect, here it is for the taking, for all of us, not just the specially gifted, but all of us, each with our own gifts.

Thérèse acts as a perfect complement to our century's huge explosions that force power outward—into bombs, into space, across new frontiers. Thérèse shows us explosions of energy inward, into inner space, and a spirit so powerful it spills over into relationships with others, near and far. She uncovers an energy of tremendous intensity in daily life. We can no longer say, "Oh no, we cannot love like that; we are not members of a religious community; we know nothing of that kind of power." If we are members of Carmel we can no longer say, "We cannot love like that; we do not have Thérèse's genius; her power to love is only for the saints." Thérèse closes all those escape hatches. She says, "Yes you can, any moment of any day; here, now, this afternoon, we can know the mysterious and wonderful exchanges of love."

Another aspect of our century is its horrible denial of the person. As we know, guards even pried the gold fillings out of the teeth of concentration camp victims. Living breathing persons were treated as objects of medical experiments, or outright sadistic torment. People by the hundreds of thousands have been thrown into prisons, dungeons, gulags, and left there to rot. The mysterious center that makes up the person has been ruthlessly attacked, canceled, obliterated. Even in less dramatic circumstances, the ordinary commerce of everyday life, we suffer nullification of personhood. We know perfectly well we did not buy what the computer printout stubbornly, repetitiously reports we did buy. We write the company; we phone; we write again. The bills keep spitting out of the machines, as if what we wrote or said never was heard, or if heard, made no difference.

In this century, where on every side we feel personhood diminished, questioned, anything but seen, held, and cherished, this young woman, this girl, this wise woman makes us see that each of us is precious as a center of being. She shows us we are held in the sight of God, precious to the Lord, precious to one another. She links through the chain of love our nearest neighbor and our most distant neighbor.

Thérèse's own immediate leaps into spiritual maturity are worth noting. At thirteen, as she was running to look for Christmas gifts that had been put into her slippers, she overheard her father sigh, weary of preparing presents once again. She fled to her room and howled with hurt and disappointment. But quickly she gave up her tears and in a leap recovered *la force d'âme,* the strength of mind and soul that she had lost.[1] The summer after that Christmas leap, she leapt again. Starting then with her nearest neighbor, her father, she reached in that summer to her farthest one, the murderer named Pranzini who was about to be executed. She felt herself wounded now, not by another's weariness in meting out pleasures, but with the indifference of the world to its Redeemer. Praying as intercessor for Pranzini, she felt God's love break through. The moment before his execution, he was reported to have seized the crucifix and kissed it. Barry Ulanov describes her intercessory action: "She would gather up the blood that was being wasted. She would give it to those who needed it. She heard her Lord's cry, 'I thirst,' as if it was addressed to her, and she determined to respond to it by giving him souls for which he thirsted, sinners...she longed to save...."[2]

Thérèse herself summed it up: "It was a true exchange of love. To souls I offered the blood of Jesus; to Jesus I offered the same souls, brought to life again by the dew of his precious blood...."[3]

Thérèse recovers for us in our time the mystery of love in person, between persons, between persons and God. That somehow threatens us. Hence the accusations that pile up against her—hers is too much feeling, too much an embrace of suffering. She gives us her gift of self-assurance, of completeness in love, of a courage to act that overflows out of that love. In return, we accuse her of sentimentality and masochism. We look to protect ourselves from the power she puts into our hands.

PSYCHOANALYTIC THEORIES OF MASOCHISM

Psychoanalytical theory offers three approaches to what is called masochism. Masochism is not something we do; it is a suffering, an affliction, and a very painful one. Three types of theoretical understanding of masochism act as maps that outline this country of pain. Some of us have ventured into that country and know that the experience is quite different from the maps. Most of us know something about it. We may also know that the great temptation in the psychological, as in the spiritual life, is to rest content with the map and never go into the country that it charts. Then we think we can stay in control. So I will state these theories in ways that may evoke the actual painful experience they describe and its temptations and difficulties.

The first of the three approaches to masochism sees it as a manifestation of the death instinct; the second, as a defensive strategy of the ego; the last, as a means of hiding a missing piece of ourselves and a reflection of our need to venerate something transcendent, beyond ourselves. The first originates with Freud and is shared by Melanie Klein. They in turn distinguish among an erotogenic masochism, where pleasure is mixed with pain, a feminine masochism where aggression is directed inward, and moral masochism, the one most relevant to my purposes, in which we submit our ego to a sadistically critical superego as our ruling moral authority.[4] In this submission we accept almost gladly what anyone accuses us of; we take unconscious pleasure in confessing to others' sins; we submit to an inner punitive voice that says in effect that we are no good, that we are never enough, that we are fools. The ego cooperates and develops chronic low self-esteem, a habit of excessive self-criticism, and timid behavior.

An extreme example of such behavior can be seen in the willingness some years ago of people around Jim Jones in Guyana to drink poisoned grape juice and die, simply because he had told them to do so. Less extreme examples, and ones that need all our attention to discern whether people are veering toward masochism or moving into real dedication or devotion, are to be found in the vows of obedience we make to a religious or military supervisor, that a young person does in effect to a teacher or a coach, that is shown in a lover's fealty to a beloved.

The second way of mapping the suffering of masochism moves from instinct to defense of the ego, to strategies we develop to protect ourselves. We use masochistic attitudes and actions to protect our ego from the threat of being annihilated. Horney, Berliner, and Esther Menaker represent this view. In its terms, we relinquish our self to avoid anxious conflict with the person, usually a parent, on whom we depend for our very life. We accept suffering from the hands of the other as if it were love. We confuse love and hate. Masochism here is an adaptation of the ego into chronic and exaggerated self-critical, self-abasing behavior because we are terrified of being abandoned by someone on whom we depend, without whom we feel we cannot survive. And so we demean ourselves to appease, placate, propitiate the other whom we need so much. We are even willing to give up a center of awareness in ourselves, our place of willing, our capacity to grow independent and use our energy for creative self-expression in the world, in order to preserve our dependent bond on this other before whom we feel so helpless. We will even distort the reality of what we perceive to preserve this bond, confusing unkind and cruel actions of the other with affection and support. Thus we collude in denying our own value as a person. We take into ourselves the disparaging attitude of the other toward us and identify with it. That keeps us mired in frustrating repetitious behavior. The only sound we hear inside us is a same harsh critical voice. Thus our egos cannot develop new and different perceptions of ourselves as achieving, willing, creative.[5] Our ego, stuck in the repeated experiences of feeling small, unable, unworthy, is passively dependent on the other. We conclude we can never accomplish anything. We will accuse ourselves of everything to maintain the illusion of connection to the idealized other. We refuse to recognize the other's flaws and problems.

Somewhere, however, we know this is no good. Somewhere, we see and feel the unkindness and cruelty of the other. We get angry. We want to use our aggression to strike back, with all the aggression that is natural to us. All that we have left unconscious and unchannelled is stirred up in fantastic ways because we have developed no weapons of self-assertion or verbal aggression with which to fight or argue our case. Instead of responding positively to the previous aggression, we are afraid and feel guilty. We even feel we deserve punishment for our hostile feelings. Thus our masochistic self-belittlement increases. We give our power away to those who make us angry. Secretly, we hope this maneuver, forcing them into a superior position over us, will also prove a means of obliging them to keep taking care of us.

In this masochistic adaptation of ego toward other, we are trying to go back to a time when no conflict existed between us. We are trying to reinstate the unambivalent pre-Oedipal time when we were young enough so that it was appropriate to depend on others to take care of us, when everything seemed sunny and good. We do not want to rebel and strike back. And so our backward yearnings keep us trapped in an age that is too young to fashion relationship with others. We always fear they will leave us. Unconsciously we devise schemes to control others to stay in protective parenting relationships with us. We fasten on to one fantasy version of ourselves as humble, weak, meek, totally devoted to others who hold all the power. We offer this to them. Then they dare not leave us. Thus we also protect ourselves from the anxiety—the dread, really—of abandonment. To preserve a false security, the ego sacrifices its whole independent development.

We can understand how people think religious life fosters such masochistic self-deprecating attitudes. All power and might, all authority and goodness are ascribed to the Almighty. Who are we but miserable offenders? This is what has been called "I-am-a-worm" theology. How often we have heard about the excesses of the flagellants, or other distortions of the sacrament of penance, and that most central appropriation to evidence of masochism in religious devotion, the One who redeems through suffering death upon a cross.

In contradistinction, Erasmus offers humorous criticism of the true groveling tendencies of religious devotees. One will "spill out a hundred bushels of hymns" in praise of God. "Another will show a voice grown hoarse with chanting; another a tongue grown dumb under his vow of silence."[6]

In the third approach to masochism, I combine the theories

of Masud Khan and Jung. Here masochism is not an instinct, nor really a defensive strategy of the ego. Rather, it is a place of protection where we are hiding something that we cannot quite bring ourselves to find and venerating something that is not big enough for our devotion. We are hiding something painful that happened to us before our egos were developed, before we had developed a real object relation, that is, sturdy relation to another.[7] What is hidden is a part of our true self, something of great value to us and our religious devotion. Such masochism involves chronic low self-esteem and accompanying action of self-abasement. These become routines, whether attitudes or actions, and hold us compulsively. We are afraid to let go, fearing what might happen to us. We become addicted to these routines, having rerouted pleasure into them, having constructed in them elaborate defense systems, hiding within them precious pieces of self that we have lost or never even found. Our masochistic habits both express and mask, try and fail to manage some pain inflicted, some suffering endured and remembered in action rather than words, in behavior rather than idea. Our perversions, such as they are, tell the story of our suffering in the only way we can tell it, through enactments of repetitious self-abasement.

Jung speaks of a religious instinct—an inherent impetus to be conscious of relationship to a Deity, to devote ourselves in that all-out lavish loving that we find so well exemplified in Thérèse of Lisieux.[8] If we do not find a way to live with this religious instinct, it will trouble us just as much as hunger or sexual instincts do if we deny them. We fall prey to disorders of the spirit as costly to us as eating disorders. We burgeon with spiritual repression at least as upsetting as sexual repression. Or we suffer religious perversions, such as masochism, if we cannot find a way to live with our urge to submit and pour ourselves into adoration.

In masochistic rituals and attitudes of self-humiliation hides an unlived religious impulse to venerate.[9] We have fixed the impulse on the wrong object, giving to another what properly belongs to the transcendent. We have blunted the impulse to devotion, mixing it with pain and degradation. We are caught in covert ways of control, of self, of other, of the religious impulse itself, refusing to give over to the source and power of being. Instead, we try to regulate the power, change the purpose of this instinct.

Jung looks at this disorder symbolically, asking what meaning the suffering of masochism bears toward us. We find in masochism a compensatory movement to the cultural picture in Western society of the ego as heroic, striving, mastering.[10] Masochistic tendencies pull us down into our unconscious psyche, where we do not understand but only suffer. We are in the passive mode, where we feel ashamed to be caught in actions and attitudes we cannot understand, master, or change. Masochism pulls us into what Jung calls our "shadow," where is to be found all that we would like to repudiate, recover from, or improve upon. We feel sick, humiliated, and stuck. But it may be just here that meaning waits to greet us. Through the shadow we may be put in touch with forces which could and should live through us if we could consent to them. Here we find archetypal energies and images that ask for relationship. The suffering of masochism hides the passion of the psyche to give over the central place of the ego to conscious relationship to power at the source of being.

RELIGIOUS DEVOTION

This brings us to the main question: What is the connection and difference between religious devotion and masochism?[11] This crucial question addresses not only a religious giant like Thérèse but any person of religious sensibility. Are we loving God in our humility, or are we avoiding the rough tasks of psychological development where we have to learn to channel our aggression? Are we devoting ourselves to the glory of God, or are we merely mealy mouthing around, rejecting God's will in fact by refusing to become the person God created us to be? Are we trying to give unselfishly in the name of Christ's love, or are we secretly controlling others by appeasement, placation, manipulations for sympathy? Are we listening in our prayers for God's word and our own true words or are we denying them out of fear and pain? Are we really serving the causes of justice and peace, or are we finding a respectable surrogate for sadism and bullying, so that those who reject our particular cause fall under our persecutory eye, all in the name of justice and peace? Are we really helping downtrodden persons, oppressed in foreign countries, or are we condemning whole generations to unemployment, and all that that involves, by insisting our American companies immediately get out of those countries? Are we really praying for the souls of the world, or are we hiding out in our churches, our convents, and our monasteries? Are we really experiencing the communal life in church, or are we filling an emptiness that we are afraid of with church suppers and community fairs?

These tough questions lie along the frontier between the disciplines of depth psychology and religious faith. We cannot precisely delineate those disciplines. We cannot precisely separate psyche from soul, nor sickness from health. Nor can we answer those questions in a nice neat formula, so that we can conclude, comfortably, "Yes, I am doing the religious thing, not the masochistic thing." Part of the suffering of masochism is that we are never quite sure. We can never guarantee in our most ardent moments of devotion that we are not also a little bit mad. Equally, in our most mad moments there may also lurk religious devotion. The contrasts that I draw now as simple and clear, then, are not like that at all. In real life they are all mixed up. What I offer is a way to think about this fascinating subject, not a replacement for going into the country itself.

When any of us is caught by the pull of moral masochism we suffer the chronic feelings of inadequacy I have been talking about. We try to relate to the other or to the transcendent through appeasement and placation, because unconsciously we feel hostile and then guilty to feel that way. This moral masochism stands in sharp contrast to Thérèse's devotion to Jesus. She does not feel low self-esteem, but loved and lovable. She is not hostile, but alive with curiosity about her divine lover. Throughout her life, she actively exercises her will, her imagination for others and for God, whether in writing poems or drawing pictures or seeking countless ways to please. Why? Because it is so pleasurable; not to appease, but to please. Her pleasure shows in her appealing image of herself as a ball, not an expensive or fancy ball, but an ordinary one for the child Jesus to kick and throw and play with because it is so much fun. Here, then, is the first difference between masochism and religious devotion, the sharp one between feelings of self-abasement and inferiority on the one hand and experiences of pleasure and love on the other.

The second contrast is between dependency and self-assertion. When we are caught in a masochistic undertow, our ego denies any perceptions of what others are doing to us that is unkind or negative. We deny the painful perception because we cannot give up others. We depend on them for our very survival. We fear abandonment which will bring on us a sense of nonbeing, of nothingness.

Thérèse certainly feels dependent on the divine object, but not in a way that cancels growth. Instead, her dependence emboldens her. She wants to grow and grow up and use her mind, energy, imagination, and aggression always to come closer to the center. Thérèse asserts herself in ways aimed at union with Jesus. She wants to enter Carmel early and secures the permission of father, confessor, even the pope! Instead of going unconscious of the way others treat her or of what is painful, she looks to become more conscious through her daily self-examinations. Instead of defending her ego, she wants to expose it again and again to the anxiety of nonbeing which the masochist both avoids and ends up wallowing in.[12] Thérèse works at emptying everything out of her mind which is not God, so that only friendship with the Lord remains, making all her desires into the desire of oneness with Jesus.[13] She does not hold herself back from suffering but embraces it as part of life, not to revel in but as a way to use her aggression to see through the pain to a fundamental truth. She saw, for example, when she was eleven, that the other girls at school did not like her very much.[14] She registered the hurt, and suffered it, and used her aggression to see through it to the truth that all affections on earth are transitory. She used her aggression not to protect herself from the blow, but to penetrate to the truth that none of us are permanently part of a group on earth. She asserted her will consciously to choose to respond to each harshness with gentleness. She chose to take the hurt of others' indifference or criticism not as proof of her inadequacy, as a masochist would, but as part of offering her little suffering to Jesus' big suffering.

The third contrast is between sacrifice and give-and-take. When masochism catches us, we disown our negative feelings and drive other people crazy. The masochist sacrifices an independent ego in order to stay passively dependent on another without the conflict of ambivalent feelings. Caught in such a position, we give up our own development for a presumed safety. We disown our aggression, leaving it untamed and unchannelled so it seeps into others. We become the guiltmakers. Hypochondria, for example, offers untold opportunities for the masochist. A hypochondriac phones. We say, "Hello," and we hear a voice sigh in response, "Not so good." Immediately we feel guilty. It is our fault others feel badly. We cannot make them healthy, young, rich, let alone cure them. Masochists manipulate us into double-duty guilt. First, we do not save them from the misery of foul weather, fatigue, illness. We are made to feel guilty that we cannot make them thin without dieting. And then, we feel guilt for the rage their manipulations engender in us. We know all this is nonsense. We are not omnipotent. How can we control the weather? We resolve not to answer the phone the next time, or if we do, will speak out, at least gurgle in protest, maybe even shriek. "Take your symptoms and..." But the cry dies in our throats. Our words strangle over new guilt, for all these murderous thoughts. What do we do? We end up staying on the phone twice as long in penance, and even asking, "How do you feel?" a question never to ask a masochist. Masochists arouse our own sadism, but we feel so guilty for our ruthlessly aggressive responses that we end up appeasing and placating, just like masochists.

In contrast, the religious person uses her aggression, does not leave it unclaimed to drive others crazy. Thérèse wanted all she could get, all the ego, all the self, in order to offer all to the God she loved. She said, *"I want to be a saint,"* thus not stinting on using her aggression.[15] She actively took everything into herself to give it back to God and gratefully received what God gave back to her. The religious person makes a different kind of sacrifice from that of the masochist who refuses to claim and develop her ego. The religious person develops the ego fully, offers it in love to God, and takes back a fuller self in love. For example, like any good French housewife who sent out betrothal announcements, Thérèse sent announcements of her forthcoming marriage to Jesus and claimed all the merits that belonged to her husband and his family. She offered the Holy Trinity all the merits of Jesus and the Virgin Mary! This is passionate, aggressive, audacious love. When she offered herself as a burnt offering to the work and glory of God, she also took what was given back to herself. Five days later she felt a wounding by the dart of love which plunged her into the fire of mystical union with her divine lover. Thérèse's power lies in this give-and-take. She expects in love not only to yield, but to reap endless grace.

The religious person does not sacrifice to get rid of the ego but to gain the self in God. The religious person does not sacrifice to avoid aggression but to harness it in service to God. The religious person does not empty out the ego in purgation in defense against fullness, but in order to fill up with God's love, which then spills over into intercession for others. Thérèse was full to overflowing.

The fourth contrast centers on pain. Both the masochist and the religious person know a lot about pain and suffering. When masochism captures us, we see pain as an end in itself. The details of pain preoccupy us, even if they concern the most minute changes in bodily symptoms, moods, or the aesthetic accents of a ritual coiled with anguish. We are caught in bondage to suffering. We repetitiously rehearse misery-sharing conversations. We are held fast in self-loathing and degrading ritual. To be enmeshed in any kind of addiction brings great humiliation. We are prisoners of literalism. The punishing attitude or action repeats itself countless times with no meaning shining through. No symbolism beckons through the ritual. It simply grinds us down.

The religious person also knows pain, but only as a byproduct of the loving union. In our attempt to reach out to the ones we love, painful things will happen. We all know this about childbirth, for example. But any creative endeavor, whether originating a new meal, a book, a sermon, a prayer, an attitude, a liturgy, brings suffering. Any time we try to create an abundance of feeling, chaos and death may attack. Any of us struggling to create know this plunge into nothingness. Sometimes these forces attack us in the body and we actually fall ill.[16] In those moments part of the greatest suffering is not to know if we have fallen into masochism or have really reached what we love. Both may have occurred. Pain is not sought, then, but is not easily avoided. Thérèse tells us simply to accept it.

The more we embrace religious life, the more our defenses wear thin. We become more vulnerable to others' suffering as our devices of tuning out and numbing ourselves in the face of pain weaken. The victims of flood and famine in Bangladesh take on the faces of our own children, our own parents, our own neighbors. We suffer with the person languishing in prison, justly or unjustly. We feel the absence of one who has died, or suddenly been killed, of the baby who should have been born but died in the womb. We can no longer so easily stand aside. We are pulled into a current where everyone's life touches ours. What do we do with this heart full of these persons' unlived lives? Pray, the saint tells us, even though praying brings us more fully to share their suffering.

Thérèse's experience goes further. She wants to join Jesus in his pain, wants to join him precisely where his disciples left him and ran away. She wants to join the women who stayed at the foot of the cross. This crucial point, subtle and decisive for anyone drawn to the religious life, provides the fifth contrast between religious devotion and masochism. Here we look for relationship with what depth psychologists call a whole object, a true other, instead of looking for a missing part of ourselves. The religious person, as Thérèse shows us, looks through pain toward the whole object, Jesus, with whom she wants to unite in love. She wants to become her whole self, her biggest self, in union with him, and at the same time to hide her little self in his. She desires this union above all else and will take anything which furthers it. She chooses this. She is free.

When we are pulled by masochistic impulses we are not free, we do not feel whole. We are compelled to look for what is missing in ourselves, the part without which we cannot be whole. We must find it and thus we repeat and repeat the rituals in which the missing part is hiding. We cannot do without this missing piece. It is essential, and yet we cannot find it. We end up substituting rituals of concealment for the whole of ourselves and of others. That substitution enslaves us. We are not free.

Religious persons' relation to suffering is a willing one. If necessary they are willing to enter that place of nothingness, whether brought on by bodily pain or psychological anguish, where we are stripped of every attachment that competes with love of God. Thérèse voluntarily takes nonbeing into herself in a small imitation of Jesus' large redemptive work. Like other religious geniuses,

Thérèse chooses to put herself in situations where she will be separated from everything that separates her from God. She chooses the suffering that comes with giving up false crosses for the sake of what shines through, what endures, for the love that is stronger than death.[17] Thérèse says, "MY VOCATION IS LOVE!" Finally, she centered her service there: "My mission [is] making others love God, as I loved Him." *"I want to spend my heaven doing good on earth,..."* She summed it up: "To love, to be loved, and to return to earth to make Love better loved."[18] When we are enmeshed in masochistic attitudes we know nothing of the shelter of love that makes all things possible. Instead, we tangle with will power, either forsaking it or struggling to achieve it. We end up sacrificing what does not belong to us, other people's peace of mind or possessions, sometimes even their lives. We even presume to substitute ourselves in such a place as Isaac's, sacrificing our sanity, our allegiance to right and wrong, to secure and control attachment to the other.

Religious persons know a very different passion, to sacrifice only what is their own. In devotion, we offer our own for God's work. We do not seek martyrdom, but if it comes, we know we must meet it, not as an end in itself, but for the sake of union with God. We offer what belongs to us into the larger whole of God's life in others. In masochism the reverse happens: we call others and God into our tiny selves and our meaningless rituals.

The last contrast guides us best in differentiating masochism and religious devotion. Here the results tell all. Our masochistic experience produces suffering, in ourselves and in those around us. Full of sighs and our own inferiority, refusing to claim the good given us, we leave a hole in the human circle, where bruising constantly repeats itself and evil jumps in. We act like a magnet, attracting and inflaming aggrieved feeling. Insult piles on injury. We examine every slight, real or imagined, as proof of our inferiority or others' neglect. Our pain causes pain in others. We manipulate and control others, make them feel responsible, helpless to help us, and guilty because they fail. Masochism leaves us stalled in our fruitlessness. We do not live the life given us. 'Round and 'round, like the squirrel in the cage, we miss the exit. Sadness clings to us, the sorrow of unlived life. It is not so much that our religion is a neurosis, but rather that our neurosis has become our religion. We are keenly aware how much that costs us and keenly suffer it.

The true religious, as Thérèse shows us so well, knows the opposite experience. Whether in suffering or willing, or in daring imaginative gestures, she always points to the center. She feels loved and grateful, spilling over out of her own little cup into actions and happiness in relationship to others. Joy ensues. If we follow her example, we feel ourselves alive to Love in all things. Intercession is the special result. In it, a religious person reaches to a love which is no longer possessive. Here, religious devotion may resemble masochism, but the substance is different. Here is a love where we lay down our arms, open our arms, put power and pride and self-preoccupation at the other's feet. This is the *agape* of 1 Corinthians 13. Here love is poured out lavishly without obstacles. This is the first commandment and the second too. Love is given. Love gives back. Thérèse was not on a constant high; she did not have an idealized solution to any of life's problems, which is what we seek when masochism ensnares us. She did not expect magical protection from all the bad as the masochist does. In masochism we are pulled to dissolve our ego in order to get a fresh start. A true religious wants to offer up the ego, to bring it as a gift of love for love given. In our masochism, we aim to remain safe by getting rid of ourselves. In the religious impulse, we aim to give all of ourselves in union with the other, so that as the eucharistic prayer puts it, "He may dwell in us and we in him."

THÉRÈSE

Thérèse is not a masochist. Why, then, is she accused of being one? Because she threatens with the intensity, power, force, and mystery of her loving, makes us conscious of our capacity for that loving that she says is available to all. She makes us conscious of our resistance. We fear what we will have to give up to serve God. Religious institutions, unhappily, abound in examples that inspire our worst fears—when people's gifts are denied in the name of obedience to God. Nuns with contemplative gifts are forced to do administration instead. A socially active monk is set to work in a library. An academic mind is sent to do manual labor for the poor. A nun with originating insight for new patterns of community living is forced to live the old institutional

way. Religions can tell people, and have, that they are disobedi-
ent if they do not comply. This sort of sadomasochistic behavior
brings suspicion on religious life. In reaction, we withdraw.

Thérèse calls us out again with sound and simple directions
for the spiritual life. Above all else, we must try to discover God's
intention with each individual soul and encourage it. She did that
when Mistress of Novices. We must accept the individual as she or
he really is, in the idiosyncratic expression of being, and accept it
with love. Barry Ulanov writes, "One must love one's own way no
matter how awkward, and in one's own words, no matter how
inadequate."[19] Then we choose what God wants for us. This is
Thérèse's image of littleness. Our little way in everyday life reveals
the great exchanges of love. We find in daily tasks the suffering of
having scrubbed off us all the dross, the inessentials, everything
that competes with the exchanges of love. Thérèse helps us find
images for our own way. She described her way as little, hidden, a
plaything of the divine child. Her specific work was intercession,
a work that still affects us and draws us today. Love plunged her
into life. She summed it up by saying she wanted to be with Jesus
in all things, to make all exchanges loving ones.

Just before she died, Thérèse could not sleep because she
was suffering too much bodily pain. Her sister Celine asked what
she was doing, and Thérèse answered she was praying. "What are
you saying to Jesus?" Celine asked. Thérèse answered, "I'm saying nothing to Him; I'm just loving Him."[20] That is the point.
That is Thérèse's gift to Him and to us.

Notes

This chapter is based on a lecture I presented at the 100th
Anniversary of Thérèse of Lisieux's Entry into Carmel, at the Carmelite
Center, Darien, Illinois (September 1988) and later published in
Carmelite Studies V (1989).

1. B. Ulanov, *The Making of a Modern Saint* (New York: Doubleday, 1966), 116.
2. Ibid., 118.
3. Ibid., 119.
4. See S. Freud, *Beyond the Pleasure Principle*, Vol. XVIII, "Mourning and Melancholia," Vol. XIV, and also "The Economic Problem of

Masochism," Vol. XIX, *The Standard Edition of The Complete Psychological Works of Sigmund Freud*, trans. James Strachey (London: Hogarth Press, 1955, 1957, 1961). See also M. Klein, *Envy and Gratitude and Other Works 1946–1963* (New York: Delacorte/Seymour Lawrence, 1975), 28.

5. See E. Menaker, *Masochism and the Emergent Ego* (New York: Human Sciences Press, 1979), 61–63. See also K. Horney, *New Ways in Psychoanalysis* (New York: Norton, 1959), ch. 15.

6. D. Erasmus, *The Praise of Folly*, trans. Hoyt Hopewell Hudson (New York: Modern Library, Random House, 1951), 87.

7. See M. M. R. Khan, *Alienation in Perversions* (New York: International Universities Press, 1979), 148, 217.

8. C. G. Jung, *Psychology and Alchemy, Collected Works* 12, trans. R. F. C. Hull (New York: Pantheon, 1953), par. 11. For discussion of religious instinct, see also A. B. Ulanov, *The Feminine in Jungian Psychology and in Christian Theology* (Evanston: Northwestern University Press, 1971), 85–96.

9. R. Gordon also writes about this view. See her "Masochism: The Shadow Side of the Archetypal Need to Venerate and Worship," *The Journal of Analytical Psychology* 32, 3 (1987).

10. See L. Cowan, *Masochism: A Jungian View* (Dallas: Spring, 1982), 5–6, 11–12, 36–37, 41–42, 61, 98.

11. See A. and B. Ulanov, *Religion and the Unconscious* (Philadelphia: Westminster, 1975), ch. 9, "Moral Masochism and Religious Submission," for additional discussion.

12. For discussion of the anxiety of being and nonbeing, see A. B. Ulanov, "The Anxiety of Being," in *The Thought of Paul Tillich*, eds. J. L. Adams, W. Pauck, R. L. Shinn (San Francisco: Harper & Row, 1985), ch. 9 of this book.

13. B. Ulanov, *Making of a Modern Saint*, 103.

14. Ibid., 104.

15. Ibid., 135.

16. My husband and I experienced this in writing about envy and about the witch. See A. and B. Ulanov, *Cinderella and Her Sisters:The Envied and the Envying* (Philadelphia: Westminster, 1983); A. and B. Ulanov, *The Witch and the Clown: Two Archetypes of Human Sexuality* (Wilmette: Chiron, 1987).

17. See A. B. Ulanov, *The Wisdom of the Psyche* (Cambridge, Mass.: Cowley, 1987), 38–46 for a discussion of the false cross.

18. B. Ulanov, *Making of a Modern Saint*, 268, 316.

19. Ibid., 225. See also 125.

20. Ibid., 324.

Chapter 12

The God You Touch

THE CONCRETE GOD

The Gospel of Luke makes palpable Jesus' appearance to his disciples after his death: As they are talking among themselves, they saw that "Jesus himself stood among them. But they were startled and frightened, and supposed that they saw a spirit. And he said to them, 'Why are you troubled, and why do questionings arise in your hearts? See my hands and feet, that it is I myself. Touch me and see, for a spirit has not flesh and bones as you see that I have.'"[1]

How different from an abstract summation that leads us away from the senses, seeing them as perishable; away from the emotions, seeing them as illusory; away from appearances, the merely phenomenal, toward the absolute, determined to get to the essence of all that is, to that which is immutable and imperishable. Here, in contrast, is the God you touch, who invites you to touch, who steps forward and says, "Touch me." This God comes into our world of senses and emotions, comes incarnate into our concrete human world, into our personal and social life.

The power of Jesus, for those of us for whom Christianity is more than a formularized religion, is the Jesus we touch and who touches us. This God literally marks the bodies of those engaged in spiritual exercises, and marks their psyches too, with major symptoms, dreams, or experiences of the numinous. This God touches the body politic, the body of the church, the body of the human community, the body of this earth.

Christian feeling is body-centered. Jesus even uses erotic language to chide those believers who prefer formulas over the passions of faith, contrasting them to the sinful but faithful woman: You did not wash my feet when I entered, but she has not left off bathing them with her tears; you did not kiss me in greeting, but she has not left off kissing me since I entered. This God moves toward the world, enters it, suffers it and stays in it—enters it as blood flowing from his wounds into its wounds, as food feeding its soul, as a tree supporting its branches, as the vine its fruit.

This is not an abstract God but a concrete one, using ordinary events to disclose the extraordinary advent of God into our midst: God as mustard seed; God as woman searching for a lost mite; God as spirit ranging across our human experience to bring us in. Into where? Into the living reality of Christ who opens us into the unfathomable mystery of God.

The concreteness of Jesus that brings us to the doorway of Christ is the offense and scandal of the God we touch. That God should be glorified in humanity, that we should proclaim with Irenaeus, "The glory of God is human beings fully alive," and "The life of human beings is the vision of God," is offensive to those of us who want God to be above our scarred, suffering, conflicted, human state, who want a God sublime in a divine unity, a God whose humanity is merely a cloak or disguise.[2]

The concreteness of the God we touch assures us of our own concreteness, positively demands we accept it and know it. We must start with who we are in our own time in history, in our own culture, with all our own issues, both personal and communal. For it is here that God comes. As C. G. Jung reminds us, deeply as we admire Eastern religions, we cannot simply graft their flower of wisdom onto our different roots grown in the soil of a different history, different culture and sense of person. We can only grow toward the other distant flowerings by firmer rooting in our own soil.[3]

To recognize the importance of the concrete is not to fight free of all danger. We are exposed now to new temptations to distort the God who comes to us in the flesh into a god we make over and reduce to fit the image of our own concrete aims, needs, and values. Only too easily, we construct a god out of the flesh of our goals, causes, plots, hopes. We reject the God who comes in fullness into our world to choose instead an empty idol out of our own cult. Christ is always betrayed by those who think they love him; it is always by a kiss that Jesus, the God incognito, is handed over to the enemy.[4] Have we not seen in the last decades Christ as red, dead, black, female, gay, revolutionary, terrorist? Do we not constantly use Jesus to embody our causes, our crimes, our virtues, our sins?

To do this to Jesus is to bypass his real existence, to make him into no more than an ideal man, just a symbol. This is to avoid facing the incomprehensible, impossible, free, and grace-filled act of God taking human flesh, the Jesus who is also the Christ, the human person who discloses God in himself.[5] Before this we fall silent. This living Word breaks our words, bringing the death of human *Logos* in God's *Logos*. Here we meet the Other who puts our being into question by making all things new, by starting everything all over again.[6]

Our efforts to bypass this absolute beginning, to change God into our images, arise from our deep fear that our connection to God has been broken. We are afraid for our world and its fate, with its hates and divisions, its petty and active malice. We fear for our souls that seem to live in darkness, not before the living Word, but in mute isolation. This fear, this malice, this loss of connection makes us turn our causes into a god, a cult idol, and promote our notion of the good, our plan for peace, into a new god for a new neighbor. We take what is concrete and particular for us and translate it into an abstract principle for an abstract everyone. Our fear makes us seize what we know and need and foist it onto others as the good that all must have and accept.

The concrete disciplines I live with in the conjoining of psychiatry and religion, the worlds of psyche and soul, offer myriad examples of this fear that besets us. A fragment of a woman's dream makes vivid how perilous is the human condition, how at any ordinary moment something wild may break in. The dream shows the dreamer working in her office waiting to see a younger woman who comes to her for advice. Her office opens onto a garden, the doors giving immediate access to the outdoors, and leaving the office unguarded and vulnerable to whatever might come in. Just as the young woman arrives the dreamer hears a frightening, snuffling, growling sound. Looking out the garden doors, she sees a huge, black, bristling animal with what is apparently its cub. Is it a bear? A boar? A wolverine? The beast is on the prowl, actively searching a way to get into the dreamer's space, exuding a fearsome, primordial threat. The beast reaches the young woman, actually comes in with her and is somehow connected to her, though she remains oblivious of it. She knows nothing of its presence, let alone that it comes at people with her arrival. Thus the beast is left roaming loose to savage others.[7] That the whole episode connects in some way to the feminine is strongly underlined in the dream, for it is a female dreamer, seeing a younger female, and a wild mother-beast with its cub trying to break in. We can speculate that the attacking fear connects to an untamed feminine element, an animal feminine force that wants to break into the conversation between the dreamer and the young woman. Or that the young woman needs advice because she is unaware of her own savage female power.

The point of this dream fragment is to show us that fear can attack us from within as well as from without, from our unconscious side as well as from our conscious life, from the archetypal layers of the psyche as well as the so-called civilized sectors of society. We see that the line between inner and outer moves back and forth, making each permeable to the other. Inner fear can translate into outer disaster, with sad and tragic results. Some summers ago, at a McDonald's restaurant in Ysidro, California,[8] a man felt shot down in his inner world because of the outer event of losing his job and with it all hope of supporting his family and achieving the security symbolized by job and money. He could not reach help. He went out, instead, and shot down others, killed them. The beast in that man was let loose on mothers carrying infants, on boys and girls riding bikes to the restaurant to buy ice cream, on men and women stopping for a hamburger. If my dreamer finds no way to house the wolverine prowling in her, it too may translate inner turmoil into outer menace.

It is into this concrete world that the God we touch comes, to give us strength to abide inside ourselves even with our fear and to reach outside ourselves to others, to touch them with life, not with death. We cannot see anything if we are lost in the darkness of our fears. We need to be exposed to ourselves and to be pulled out beyond ourselves without losing connection either to the persons we are or to the persons others are. The dangerous appeal, both psychologically and spiritually, of so many of the solutions offered in our times—the political remedy, the route of the guru, the organization that guarantees peace, all the new diets—lies in their shiny multiple appeal, looking as if they are both concrete and yet able to pull us well beyond ourselves. In fact they are only too abstract and far beneath the life of self. In contrast, the evangelists of the gospel offer us their confidence in a simple accessible divine reality: they were there, and were touched by it. Now we must ask, what is this touch? How does this happen?

THE EGO

These are the questions I take up from the concrete departure point of my own work in depth psychology and religious life. For ours is a psychological century, in which depth psychology has offered to human understanding and imagination a large additional hermeneutic for interpreting human life and religious faith.

Depth psychology stresses above all else the necessary presence among us of the concrete ego world, both individually and socially, and thus our need to come to terms with it. We cannot go beyond the ego in service of others and in love of God if we have never reached the ego. For the psyche is the flesh, in which the forces both of darkness and light take up residence. We need the human ego to assimilate, house, and channel the beyond-ego, the non-ego forces that touch us and that we are so eager to touch in turn.

R. C. Zaehner, scholar and critic of Eastern religions and Christianity, gives a frightening example, in the figure of the mass murderer Charles Manson, of the danger of neglecting the concrete psychic ego container.[9] Zaehner claims that Charles Manson underwent a genuine religious experience of the great truth emerging from the Eastern religions: that evil is transience and ignorance, and salvation release from the impermanence of this world into an eternal now where opposites do not exist. There, in an eternity of being, evil and good, the choice to kill or to be killed, are all equally unreal. Manson touched the "now" beyond the ego world of good and evil and of conscience. He could murder serenely, without remorse. And he did just that. He butchered others, strangers to him, making them into stand-ins for parts of his inner fantasy. He had no ego reality with which to assimilate the religious insight that had somehow come to him. He had no accessible human society and culture with which to domesticate and channel the enlightenment that struck him. So it struck through him to strike down others.

It is clear—we neglect the flesh of the psyche at our peril. For we too can be pulled, like Manson, through to the other side, the non-ego side, with no way back, and there discover an undifferentiated force that is let loose against others through us. Neglecting the concrete ego container that must house spiritual insight is like living with an uninsulated electrical wire of high voltage. We need the assimilating, containing capacities of the human ego world lest we become utterly assimilated only to what happens to us, both individually and communally.

In contrast to Charles Manson, another figure brought to face the issues of ego and non-ego, Ety Hillesum, a Dutch Jew in her late thirties, whose inexorable journey to the death camps of Auschwitz, narrated in her journal, *An Interrupted Life,* describes a startling development of soul. She came finally to house what happened to her and her world and thereby achieved original insight into its meaning along with her ability to extend precious human caring to those around her.

In the midst of increasing daily restrictions—Jews banned from the park, from bike riding, from stores—she found herself, to her amazement, increasingly aware of God's goodness. She became a "kneeler in training,"[10] bowing down spontaneously to give thanks for her patch of sky or a sudden scent of wild jasmine, above all to celebrate people who had it in them to carry their own crosses. In the deportation camp she says good-bye to a friend shipped out before her to the death camps: "We were both able to bear our loss....What is so desperate about this place [is that] most people are not able to bear their lot and they load it on to the shoulders of others. And that burden is more likely to break one than one's own."[11]

In carrying her own cross, this Ety Hillesum found a radical interpretation of God's presence, there, in a community of Jews held ready for extermination, waiting in a deportation camp. This is "all that really matters: that we safeguard that little piece of You, God, in ourselves. And perhaps in others as well....We must defend Your dwelling place inside us to the last....I shall never drive You from my presence."[12] That way of touching God enabled her to go out to touch those around her: "Whenever yet another poor woman broke down...or a hungry child started crying, I would go over to them and stand beside them protectively...force a smile for those huddled, shattered scraps of humanity...for what else could one do? Sometimes I might sit down beside someone, put an arm around a shoulder, say very little and just look into their eyes....People said to me, 'You must have nerves of steel to stand up to it.' I don't think I have nerves of steel...but I certainly can stand up to things. I am not afraid to look suffering straight in the eyes."[13] Her resolve is simple: "Against every new outrage and every fresh horror we shall put up one more piece of love and goodness...."[14]

Carrying her own lot, this woman found God touching her and found she could touch others. God saw her, and she saw the woman next to her. Thus do touches of goodness go one by one by one, to build a piece of firm earth in an ocean of misery and desolation. Ety Hillesum housed in her concrete self in a concrete situation the concrete God who touched her. This touch did not take her out of this world, to lose her humanity, but plunged her into it with the force and staying power of divine love taking up firm residence within her humanity.

This God who comes to us sees our humanness, sees us as persons, and strengthens the power of our personhood. This God differs vastly from the great sumptuous abstract images of deity. There is no answering recognition of us as persons in a nonpersonal god of animal force, that sees the other only as object, as food. There is no answering recognition of us in the god of the historical dynamic where the person is merely a negligible instance of generalization. There is no answering recognition of persons in the figures of gods and goddesses now being resuscitated by some in psychological terms. The woman of a revived paganism is no more than a natural force—of blood, milk, fertility—and the gods, themselves reclothed as unconscious complexes, are without relation as persons to us as persons. But the God that touched Ety Hillesum was ultimate reality revealed to her person, in a personal way seeing her hidden person, enabling her to be in touch with others as persons, even in the anterooms of hell, the camps of death.

Like her, we must find our concrete ways, personally, communally, to accept our lot and to be grateful for what we can be in it, to find God touching us there. We need this concrete ego world lest, like Charles Manson, we become assimilated to the non-ego world, blasted away from ourselves and others as persons because we cannot house what has happened to us.

We are all too keenly aware that great powers, constructive, destructive, now lie in human hands and human psyches—nuclear power, power over the environment, political power. It is no small matter to learn to house such power and assimilate it to human culture, to communal egos. Without concrete channeling the reverse of a positive assimilation occurs—human culture and community are swept into terrifying whirlwinds of unhoused energy.

CLAIMING THE EGO

An example of the kind of concrete questions raised about religion in our time is emblematic of the place of depth psychology in this context. This example symbolizes the necessity to take seriously the dangers involved in any effort, religious or otherwise, to transcend the ego.

This important set of contemporary questions comes from women.[15] Can Jesus, a male, be a savior for females? Is the Christ figure a valid symbol for women, fostering in them a healthy integration of personality and acting as their chief help in experiences of God? Or has Christianity so identified the maleness of the historical Jesus with normative humanity that femaleness automatically falls to second-class citizenship in the community of God, a status we have seen historically translated as barring women from priestly office and power? Have women by virtue of their sex alone been excluded from full representation in Christ's ministry, a sex that is somehow less important than the male in creation and redemption? Is Jesus' maleness so precisely identified with the divine *Logos* that femaleness is excluded from divine status and participation?

These sorts of questions express concrete issues individual women and women in groups have experienced burningly. They cannot be dismissed. From the point of view of a depth psychologist the significance of these questions lies in the attempt to recover to full consciousness—both individual and collective consciousness—the tangible reality of women's experiences and the symbolic reality of the feminine. These questions reach to find the forgotten or neglected element, the lost sheep, the missing mite in the widow's house. These questions aid incomparably in establishing and confirming the ego identity of women as female believers and the ego-consciousness in our social life as it is identified with the feminine mode of being human and of seeking the divine.

Claiming the ego is important. The simple truth is that we cannot go beyond it until we have first arrived there, cannot transcend it if we have not found it, cannot go out of it in an askesis of disidentification and oblation until we first have possessed it.

Women's questions here are more than questions. They are efforts to feel God's touch in the concrete existence of all sorts of people in our society: God in relation to persons of different races, in relation to persons of different economic classes, in relation to persons of different political beliefs and differing political powers, in relation to persons in different countries around the world, in relation to persons of different sexual attitudes and experiences. We live in a time when collectively and individually we see the God we touch and who touches us in all the places we live. The questions of women here are an attempt to see and to feel and to know the most sublime and divine figure in relation to the most near and pressing issues of ego identity.

In that attempt, women's questions symbolize the dangers we all face when we seek concrete ego definition. Our concrete ego status—whether individually or in groups—can usurp first place for us, ahead of, before God. The question to the Jesus figure changes from Who are you? to Who are you for me? For us? The ego reality of persons, with its demanding need to be secure, to achieve, to make a grand mark, can so dominate us that soon our address to God is not to God but to what we need God to be. The utilitarian attitude that inevitably accompanies the rise of contents to ego-consciousness can become our sole focus, so that our whole congress with the divine fastens around the way God might empower us or our group. Have we not seen such a preoccupation in recent definitions of God according to sex, color, political, or sexual orientation?

When this danger encaptures us—the danger of putting our value in place of God's coming into the world—the symbol of the Christ who unites what we know with what we do not know collapses into a symbolic equation of the Christ figure with whatever our group norm is. We take to ourselves the decision whether or not the symbol of Jesus Christ is a valid one anymore, forgetting what Jung so sharply reminds us of: "Christ is still the valid symbol. Only God...can 'invalidate' him through the Paraclete."[16]

In this way our concrete world and its important values elevates itself to cult-and-idol status. Sin creeps in, establishing itself in the citadel of our most cherished values. We look to the Christ figure with a new demand, that he conform to our concrete reality and values, instead of listening to his concrete word in text, in prayer, in parable, and presence.

It is the very concreteness of Jesus, ironically, that will rescue us from this idolatry. Women, again with their questions, represent the shock we all feel in the face of this astonishing figure, specific, concrete, particular, who stands over against every definition and every abstraction we thrust upon him. The scandal of Jesus' particularity for women is that he is male. That is his offense. Further, this Jesus who is a man is manly—virile not limp, related not brutish, commanding not patronizing, suffering not detached. Nowhere in the texts of scripture do we find Jesus treating women in degrading ways. Not once. Indeed, we find the opposite. To the Samaritan woman he announces that he is life-giving water. To Martha, he is the coming resurrection. To the Magdalene, he is risen. He speaks theology with women, as well as summoning them, judging them, comforting them, using them to represent God in parables. He shares his intimacy with women, praises them, forgives them, knows them. He really knew women's lives, really spoke to them, called them out to follow him.

The concreteness of this person stands boldly against the ways we try to cover him, make use of him for cause, party, or platform as we abstract his particularity to illustrate our values. Looking at who Jesus is in scripture is to liberate him from false abstraction. He is the one who emptied himself to take on our humanity and bring a new humanity. What women face here so

strongly is the journey of faith facing all of us. The question is,
How do we bring our concreteness to God, to look at and to hear
whom it is God sent to us?

What, in fact, does Jesus show us concretely? He shows us
the depths of the Christ who opens onto the infinity of God, the
Christ in whom there is no male and female, the Christ who presides over all maleness and femaleness. Responding to the concrete concerns of feminism, Jesus liberates us from the
caricatures of patriarchy, revealing a living God who breaks
through and transcends the divisions of sex among us, where
being male does not equal excluding female. Here is an all-inclu-
sive love and power that makes us one out of our distinct opposite parts. Thus we can grasp the experience of the saints who
found in Jesus breasts, mothering, birthing—Bernard of Clair-
vaux, Julian of Norwich, Gherardesca of Pisa, Umilita and Mar-
garita of Faenza, Aldobrandesca of Siena, to name just a few.

TRANSCENDING THE EGO AND INCLUDING THE GAP

If the first thing depth psychology teaches us is the necessity of a
concrete ego, both personal and collective, in order to touch
God and to receive God's touch, the second thing it teaches us is
that there exists in the human psyche and soul a surge toward a
sense of I-ness that transcends mere ego functioning.[17] To flour-
ish, this sense of I-ness depends upon relation to an other, a non-
ego, a beyond-ego subject that exists in its own right. Such a
sense of self is born out of the relationship of ego to other. It
unfolds in the space between ego and other and continues with
us all our life long. We find our sense of self in the mutual recognition of parents and children, of lovers, of friends, of soul and
creator God. Such experience of I-ness transcends the divisions
of the psyche into id, ego, superego, into unconscious and conscious. It reaches to include all parts of our experience, the mad
ones too. We cannot reach a sense of self without including the
least parts of our experience, or the most upset.

Grasping the centrality and large grasp of this sense of I-
ness rearranges our understanding of madness. It no longer contrasts with health for us. Rather, we see health and madness both

belong to a sense of self and oppose the experience of not being really alive. D. W. Winnicott articulates our debt to persons suffering madness, who make us face the question of what life is about. "You may cure your patient and not know what it is that makes him or her go on living. It is of first importance for us to acknowledge openly that absence of psychoneurotic illness may be health, but it is not life. Psychotic patients who are all the time hovering between living and not living force us to look at this problem, one that really belongs not to psychoneurotics but to all human beings."[18]

Masud Khan, Winnicott's editor and a distinguished analyst in his own right, goes further: "In our clinical work, sometimes, it is more important to sustain a person in living than to rid him of his illness....The patient is willing to stay ill and suffer the consequences so long as he or she is 'living' or 'not' living."[19] Madness can be best described as a gap in our being. Khan says these pockets of madness come from not being able to translate into psychic experience what happens to us. As a result of our psychological inactivity, what we do experience goes into oblivion only to turn up later in private mad states of being. Thus, "the need of the mad is not so much to know as to *be* and speak."[20] For madness, like health, contains its own sense of I-ness, its own way of knowing and elaborating inner and outer worlds. In the gaps of madness lies a creative potential for individual and social living. In an adult life we experience and actualize this madness through art, literature, through a sharing mutuality with an other, and through mystic states.[21] We seek in madness that same precious sense of I-ness which transcends the merely adequate ego functioning so often equated with health.

Khan gives an example of a young rock musician who consulted him with a strong complaint: "I am with life but not in it....I am an onlooker." Only on drug trips and when asleep could he get near the sense of I-ness which he so prized that he then stayed drugged, in a somnambulistic state, in order to find again a sense of self. He described fleeting glimpses of what he sought—this sense of I-ness that transcends mere functioning, that depends on relation to something beyond the self while also preserving and fulfilling it. This experience came to him through his music: "When I hear the right tune in that state I *am* the tune, which I am also hearing....There are four of us: the tune, me listening to the tune, and the tune and me as one. And yet again we are also all one. That is the joy of it."[22]

It is that joy to which both Buddhist and Christian ways lead. But we do not reach it without including everything in those ways, even our madness.

Our task, individually and socially, is to make space for all the gaps in our being, and thus to include the mad parts. We must face how hard we make it in our society for our mad parts to speak and to be. Either individuals are drugged in mental hospitals, going without speaking for weeks, or by an act of a legislature are dumped back onto city streets, unhoused and unheard, despite their yelling out at us at street corners. Madness, like health, is a way of living in both inner and outer worlds. If we do not make space for it, it will translate itself into homicide, suicide, every physical symptom, all the terrors, like the amassing of pressures around the heart, or the amassing of weapons in countries. It will reduce itself like the translation of complexities into oversimplified ultimatums of the "all or nothing" variety—diet plans, unbreakable prayer schedules, the dictated conditions that must precede people sitting down at peace tables.

It is this self, concrete, mad and sane, this sense of I-ness, that touches God and that God touches.

What is this touching like? It is pain and it is joy.

We not only may seek, we are forced to seek that concrete sense of I-ness in touch with the transcendent through the compulsion of illness, obsessive fantasy, entrapping depression, or disintegrating anxiety. We can be brought to a sense of I-ness through health or madness, but not through that conformity where we forsake our vocation, or turn away from the summons to be in the concrete place before us with its concrete tasks. The parts of ourselves and of our world press to be gathered in, to be made into self and world. To refuse that gathering and the tasks it imposes is to turn from the will of God that wants to be realized right here in the doubt and insecurity of our concrete self and concrete world. We are called to accept without reservations the particular concrete situation in which we find ourselves, to consent to make order in the chaos into which we are born.[23] That is our cross, and we must carry it.

To try to gather all these parts means pain, because some of the parts are missing, some even lost, a few banished. To set out to collect them means looking for the thing in ourselves we despised or feared, the thing in the world we avoided. It feels like opening a door to a horde of barbarians, to the beast in the garden, to all the crude, unthinking, impulsive needs, dreads, and hurts hiding in the unconscious. That is painful. Even more painful is what follows, because when unconscious contents become conscious, they transform themselves into concrete tasks and obligations.[24] Here is an example.

A man dreamt that he was present at the crucifixion of Jesus: "I could not see but I could hear. And I heard Jesus yelling out and cursing in his agony of suffering. I was afraid. I thought, they never tell you this part. I felt I was admitted to an awesome secret." For the dreamer, the Christ figure was doing what the dreamer needed to do and was avoiding— registering consciously his pain, the yelling and cursing pain itself, and with it the outrage that such a pain could exist. This was the missing part for the dreamer. This was the pain he was avoiding. For he was undergoing the death and rebirth of his whole religious orientation. But he wanted to duck the suffering, to repress it, which only paralyzed his action. He rationalized his experience as not important, because he was there to serve others, which paralyzed his emotions and, far from serving them, foisted his unconscious pain onto others around him. His task was to take up his missing part and feel it, to submit to his own pain.

This task confronts all of us, to deal with what touches us and not avoid it, to collect our missing parts: the neglected and overlooked and banished parts of our inner and outer populations. We are never touched in the abstract, only in the flesh. The marks of our own frown lines, our overweight, our sleepless nights, our neighborhood crime, our neglected land or polluted air reveal this truth. God waits in those parts, waits for us to visit the part left in the prison of repression, waits for us to offer some life-giving water to outcast sexual parts, to give food to starving parts. All these bits must be gathered in and nourished. As Lady Julian puts it, All must be knit in, must be one with God.

So the first avenue of pain leads to our opening up to our outcast parts, to our learning to make room for the mad bits, the gaps, like the dreamer with the beast, needing to find room for its prowling savagery.

A second avenue of pain opens from the first, from our weakened defenses. When we try to collect all the parts of ourselves and our world into consciousness, we can no longer so easily protect ourselves through denial of the suffering around us and within us. We can no longer succeed in blocking out what is there. We cannot split away from it. We cannot disown what is painful as if it did not touch us. Now we are touched. We can see what others go through. The hungry child of another continent bears our own child's face. We can no longer just blame our neighbor for everything, saying, in effect, the beast is yours, not mine. The stone we cast hits us as well. We see how we are all touched by evil and how we must struggle to help one another. Our old opaqueness to suffering is diluted to a palpable transparency, and our pain increases.

How odd and how paradoxical! Our work, in order to receive all parts of our psyche without segregating any, both liberates and unifies us. It makes us stronger, yet also delivers us into pain. For now we feel more immediately what we go through, and what other people endure, all of which opens us to more pain, and to more grace, as we disidentify from any and all of the parts. Being open now to the whole, to including all the parts, detaches us from the false security of identifying with any one of the parts as if it were the whole truth.

When we identify with a part-object in that way, it does not feel false, but rather secure, a certainty. We know the truth, we assure ourselves; we know the plan; we possess the answer. To realize now that this part is but one among others and that our earlier security was false is to embark on a new and often greatly painful askesis. The order now is detachment, disidentification, a sacrifice of the security of being in control. It means, for example, that we must give up the luxury of lecturing our neighbors, even accusing them of major failings if they do not identify with our point of view. Now we must listen to our neighbors, both outside ourselves and inside. In social terms, it means seeing that true community includes all parts, that we need each other's parts to make up a whole group. It means recognizing that our differences enlarge us. The inner venture, in the same way, in order to collect all the parts, matches the outer venture in its industrious efforts to include all the parts in the wholeness of the human family.

When we think of this disidentification in concrete terms, the pain and the purpose become evident. To take the sexism of society, for example, as the only lens through which to view reality, is exposed as simply one part, one means of interpretation, which will turn false and deluding if taken as the sole part, the only way. It means, then, renouncing the power-fixated philosophy that inevitably springs from psychologically identifying with a single perspective. Similarly, if we take the psychological as the defining perspective, or, even more popular today, the political view as definitive, reducing all parts to this one, we distort the parts and, thus, inevitably, the whole. Identification with a single point of view must be sacrificed along with all the false power and false security that came with it.

If we take seriously the pull of both psyche and soul, we will be pulled out of such identifications. This does not mean the question of sexism is not real and significant; it does not mean the psychological dimension does not exist; it does not mean that the political factor does not pertain. Their reality is made all the more vivid as their proportionate place is more truly estimated. What is exposed to our understanding is that these perspectives are not ultimate, but contingent, like all the rest of human life.

If we take seriously the pull of psyche and soul, our temptation to make cult idols is exposed. We see how we abstract the concrete issues that touch us when we try to impose them on everyone, instead of respecting the concrete ways others are touched in their psyches and souls. In religious terms, we may be moved to make an act of oblation, to offer up to the really ultimate, to the God who touches us, these precious and valuable points of view by which we are so concretely touched.

We might well ask how far does this go? Religious exercises, both East and West, tell us it goes relentlessly forward even unto death—the death of the ego.

The process of identification and disidentification can be seen as a ceaseless motion of psyche and soul. We collect bits and pieces of what matters to us and realize again and again how much they matter while simultaneously realizing how contingent and partial they are. In some final sense they do not matter or matter only as a part of the whole. Hence we offer them up, transcend our identification of ourselves with those values, and move out of this concentration on parts to a whole larger than ourselves.

In the process we are pulled loose not just from our problems but even from attachment to our highest values, to the theories we cherish most or the national causes to which we give energy and money or the goals we have approached with such devotion. The deeper we go into seeing and accepting the concrete, the more we see its partiality. This single value, this particular cause, cannot be equated with the center of existence. It matters, but it cannot be identified with the source of everything that matters.

Mystics tell us that when God draws near and acts directly on the soul, the soul is pulled loose from all it has loved in place of God. Psychologically and spiritually we experience the transcendent God as darkness, as an unavoidable gap between us and the ultimate. In Christian language, the gospel makes clear we do not get to God from our human side. Our images of God and traditional doctrines do not give us God. At best, they simply point to divine reality. Our images cannot be equated with God. Indeed, in God's drawing near, it is precisely those images that are abrogated, broken through, transcended. In Buddhist language, even the notion of imagelessness is an image that must be discarded, as we are handed over into the silent still point at the center of all. This is a perilous passage for any believer.

A woman advanced in spiritual exercise and in Jung's method of active imagination put herself into the New Testament story of the woman who had hemorrhaged for twelve years, the one who secretly reached out to touch Jesus in the crowd, whom Jesus in turn demanded to know, calling out, "Who was it that touched me?" This woman envisioned herself in a Palestinian village, dragging herself across a hot and dusty street toward the crowd that surrounded Jesus, to reach out and touch him so she could be healed. But the fantasy took its own self-directing turn. It was too crowded for her to reach Jesus. She gave up and lay in the dust. The crowd broke up and Jesus prepared to leave. Suddenly he turned and called to her, "What do you want?" She fumbled and stammered, saying, "I suffer, I am divided, pulled apart." Jesus looked at her directly and said, "That is your cross and you will have to bear it!" "Bear it!" she screamed in anger, "You talk! You will be crucified and many others will be killed in your name!" With that, she said, "I drew out an axe and threw it at Jesus, intending to strike him." But Jesus reached up effortlessly and caught the axe lightly in his hand, then turned and walked away. End of vision. No tender solicitation here, no traditional healing touch. Not only is the woman made to claim her own aggressive strength and anger, but she is confronted with a Jesus entirely other than her expectations. They were broken.

In any serious spiritual life, we must come to a gulf that cannot be crossed from our side. We must find ourselves stripped of all expectations and aids, all human programs and procedures, as we stand at the edge of the ocean of infinity. Our finite ladders—of theology, of spiritual exercises, of psychological theory and political programs—do not reach across to the other side. The gap is not bridged from where we stand. We are emptied of all we possess. We discover our true poverty, our radical dependence on God.

Paradoxically, we never reach this point unless, taking the concrete seriously, we do identify what we love and need and even plot. But in doing so we will find we have moved out, disidentified, as we come to see that nothing human delivers us across the gap to the other side. Here the mystery of the two natures of Jesus bears in upon us, for there is no Christ without Jesus, but it is Jesus who comes to show us the Christ who lives in God.

The coming of the Holy One inevitably brings with it that darkening and emptying of the ego world which empties out the collective ego world too. What happens to the individual psyche must happen to the collective consciousness of society. We are brought to the great gap, to the end of our plans for saving the world. In these perilous times, when we worry about the survival of our planet, our country, our culture, perhaps the darkness and remoteness of God is only the effect of God drawing near. Like the mystic whose soul the divine presence darkens, making human will, intellect, even imagination no longer effective, the soul sitting in the dark, aware of a greater presence, but unable to do anything but wait upon it to be drawn into it, so it may be with our collective ego, our social state. The *umbra Dei* draws near, pulling us out of identification with our social plans, making us feel the death of our ways of saving and perfecting the world. Perhaps it is upon that dark presence we must attend, as it transcends our collective ego and pushes it from center stage.

The female way may be our best guide here. We should remember that gaggle of Marys left at the foot of the cross, the only ones of Jesus' followers who endured the stripping of all hope and expectation about what he was to each of them— teacher, brother, lover—and what he was to be for the world— priest, prophet, king, overthrower of the established order. All that is stripped away, annihilated, made into nothing. Yet still the women remain, near the concrete person, wanting to tend the concrete body. They stay through the death of their projections, through the suffering of their disidentifications, stay on through a painful, ignorant, frightened waiting, wanting to receive the utterly new, even if afraid, waiting and wanting even unto the dark coming of his death. They stay on in the dark and through and beyond the dark. And so it is to women that the resurrection is first announced.

THE EGO FOUND

To the emptied, waiting, disidentified ego, keenly aware of its poverty and its dependence, something special happens. Someone comes. Psychologically, we describe this as the subjective character of the human ego being taken over by a greater subject. Jung calls it "the breaking in of the Self" upon the ego, moving the ego over, away from the center of things. One's psychic universe is thus radically rearranged so that the unconscious can now get in. Consciousness is opened for good. The ego is not knocked out, but simply moved over, made porous, made permeable to a larger subject, which takes up residence in the middle of our sense of I-ness. We are clear now in our disidentification with the center, that we only work on the ship, no longer are its captain. The sense of I-ness, of which the ego is a part, also opens onto the unknown and lives comfortably with it. We know the unknown is there and can touch us at any time and we accept that is the way things are.

In religious practices of East and West, this is the state of consciousness aimed for. The ego is pleased to empty itself and open to another influence, not felt as our own activity, even though it operates within us. Rather, we feel the presence of an other, a non-ego, a subject objectively there that takes our own ego as the object of its attention and care. This is the summons and this is the task. For the other lays hold of us here and asks everything, asks our constant presence. Paradoxically, it is just in the death of an ego-centered existence that a sturdy concrete ego is also needed to receive the One who comes, lest like Charles Manson that touch destroy the ego because it is not tough enough really to respond but can only identify. Such identification is totally inappropriate, like a mouse identifying with an elephant that with its touch can only crush the mouse.

Christian and Buddhist exercises draw close, at this point of breakthrough to another dimension of consciousness beyond the ego. In both systems, the ego feels it has undergone a death, that it has been supplanted by a new and different kind of awareness. In neither system, however, does the ego feel it has brought about its transformation, despite all its readying practices, ascetic exercises, meditations, and prayers. The ego knows it has not itself caused this to happen. Christian discipline specifically stresses that the ego is not the author of this transformation, only one part in a large plotting. The author of all things transcends the ego's consciousness, breaks in upon it, invades it to liberate it, to bestow upon it as a gift a new center which itself will author a new life for us. Indeed this presence that comes does not even offer the ego a set of choices to which it must respond, but instead changes the whole story entirely, so that what the ego had thought was its own crucial questions are now revealed to be mere fumbling answers to anterior questions put to it. The ego is like Job, who pressed his questions on the Almighty only to discover when Yahweh answered that the answers came as prior questions addressed to him. It breaks in on Job that his view is so small, so partial, so limited as he tries to grasp the perspective emanating from this large center. So Job gives up his questions, offers them up, moves to renounce his narcissistic point of view in his love for the whole.

It is precisely at this point of offering, this stirring to gratitude by the generosity of the gift, that we want to give something back, to bestow somewhere, somehow our small concrete ego and our sense of I-ness. Thus do we enter the mysterious exchange called love, an entrance that brings the psychological dimension to its fitting end. Like any concrete human dimension, however valuable, it is not omnipotent or ultimate. And so depth psychology comes to a stop at its own borders.[25] To go further we must seek theological categories. We do not want to make a cult idol out of a psychological system.

Depth psychology's great work is to unshackle us, to help remove obstacles in the life of the psyche, to help us find the secret life hiding away in the bits of madness that we suffer. But when it comes to embracing that life and living on into it, psychology must be transcended. We enter into the space of a relationship between our experience of I-ness and the transcendent Other. The psychological question now is, How do we house this greater subject that takes up residence in us, radically altering the center from which we live? How do we accommodate this "tremendous stranger," or this "mysterious density of being"?[26] How do we, how can we, live in relation to it?

The theological questions ask, Who has taken up residence within and among us? Who is this One? Christian faith answers, The One with the largest sense of I-ness. The One who is like us and yet opens onto God. Jesus, the concrete person who is the Christ, the self-giving, the self-suffering love of God. This is what now lives in us, this active love pouring itself out into the world.

The psychological questions are, What is this experience like? How can we understand it? How do we house this swift running current? What is it like to live this way? They complement the theological questions that ask, To whom do we live in relation and who do we thus discover ourselves to be? Are we like Mary now, asked to house and bring forth into the world this God who awoke the heart of a girl in Nazareth as he moved within her like a giant?[27] Does the incarnation mean God's life will be ours? Does it mean our life will be caught up in a ceaseless love bursting out into the world, bringing being, sustaining being, glorifying being? Is this the Trinity's secret, that the unending exchange of love to love to love, of love begetting, begotten, bestowed, is housed now on earth? Are we then the female earth, the concrete earth, that houses this love and provides residence for the three-personed God in our own particular personal lives?

Psychologically we can describe something of this new life, and theologically we can define it as our small selves living now in the largeness of Christ. Psychologically this experience of being is an experience of our own particular I-ness made possible, supported, caught up in something greater than ourselves.[28] We feel our I-ness in touch with what is, what matters at the heart of things; we feel united around a core. We know ourselves linked up with a greater being, one which is endless and unfathomable, so that we cannot define it but can only walk around it, telling of it. A feeling of spaciousness pervades, of circulating life and breath, indeed of something breathing into and through our own breath, making us feel alive in body, mind, heart. The dualities of subject and object are softened, made unimportant. We live in an other and that other lives in and through us, yet a sense of self relating to other—not becoming other—persists vibrantly. A joyous sense of being alive and living creatively exists, the parts connected, linked up, where ideas and emotions, bodily instincts and spiritual aspirations connect. New things happen. New thoughts appear. New feelings begin and a sense of dwelling in and with all others grows. And so we feel touched and deeply in touch with others in a world of shared existence, knowing with them a caring solicitude and a sense of inherence. What afflicts our neighbor is also our affliction. Henceforth we do not do good works or act helpful but rather live, one with another, in the presence of this live center that holds us all together and in being. From this joy spring acts and attitudes toward others and the world, spring small, concrete, significant acts to share this joy, to gladden in it with others. Our motivation for the good thus differs radically from good works done out of guilt, fear, aggrandizement, or urges to power.

Theology describes this experience as grace, that which nullifies the divisions and polarizations of male and female, Jew and Greek, slave and free person. Dualism gets broken, dissolved, set aside, knit into a new state that is one and with which we are one. Yet, being caught up in this current of connectedness quickens our awareness of evil, too, the evil let loose by this very connectedness, an evil that would break this current, interrupt it, supplant it with separation, dominating distinctions that would violate the very possibility of being. Evil widens the gaps, makes holes in the fabric of being. Above all, evil looks to kill the simple happiness in being that this new consciousness confers.

In theological language, this current of connectedness besieged by evil is the piercing of Jesus whose blood flows out into the world. When we are caught up in this divine life, its piercing strength flows through us into the world and the blood of God too, from suffering to suffering, from forsaken to forsaken. François Mauriac says we imitate not Christ but his executioners.[29] We can understand why. Christ brings an experience of being, its new creation, not a new government, not a new world religion or rearrangement of the sexes. He brings the antecedent experience of our being connected up, linked to the source, no matter how frail, flawed, fagged, or failed we may be. From that anterior connection to being flows the experience of I-ness and we-ness that makes possible justice and peace and a fullness of life, religious, sexual, or whatever, establishing the conditions for their coming into being. But we always begin with those values of justice, peace, health, which we prize as our best human values. Adhering always to those old, nagging departure points—our causes, our cult idols—keeps us outside the sphere of Christ's new being, this zone of new creation, making it impossible for us to penetrate it. That is the judgment, and the shadow side of grace. Thus Christ's good releases evil, because it does not automatically produce our values for us nor meet our terms and we hate that. Thus, frustrated rather than fulfilled, we join in wanting to kill simple happiness in being.

From a theological perspective, the contrary attitude and experience, a reveling in the happiness of being, is the point and the way God is glorified. This is the transformation that religious experience works. God is no longer an object for our contemplation, nor an idea to be thought about, but instead a living presence whose hallmark is joy. The medium here is our particular concrete souls and psyches and shared existence together. God living in us, among us, immediately present to us.

Looking back, we understand now the pain of the ego disidentifying from the things it put in place of God, and the even greater pain as it disidentified itself from those things that mediated God to it. All those things get taken apart, are broken into pieces, to fall into the gap between us and God. What the ego is moved to and made ready for is to be filled by God's immediate presence, no longer mediated to us by concept, cause, image, or ritual. God is here in the flesh, burning in us.

This flame makes us want to disidentify with our little gods because we want to be touched by the unknown God. Yet the unknown God we want to touch us is not utterly unknown—for it is known in Jesus, and the worship, theology and art that portray him. This God—known and knowable however unknown—burns in us.

It is this flame that makes the soul go out of itself into the world in loving acts and attitudes. For who is it that the soul experiences, that the psyche struggles to house? It is the inner being of the divine, circulating, linking up humanity into the inner life of God. To live there is to glorify God, God in the concrete, the God who touches you and thus the God you touch.

Notes

This chapter was originally presented to the Middlebury College Conference on The Christ and The Bodhisattva with the Dalai Lama, Middlebury, Vermont, in 1984. The papers were later published in *The Christ and The Bodhisattva*, eds. D. S. Lopez, Jr. and S. C. Rockefeller (Albany, N.Y.: State University of New York Press, 1987).

1. Luke 24:36–39, Revised Standard Version and Knox translation, *Bible* (New York: Sheed & Ward, 1950).

2. Irenaeus, *Adversus Haereses* IV, 20, 7, cited by D. Carmody, *Feminism and Christianity* (Nashville: Abingdon, 1982), 35.

3. See C. G. Jung, "Foreword to 'Introduction to Zen Buddhism,'" *Psychology and Religion: West and East, Collected Works* 11, trans. R. F. C. Hull (New York: Pantheon 1939/1958), par. 905.

4. See D. Bonhoeffer, *Christ the Center*, trans. J. Bowden (New York: Harper & Row, 1960), 36.

5. Ibid., 84.

6. Ibid., 27–28.

7. All psychological material, unless otherwise noted, is taken from my practice as a psychoanalyst, with gratitude to those persons for their generosity.

8. James Oliver Huberty, aged forty-one, an unemployed security guard, killed twenty-one people and wounded nineteen others at McDonald's Restaurant in Ysidro, California, in July 1984.

9. See R. C. Zaehner, "The Wickedness of Evil," in *The City Within the Heart* (New York: Crossroad, 1981), ch. 3.

10. E. Hillesum, *An Interrupted Life*, trans. Arno Pomerans (New York: Pantheon, 1983), 62.

11. Ibid., 201.

12. Ibid., 151.

13. Ibid., 192.

14. Ibid., 198.

15. See Carmody, *Feminism and Christianity,* 21; see also R. R. Reuther, *Sexism and God-Talk* (Boston: Beacon, 1983), 135; see also E. S. Fiorenza, *In Memory of Her: A Feminist Theological Reconstruction of Christian Origins* (New York: Crossroad, 1983), xviii. See also E. Moltmann-Wendel and J. Moltmann, *Humanity in God* (New York: The Pilgrim Press, 1983).

16. C. G. Jung, *Letters*, 2 vols., eds. G. Adler and A. Jaffé, trans. R. F. C. Hull (Princeton: Princeton University Press, 1973 and 1975), II, 24 November 1953, 138.

17. Psychoanalysts from different perspectives recognize the fact of this larger "self." See H. Kohut, *The Analysis of the Self* (New York: International Universities Press, 1971), xiii–xv; see also H. Kohut, *The Restoration of the Self* (New York: International Universities Press, 1977), 99, 133, 310–12. See also D. W. Winnicott, *Playing and Reality* (New York: Basic Books, 1971), ch. 4.

18. Winnicott, *Playing and Reality,* 100.

19. M. M. R. Khan, *Hidden Selves: Between Theory and Practice in Psychoanalysis* (New York: International Universities Press, 1983), 97.

20. Ibid., 85.

21. Ibid., 181.

22. Ibid., 48.

23. Jung writes, "Doubt and insecurity are indispensable components of a complete life. Only those who can lose this life *really*, can gain it. A 'complete' life...[consists] in the fact that one accepts, without reservation, the particular fatal tissue in which one finds oneself embedded, and that one tries to make sense of it or to create a cosmos

from the chaotic mess into which one is born." Jung, *Letters*, II, 10 April 1954, 171.

24. Ibid., 172.

25. See C. G. Jung, "Psychology of the Transference," *The Practice of Psychotherapy, Collected Works* 16, trans. R. F. C. Hull (New York: Pantheon, 1946/1954), 192n.

26. T. Merton, *The Ascent to Truth* (New York: Harcourt, Brace & Co., 1951), 298–99; see also L. Dupré, *The Deeper Life* (New York: Crossroad, 1981), especially chs. 3 and 4.

27. Merton, *Ascent to Truth,* 317.

28. An example of one's own self being concretely in touch with something greater was given on the ABC television interview with Valerie Brisco-Hooks, Olympic Gold Medal winner for short-distance running, 1984. She said of running: "When it's right, you slip in between space and time and it's better than anything else on earth."

29. See F. Mauriac, *The Son of Man*, trans. Bernard Murchland (New York: Collier Books, 1960), 88, 90.

Chapter 13

Being and Space

Space is a category we must look at much more closely if we are to understand being—*our* being, as persons. Described in its simplest terms, the discipline I profess, psychiatry and religion, focuses on making space for persons, an enabling space for us to be persons in relation to the collective forces of our unconscious life and the crushing pressures of mass-mindedness of today's world.

Is it a luxury to place our small persons at the center of attention in a world afflicted with war, famine, and political strife? I think not. For without our being persons, persons together, persons responding to persons around the whole inhabited world, we have no world, we have no future. Without the space to be persons, our being cannot fill up with value; we cannot have being; we cannot be.

BEING AND VALUE

Value gives us a sense of being, not abstract being, but here-and-now being, as the specific persons we are. Value gives a center to our being. But to have the being that we can fill with value, we need space, a living space of our own that is contained, yet not crowded in upon or invaded.

Depth psychologists of all schools recognize the primordial importance of the female as mother in establishing our first space to be human. For example, Alexander Lowen of the Bioenergetic school of depth psychology stresses that an infant's experience of body space in relation to the mother's body in the act of feeding is the first exposure to being as unconditionally accepting, or as non-accepting. Without this experience of acceptance or a later experience that fills this gap, we never really inhabit that first and last space of human existence—our body. Melanie Klein, who takes Freud's research into the superego—that great executor of value—as far back as possible into earliest infancy, asserts that we get our first tastes of goodness and badness in the eating rituals established between mother and child. D. W. Winnicott uses the image of a mirror to describe a mother making space available to her child. In looking into the mother's face as she looks at her child, the child sees its own face reflected there, and finds in that reflection a space in which to discover its being, its "I am." There is an unexpected correlation between Winnicott and the theologian Karl Barth who uses the same image: Christ is our mirror, asserts Barth, in whom we see reflected the image of our true being.[1]

In these examples we see recognition of the tremendous impact women have on the foundations of our being human. The feminine virtue of nurturing value through making space is exercised by men and women alike, not only for infants just born, but for the many kinds of birth experiences that occur throughout our lives—in education, in worship, in the processes through which we gain insight in analysis, or the ways we learn to build something new—an idea, a love relationship, a prayer, an act of courage.

The beginnings of personal being come from shared space. For space is the category of relationship. We have no space of our own except as it is defined in relationship to other spaces, the multiple and interpenetrating spaces of our unconscious life, our life together in society, and our life in relation to Being itself, to what we call God. Depth psychology speaks to these three spaces.

THE SPACES OF THE UNCONSCIOUS

Depth psychology opens the spaces of our unconscious to us in its focus on the shaping power of our fantasies, our dreams, our wishes. The existentialist Medard Boss insists that the space of our dreams possesses its own authentic existence that we must come to meet and allow to live on its own terms.[2] We should not, he says, always approach our dreams in terms of conscious reality, translating their meaning into the vocabulary of consciousness.

Rather we should live there in our dream as fully as we try to live in waking life.

If, for example, we meet a tiger in a dream, as one man did, we need to live out that encounter.[3] We must not on waking take refuge in translating the tiger's reality into the terms of another space, saying, for example, that the tiger is really only our repressed aggression or our animal instincts. No, the tiger is the tiger. We must not destroy it in our psyche by exploiting its existence for our conscious use, any more than we can condone the killing of real tigers to steal their skins for fur coats. We need to work out the space of a living arrangement with our psychological tiger that permits it to be itself and permits us to reflect on it without destroying it.

We must see that effective ecology and the preservation of the natural nonhuman environment begins in the most intimate terms of our unconscious space.[4] Failing to respect the life of imaginary nature as it inhabits us psychologically spills over into an inability to respect the life of actual physical nature in the world. We invade our environment with conscious intentions to translate its life into something for our use. We need to build a large enough space to accommodate the terms of life of both the human and the nonhuman.

SOCIAL SPACE

Psychiatry and Religion as a discipline speaks of social space in terms that break down traditional dichotomies of the public and the private, of group and individual. Harry Stack Sullivan puts it aptly: There is no self in isolation; our self at its core is social; our sense of who we are grows out of the space we share with others.[5]

Moreover, when we fail to establish our own space as persons, our world becomes increasingly depersonalized. We speed on highways without thought of our neighbor in the next car or the pollution we build up in the atmosphere. We shove our anger into aggressive stances from which we assault each other. Instead of working through the anger, we spread it around, making people mad at us and us at them. Our disagreements then become a series of disjunctures in space. We speak of communication gaps, generation gaps, ideological gaps. We create a social space that has holes in it that we cannot fill up with feeling nor make a human bridge across.

We may leave our aggression inert and unharnessed for human use. We can become "spaced out" in a hundred different fashions. We quit the world. Or we use our social space to work out what remains unlived in our personal space. From the inside we feel crowded in upon by unconscious forces that seem to flood our space, pushing us even into murder. Our frustration, grief, and anger may all run together, reaching such an intensity that they must burst into social space. Then innocent persons are pulled into new spaces as "hostages," trapped in buildings, in planes, in trains, or in the sight of a sniper's rifle. These persons have lost their own space and become sucked into the spaces of someone else's madness, as stand-ins for the terrorist's acting out of a drama with unconscious forces. Need we even remind ourselves of the horror of a whole social space overtaken by madness as in the Holocaust of World War II?

SPACE FOR MEANING

Subjective space is not easily reified until we fear we may lose it. Enough pressure can overwhelm that space, as totalitarian systems and invasion by unconscious forces have demonstrated again and again.

The impact of the meeting of depth psychology and religion is to move us to find space for the poor and outcast parts of ourselves as well as for the poor and outcast of our world. One enables the other. We learn to make space for our fear, anxiety, and hate, and for the suffering that lies hidden behind the hate.

We learn to make room also for possibilities of being. We discover that our anxiety often stems not from nonbeing—over what fails to be there—but rather from what we feel when confronted with the face of the being that is there, waiting to be lived. We suffer the *anxiety of being*—anxious over our daring to live openly with others, our daring to risk a confidence in ourselves, to love, to trust, to try to make our world a better place in which to live.

We learn to make space for meaning and to know that the life of faith grows down as well as up, down into the spaces of unconscious mental processes, to take root there. That rootedness alone protects religion from becoming an instrument of sadism that cramps the space of the soul because too much life has been repressed out of it. Here Tillich's use of the phrase "the ground of being" carries force. We experience God as grounded in the specific concrete spaces of our lives—our unconscious lives, our lives with others, our lives around what we value, all that matters to us.

In making space for these relationships, we are sometimes opened to the grace of being in such a way that we are able to accept what in fact we are, our "real self" in contrast to what Karen Horney calls our "glorified self," composed of sentimental wishing and power demands dictating what we should be.[6]

With this groundedness, we may come to see that grace itself takes on spatial dimensions. Grace breaks in upon us, rearranging our living space, quietly enlarging it, always working to make it more spacious.

VISIONS OF SPACE

I am going to pause here, because as T. S. Eliot says, "Words strain, crack, and sometimes break...slip, slide, and will not stay in place."[7] So we are going to look at some pictures of space. Artists have known how to express spaces which words do not always describe as well. Artists give value to space, confirm and deepen the images we see. The pictures come in five groups. The first shows large spaces that house the human:

> Turner: *The Old Chain Pier*
> Monet: *Gare St. Lazare*
> Pissarro: *Paris Boulevard*
> Cezanne: *Boats on Shore*

The second group shows religious spaces, ritual spaces:

> Grünewald: *Isenheim Altarpiece*
> Dürer: *Adam and Eve*
> Titian: *Altar of the Vendramin Family*
> Van Gogh: *Pieta*

The third group shows the spaces of madness:

Blake: *The House of Death*
Goya: *Witches' Sabbath*
Fuseli: *The Nightmare*

The fourth group shows the spaces of painting and design which capture the textures of our unconscious life:

Mondrian: *The Red Tree*
Mondrian: *Broadway Boogie Woogie*
Gorky: *Agony*
Pollock: *Blue Poles*
Hofmann: *Push and Pull No. 3*
Picasso: *Young Girl at a Mirror*
De Kooning: *Woman No. 2*

The last group shows us crafted space, made to accommodate human beings. One way or another, these pictures proclaim the value of being human. They offer ease to our physical being:

Paris Metro Entrance
Mies van der Rohe: Chicago Apartments
Wright: *Falling Water*
Oud: Stuttgart Row Houses
Mies van der Rohe: Farnsworth House
Alberti: Sant' Andrea, Rimini
Wright: Johnson Wax Company Building
Van Gogh: *The Chair*
Braque: *The Chair*

FINITE SPACE: THE EGO AS CONTAINER

One of our lifelong tasks is to find our own space in this world, to find what an illustrious line of depth psychologists call our "ego." The ego is the space of our finitude, the space for our human identity. The ego is our container, out of which we relate to others, to unconscious processes, and to transcendent meaning. At its best, our ego takes on spatial dimensions, enabling us to experience our three-dimensionality in the world, confirming the fact that we have height, width, depth, texture, surface. We are in space together, next to each other, taking up space as palpable, visible presences. In good love relations we know the mystery of mingled space.

Central to our ego container is our body-space, our tangible way of being who we are, or of not being who we are, of abandoning our space. Most of us suffer at one time or another this invasion of body-space by negative self-images, often engendered by cultural stereotypes, particularly sexual ones, that dictate one image of an ideal man or ideal woman. Thus we endure our "fat" days or "ugly" days, when we attack our bodies as too bulging or too round, too big or too thick, too small or too flat.

The rapid growth of emotional illnesses clustered around our body-ego shows us a litany of ways we feel ejected from our own body-space. The alternation of anorexia and bulimia (starving or stuffing ourselves), the freezing of sexual response and the frenzied search for sexual sensation, the spiritual greed of gorging on ever new ways to meditate and to hallucinate without ever satisfying the soul's hunger—all make plain to us that we live in troubled times.

Our time is not without its bits of light, however. One touching enlargement of ego space comes from women, traditionally the carriers of images of space, for home and rest, for refuge from the world's harassments, for pleasure, for new life in pregnancy, for the uniting of spirit and feeling. In our time there have been many women who have changed our images of body-space. There are, for example, the women who made public their private battles with cancer and the invasion of their body-space first by disease and then by a surgeon's knife in a mastectomy operation. They tell us through *their* experience that *we* can rescue our value as persons from the pressure of fashion images that dictate a stereotyped shape for all women. These brave women show us the potential flexibility of even our most intimate body spaces. These women, who go on living with the mark of the anxiety of dying on their bodies, help all of us with our own fear of death. They show us that we may find ego containment even next to the seemingly uncontainable spaces of death.

Central to our ego container, too, is the precious force of consciousness. Consciousness in one of its major roles is the power to make space for what we used to call as children "me, myself, and I." There we can sort through feelings, turn over ideas, become aware of needs, plan actions. At best the gift of consciousness extends our space in the world. Our ego container enlarges in good conversation with friends. We exchange perceptions and mix what we inherit from tradition with the new and original insights we conceive.

One man's dream conveyed to him the power of consciousness. He dreamt he was in a church at a holy water basin. The basin was at the end of a long channel that seemed to go downward into the cellar. The water rose from below, against gravity. He looked down into the channel to see where the water was coming from and saw instead a mirror that did not reflect his face but rather reflected the mysterious source of the water. When he awoke, the mirror seemed to him an image of the power of consciousness to reflect on the source of things.

Many of us abuse this power. We do not meditate on the link between the largeness of Being and the small containers in which we catch it. Instead we build airtight ego systems. We leave no space for unanswered questions or unfelt feelings. Theology calls this "making idols." We see it sometimes in large, tightly packed theological schemas. We see the same thing in the current fad of political religions that would turn hard stubborn mysteries into problems that will be solved, that must be solved, if we could only strike the right attitude. We see it in some psychoanalytic theories—and that is the greatest irony of all. Theories that set out to support the value of the person end up leaving no space for the human being. The person gets lost in the terminological and structural overhead. We try to take ourselves apart like machines. We detect the way our narcissism, in its secondary mode, constricts our object-relations which, in turn, shape our internalized ego ideal that has undergone splitting, so that we find ourselves trapped in the persecutory position unable to move on to the depressive modes. Before we know it, we are nowhere to be found.

THE SPACES OF MADNESS: SIEVE

When we talk about ego containment, the centrality of our bodies and our minds, we must also talk about what attacks and weakens them: the spaces of madness.

Madness afflicts most people. How many of us know firsthand its disintegrating effects? To characterize this experience, one patient used to say she felt as if her insides were "sweating."

At one extreme, madness makes us feel our ego container is like a sieve. The stuff of life seems to slip through all our attempts to hold it. We feel holes in our sanity, gaps in our ability to be present to ourselves or to others. Into those holes and gaps floods anxiety, which makes us feel that nothing will ever stick to the core of our lives. The world drops away; we disintegrate into bits.

Under such pressure we come to know firsthand the psalmist's description of being lost, of lost being, of living in exile from the human family, from the place of meaning. We know firsthand what theologians and philosophers write of as the abyss of nonbeing, the void, Heidegger's "nothingness." And worse, we know we are capable of living a counterfeit life, of creating a false self in order to flee from the terror of being swallowed up in spacelessness. As the existentialist analyst Ronald Laing puts it, we become "impersonations" because we do not take hold of our own person.[8] We give away our souls in adapting to others' expectations. We commit perjury against our own truth, which is true and ours, however small and odd and eccentric it may be.

Madness is not a private phenomenon. Because our self is social, the madness that afflicts us seeps into the social sphere as well, and social madness oozes into our self.

In our sieve-like state we create vacuums in our social space. Where there should be presence and exchange among us, we insert anxious resentment. If someone extends a hand to us, we recoil, feeling invaded. If no hand is offered us, we resent being neglected. We have no container in which to hold our own excitement. So the excitement turns into incitement and anxiety, and we turn against the very persons or ideas that first excited us. We are consumed with envy and fear. We are unable to respond with feeling.

We know something of the apocalyptic emptiness of

Dante's circle of hell reserved for the trimmers. Jesus spoke of trimmers and their inability to accept being, their refusal to take hold: "To what shall I compare this generation? It is like children sitting in the market places calling to their playmates: 'We piped and you would not dance; we wept and you would not mourn.'"[9]

In the throes of trimmerdom, we refuse being. Failing to take hold in our personal space, we spin into spirals of madness, from rejection to rejection, pushed to the borders of human community.

What rescues us? The person-to-person container. The therapeutic partnership is just one example of this: one person reaching to another. Together, between them, they make a space in which an ego container can be constructed, or the missing pieces of ego can be found and reunited.

An example of such a missing piece of ego reality is given in a woman's dream image. This woman possesses many gifts, but she lives unsure of herself. Often she falls into anxious, painful self-doubt. She dreamt she was with a group of people and with her, belonging to her, was a convulsive child who could not speak but only writhe helplessly on the floor. There is no question of "analyzing" this left-out, helpless part of herself. The first task is to make a space for it, to contain it within a human relationship.

From the analyst's side, we discover again and again that in reaching out, we are reached too; in finding missing pieces of another's ego, we discover missing pieces of ourselves as well.

THE SPACES OF MADNESS: DENSITY

If one way we fall into madness is through the holes of a sieve-like ego container, an opposite way we suffer madness results from our ego taking on too much density. In a sieve-like state we lack firm boundaries and possess no containing space to hold what happens to us; we suffer from "insufficient finitude," as Kierkegaard would say. At the opposite extreme we close up tightly into what Kierkegaard calls a state of "shutupness," a mute density, opaque and defended, with no egress into life, an "insufficient infinity."[10] Here we try to guard our lives only to learn the truth of the scriptural passage: In finding ourselves we lose ourselves and in losing them we find them.

One man, as an adult in analysis, remembered that when he played the game of hide-and-seek as a boy he was wildly anxious to play well and to keep himself firmly in hand. But he hid so thoroughly that his playmates could not find him and they gave up and went home.

For many of us it is the blows of fate that force us to contract our ego space into too narrow a focus. Blows of fate all but break us, leaving little space for feeling, remorse, or mourning. Our child dies, driving us nearly to madness with grief, or into congealed rage at our helplessness in the face of death. Our marriages break up. We lose our jobs. We lose heart, and are unable to live with zest or imagination anymore. We lose our faith in God. Our visions for the future space of our nation are violated and ended by assassins' bullets, by senseless war. Our earth space is ripped up and plundered, leaving no assurance that those we love who live after us will have breathing and planting space in which to grow psychological roots as well as food.

We may fasten on hate as a way to survive, hate of someone we hold responsible for the death of our loved one, hate against a system of government, hate against a particular class in society— the rich, the poor, the bourgeois. Our intensity of hate is a way to hold onto our sanity, or at least try to, by closing the door against large emotions we cannot contain, emotions of sadness, perplexity, or helplessness. Hate makes us contract our egos into a posture of tight closure, like a clenched fist.

Such density in our own egos produces its own brand of social madness. We hold on too hard to theories, to the point of fanaticism. We become purveyors of systems or of antisystems. We become Freudians or Jungians or Marxists, preferring abstract theories to the concrete persons that hold them or the human beings about whom they have been fashioned. Our systems divide up our social space into areas of *us* and *them,* segregating people into separate spaces. We lay the foundation for building a scapegoat psychology where we make the *thems* responsible for the suffering that has come to *us.* Or we cover our lack of space by asserting a cult of nothingness—insisting that life is full only of despair with no place for laughing, for eating together, or for human friendship. We make our space in the nonspace of the alienated life—antipsychology, antipolitics, antiliterature, antihope, a world of antiheroes sinking into the dissociated space of extreme passivity.

We become mere adversaries or advocates, forgetting as we become helpers of the poor that we too are the poor. Equally, in attacking the rich we forget that we too are the rich. And in becoming practitioners of mental health what do we forget? That we too are among the ill, and are the receivers of health from the ill.

Masud Khan writes of the lethal effects on society of our inability to make use of our dream space. When we cannot establish a dream space in our inner reality, we tend instead to exploit our social space and our relations to others, to act out there the tensions pictured in our dreams.[11] We lack what my husband and I called in the book we wrote together an "intercessory ego" that stands between our unconscious instincts and our shared life with others. As a result, we then experience our instincts at the expense of other people.[12]

In a similar way, if we fail to entertain our fantasies as fantasies, we are robbed of both fantasy and reality. We have no fantasy space. We live out our fantasies as if they were reality.

Again we see the interrelatedness of our selves and society. For this mixing up of fantasy and reality, so encouraged in a world that leaves too little space for the person, provides one of the principal dynamisms for acts of social and political terrorism. Lacking an ego container, we turn the world into a battlefield in which to work out our rage and frustration. Having lost our subjectivity at the world's hands, we lose our capacity for objectivity at the world's expense. It does not matter, for example, who specifically is killed on a hijacked plane, who specifically dies in a building wired for bombs. There is no specific subjectivity. We no longer perceive concrete subjects; they have become mere objects for our own subjective drama, which has merged with a political cause. We grab at other people's space because we feel robbed by others of our own space. As victims, we victimize others. Other people have no name because we have lost our own name. The world becomes our private container and ceases to be a world for others.

This is what gives politics a bad name and makes religion not a force for social justice, but an opiate to deny our personal anger by merging it with political slogans. This is why good people and bad come together in times of violent revolution, in the collaborations of terrorism, and why we live in a world in which there is so much of both.

To the genuine problems existing in our shared space, we add our personal problems. We avoid tackling our own problems by merging them with social issues, which only compounds the complexity of the social issue. We refuse, for example, to look at personal causes of our anger. Instead we hide our problem with anger in the justified anger that actual social injustice engenders in most of us. Thus we betray the causes we endorse. For we use them as hiding places for problems we will not face in ourselves. Just as involving ourselves in social causes cannot wait until we are "healthy," our facing personal problems cannot wait until all social problems are solved. This way we invade the new space we are trying to create with old bureaucracies that squeeze out the life in the space. We set up administrative procedures that have an ersatz eternal life of their own, so that even when we work hard to solve a problem and reach a solution we never really solve it. Up it comes again later, to be discussed all over again from the start, with all the old disguises and bureaucratic obfuscations. Thus we demoralize ourselves. We talk progress while going 'round and 'round in a squirrel cage, never really beginning or ending anything. Space becomes cyclical. As Freud would say, we have achieved "a monotonous return of our origins," never clearly finite with precise boundaries able to act as a container for us.[13]

When we mix up our personal and shared spaces, our fantasy and reality spaces, we damage our communal space. Fantasy is a place of play, a space to relax, to rest from the demands of reality, to let off steam. Laughing is a balm even to great soreness and suffering.

Religion at its best, with its tradition of imagery and ritual, constructs a communal space to contain our shared fantasies and wishes for a better world. There we find a place for the primitive parts of ourselves to live alongside our reality as adults. In the ritual of the Eucharist, for example, we have space to express our unconscious cannibalistic wishes, and our deep need to relate to goodness by eating it, not only to envision God as the "bread of life," but actually to lay hold of the bread inside ourselves.

The task that confronts us is to find space for the person within the life of the group and space for the group within the life of the person as firmly and clearly as we grasp the palpable, edible, digestible divine bread. Freedom is found only in putting ourself at the disposal of others in unmistakable openness, to act with love, in the world. The rest is merely spreading neurosis around.

The really different course, the promise of genuine change, comes only in person-to-person contact. In mental illness, for example, the only saving gestures take place in the space created in a relationship between one person and the next. We may complain that building personal relationships seems too meager and too slow, given all the problems of our times and all the people suffering from lack of personhood. Maybe so. But this works. And once it works, we do not have to repeat it. Being is there.

Human space restores humanization. Like the parable of the Good Samaritan, our neighbor is the person right next to us, people we know, people within reach to whom we can make a difference. This may be slow, but it is possessed of endless bountiful effects, like the mustard seed that grows into a resting place for birds and animals and people alike. The communion of saints is the group that provides space for the person, for *each* person.

SOUNDS OF SPACE

I pause again, now to play music, to permit us to hear how we fill up our space with sound. Musicians give value to our space, to the images we hear. All the sounds we shall hear approximate, one way or another, states of being, reflecting our multiple states of being.

From Mahler's *Sixth Symphony,* we hear contrasting sounds of serenity and the impending horror of this century glimpsed by the composer in its first years.

From Brahms's *Trio No. 1,* we hear the sounds of different voices which must speak together in order to speak at all.

Earl Hines and Johnny Hodges in *Caution Blues* open up to us an ambling through space, with humor. They recall Richard

Wright's definition of the blues: We go around a chair clockwise. Then we go around the chair counterclockwise. Finally, we stand aside and sum up the value of what we see.[14]

From Varese's *Poeme Electronique* a speaking of strange space, disordered, as he writes, by "tragedy and inquisition."

From the *Sanctus* of Stravinsky's Mass comes a bold human salute to the spaces of holiness.

Finally, Mozart in his *Ave Verum Corpus,* almost at the end of his life, in his own misery, proclaims the immensity and joy of Being made incarnate. The Holy is honored in finite space and in human voice as the true body of Christ.

INCARNATE SPACE

Life together becomes possible as we open our personal ego containers to space beyond the ego. Like the philosopher Husserl, who claims that concentration on the phenomenon leads to depth rather than a veering away from it, so depth psychology finds that we are drawn through our ego containers into what is beyond them without losing any significant part of this world.

Freud writes of being able to break through the world of illusion into the realities of love and work. Edith Weigert writes of shedding our "as-if" self for the sake of embracing our true self in authentic living. Jung writes eloquently of our ego container, as the center of our conscious life, establishing connection with the Self as the center of our whole psyche, conscious and unconscious. Jung's description of the Self recalls that of Bonaventure, that champion of anti-necessitarian space, of space which is no specific space but a circle whose center is everywhere and whose circumference is nowhere.

Here the question of value takes on shape. Here we ask not only who we are, and who we are in relation to others, but also, who we are for. Where and to what do we devote ourselves? For what meaning, for what love, do we empty our space to make room for new being?

Psychologically, value operates as the reason we get well, or, for lack of it, the reason we fall ill. Judeo-Christian tradition describes this as incarnate space: it is the space of the person that God enters and fills, rearranging our contours, making new things possible.

Paradox marks this incarnate space. We find our ego containers as we open them to what is beyond our ego—to the unconscious, to others, to transcendent meaning, to the fullness of Being. It is precisely this opening of our ego container to a spaceless dimension that solidifies its own dimensions in concrete space here and now. Our ego must both open to and be opened by the space of the infinite if our ego is to be a secure finite container. We do not first secure an ego before we have any experience of the worlds beyond it. One woman put it trenchantly when she came for therapy: "I am not here to get 'mental health'!" No indeed. Finally and basically, we do not want to feel healthy but real, not well adjusted but alive. Health finally is not enough. We want a life with value.

In our own small ways, we partake of the paradox written about in Philippians 2 of the New Testament with its mysterious descriptions of God's emptying of the immensity of Being to take on the contained space of concrete human life. Similarly, we too find our freedom to be all of ourselves, to be all we are or can be, in such a *kenosis*, a pouring out of what we have, an opening of containment to space.

One of the ways we experience this paradox of infinite space in finite space is in the interchange of self and society. We bring into the social sphere the values of being a person, and experiencing the fact that God dwells among us in our shared space.

One example is found in architectural arrangements of space, for instance in building new kinds of city housing projects. A traditional style clustered several very tall buildings together, each of which had many apartments to a floor. The crime rate in such an environment was quickly found to be high; people living there lived in fear of their space being violated. A new architectural design arranged living space in smaller units—buildings of seven floors with four apartments to a floor. Each building was surrounded with a small park, with benches and trees. The crime rate dropped to less than half of its former total. The reason? People living there felt their personal ego space extended to include their neighbors on their floor in the building and in its surrounding small park. People felt an active and willing responsibility for each other and their shared space. Not only was the physical space less a breeding ground for crime; the architectural arrangement of psychological space provided the conditions for the growth of human relations.

Another aspect of living with paradox recalls some words of our religious tradition from Psalm 118:22: The stone the builders rejected has become the cornerstone. These words take on special psychological meaning. We see that the problems with ego containment that we experience as liabilities and as negative forces may also show themselves as positive. Our liability, our negation, becomes a paradigm of our possibility of being.

The problem we face when our egos become like sieves, full of holes of madness and anxiety, may also take on positive meaning. These holes can become entry points for something positive to shine through. Through the holes another presence may appear to our absence, a sanity to our insanity, a space to breathe surrounding our constricting fear. Our experience of falling away to nothingness we may now feel as a means of giving way, of consenting to a larger framework beyond our ego's control, where we may come to know something of the grace of being accepted as we are—broken and with problems—*before* we "get healthy."

One man put it succinctly: "We are able to accept all this junk in ourselves because we are loved by God." His statement came out of his experience of being plagued by attacks of confusion when he literally would feel himself sink into nothingness, often falling asleep in the company of others or when working. He felt himself as dissolving, slipping away from consciousness into a formless state. Like a sieve, everything fell through the holes of his ego-consciousness. This very attack of confusion, that he wanted to reject and "get cured from" if he could, became the cornerstone for his opening his ego container to a larger scope of being. Now when he felt this confusion coming over him he answered it in a new way. He went into his room, shut the door, lay on his bed, and did nothing; absolutely nothing. He emptied out. Instead of falling helplessly into a void, he entered it by choice. After a time, he would feel "being begin to seep into me from the ground up." What looked like laziness actually was his dwelling in silence, a contained awe before what he came to feel was the mystery of being. In one of these times he had a short dream that made the statement: "When *you* are here, *It* is *there*."

Our problems with too dense an ego, with holding on too tightly in order to survive, so that we become hard, compact persons, may paradoxically be a means of leading us toward its own solution. As we consolidate, condense, become more opaque, with less light and less lightness, we may enter our own place of dread, our own hour of Gethsemane, with no way out.

Thomas Merton claims that all serious prayer leads us to this experience: to explore that inner wasteland of being that is also mirrored in the world around us. In that desert we explore the ground of dread—not the dread of violating superego taboos or social norms, not the dread of id instincts overtaking us, not the dread of external dangers. We come face to face instead with "a profound awareness that we are capable of ultimate bad faith with ourselves and with others; that we are capable of living a lie."[15] In our strategies to save our lives, we have lost what really matters.

In that silence, that darkness of Being, before God, we let go. We give up holding onto ourselves. We open our clenched fist and offer the little we have—the self we would preserve, the ego we would save, the pattern of self-transformation we would follow, the past we would change and the future we would engineer, letting go to a mysterious presence, a love that survives dread.

In less exalted language, one woman describes this motion of soul with a homely analogy: "It is as if I were a bunch of flowers packed too tightly into a vase. I have to take my hands and pull the flowers up and out a little to make spaces between them for the light to get through."

THE SAVING SPACE

Opening our ego containers to value, to a devotion to what is beyond ourselves, gives us a sense of the saving space of God. We do not get to God by subtraction, by narrowing ourselves to a condensed dot, nor by losing ourselves through the spaces between our fingers. We get to God by enlarging, opening our ego container, letting God get to us, pouring out of ourselves into the lives of others, and being filled in our emptiness by an accrual of being that enters from God's side.

The incarnate space is the saving space we make for each

other, which is made for us when grace breaks in upon us. Then we know we have a space of our own and we enjoy it here and now. We know an end to envy. We do not want to deny anyone else his or her own space. We enjoy others' occupation of their space. We have a basis for freedom that we get to, not by sizing up the world around us, but by sensing where and what our own space is and how it opens and is opened by what is beyond ourselves.

Saving space is where we confront the largeness of Being, paradoxically, in the small container of our self. At its best, the church and our tradition of religion honors this space and guards it as a refuge from the world and as the entry point by which God comes into the world.

In such experience of saving space we have intimations of the space of resurrection. Out of this broken space—where illness paradoxically also shows us a way to understand health, where violence marks off the preciousness of peace, where our body-ego with all its frailties also is the locus of incarnation of being in space and time, where our limited consciousness also gives us a mirror by which to reflect on the infinite—here we catch a glimpse of our identity in the space of resurrection. This is not the space of decay now, but the space where time is arrested, where we glimpse eternity as space outside of time.

Notes

This chapter originally was given as a lecture at my inauguration as Professor of Psychiatry and Religion at Union Theological Seminary, New York City, delivered on March 22, 1977.

1. See A. Lowen, *Depression and the Body* (Baltimore: Penguin, 1972); M. Klein, *Love, Guilt and Reparation and Other Works, 1921–1945* (New York: Delacorte Press/Seymour Lawrence, 1975); D. W. Winnicott, *Playing and Reality* (New York: Basic Books, 1971); K. Barth, *Church Dogmatics*, Vol. III, Part 3: *The Doctrine of Creation* (Edinburgh: T&T Clark, 1960), 49ff.

2. See M. Boss, *The Analysis of Dreams*, trans. A. J. Pomerans (New York: Philosophical Library, 1958).

3. All psychological material is taken from my private practice as a psychoanalyst unless otherwise noted, with gratitude to those persons who generously gave me permission to use their examples.

4. See H. F. Searles, *The NonHuman Environment* (New York: International Universities Press, 1960), ch. 3.

5. See H. S. Sullivan, *The Interpersonal Theory of Psychiatry* (New York: Norton, 1953).

6. See K. Horney, *Neurosis and Human Growth* (New York: Norton, 1950), ch. 3.

7. T. S. Eliot, "Burnt Norton," *Four Quartets*, in *The Complete Poems and Plays, 1909–1950* (New York: Harcourt Brace, 1952), 121.

8. See R. D. Laing, *The Divided Self* (Baltimore: Penguin Books, 1965), 72.

9. Matthew 11:16–17.

10. See S. Kierkegaard, *Sickness Unto Death*, trans. Walter Lowrie (New York: Doubleday Anchor Book, 1954), 162–68.

11. M. M. R. Kahn, *The Privacy of Self* (New York: International Universities Press, 1974), chapter 21.

12. A. and B. Ulanov, *Religion and the Unconscious* (Philadelphia: Westminster, 1975), 235–42.

13. See S. Freud, "The Return of Totemism in Childhood," *Totem and Taboo*, in *The Standard Edition of the Complete Psychological Works of Sigmund Freud*, Vol. XIII, trans. and ed. James Strachey (London: Hogarth, 1973), 140–61.

14. See B. Ulanov, *The History of Jazz in America* (New York: Viking, 1952), 27.

15. T. Merton, *The Climate of Monastic Prayer* (Spencer, Mass.: Cistercian Publications, 1969), 36.